D0079456

Field Marshal Bernard Law Montgomery, 1887–1976

Recent Titles in
Bibliographies of Battles and Leaders

The Pusan Perimeter, Korea, 1950: An Annotated Bibliography
Paul M. Edwards

General Douglas MacArthur, 1880–1964: Historiography and Annotated Bibliography
Eugene L. Rasor

The Inchon Landing, Korea, 1950: An Annotated Bibliography
Paul M. Edwards

Dangerous Sky: A Resource Guide to the Battle of Britain
Eunice Wilson

The War of the Spanish Succession, 1702–1713
W. Calvin Dickinson and Eloise R. Hitchcock

The War in North Africa, 1940–1943: A Selected Bibliography
Colin F. Baxter

The Battles of the Somme, 1916: Historiography and Annotated Bibliography
Fred R. van Hartesveldt, compiler

Signals Intelligence in World War II: A Research Guide
Donal J. Sexton, Jr., compiler

The Southwest Pacific Campaign, 1941–1945: Historiography and Annotated Bibliography
Eugene L. Rasor

The Solomon Islands Campaign, Guadalcanal to Rabaul: Historiography and Annotated
Bibliography
Eugene L. Rasor

The Dardanelles Campaign, 1915: Historiography and Annotated Bibliography
Fred R. van Hartesveldt, compiler

The China-Burma-India Campaign, 1931–1945: Historiography and Annotated
Bibliography
Eugene L. Rasor

Field Marshal Bernard Law Montgomery, 1887–1976

A Selected Bibliography

Compiled by
Colin F. Baxter

Bibliographies of Battles and Leaders, Number 23
Myron J. Smith, Jr., *Series Adviser*

GREENWOOD PRESS
Westport, Connecticut • London

Library of Congress Cataloging-in-Publication Data

Baxter, Colin F., 1942–
    Field Marshal Bernard Law Montgomery, 1887–1976 : a selected
bibliography / compiled by Colin F. Baxter.
        p.   cm.—(Bibliographies of battles and leaders, ISSN
1056–7410 ; no. 23)
    Includes index.
    ISBN 0–313–29119–5 (alk. paper)
    1. Montgomery of Alamein, Bernard Law Montgomery, Viscount,
1887–1976 Bibliography.   2. Great Britain—History, Military—20th
century Bibliography.   I. Title.   II. Series.
Z8591.3.B39   2000
[DA69.3.M56]
016.355′0092—dc21   99–33434

British Library Cataloguing in Publication Data is available.

Copyright © 1999 by Colin F. Baxter

All rights reserved. No portion of this book may be
reproduced, by any process or technique, without the
express written consent of the publisher.

Library of Congress Catalog Card Number: 99–33434
ISBN: 0–313–29119–5
ISSN: 1056–7410

First published in 1999

Greenwood Press, 88 Post Road West, Westport, CT 06881
An imprint of Greenwood Publishing Group, Inc.
www.greenwood.com

Printed in the United States of America

∞™

The paper used in this book complies with the
Permanent Paper Standard issued by the National
Information Standards Organization (Z39.48–1984).

10 9 8 7 6 5 4 3 2 1

The author and publisher acknowledge Viscount Montgomery
of Alamein for his gracious permission to reprint excerpts from
Field Marshal Montgomery's *Memoirs*.

Contents

Series Foreword

The Greeks at Thermopylae, the Crusades, the Armada campaign, Trafalgar, Verdun, Gettysburg, El Alamein, Pork Chop Hill, Khe Sahn, the Falklands, and "Desert Storm" are only a few of the many campaigns and battles, large and small, which have been fought down through the ages. Of course, each of these operations had leaders ranging in quality from Leonidas at Thermopylae to the group think of Vietnam and all featured diverse strategy, tactics, and weaponry. It appears to be mankind's unhappy lot that war has been and apparently will for sometime continue to be a growth industry, despite centuries of horror-filled record-keeping and preventative lessons available for the learning. With only a few exceptions, monographic bibliographies of individual battles and leaders (our series title admittedly, is borrowed from the famous American Civil War history), campaigns and weapons have not been compiled previously. Contributors to this series while thus breaking, new around have also constructed works suitable for wide general audiences. These tools may profitably be employed at every level from high school through graduate university and by the casual researcher/buff as well as the dedicated scholar.

Each volume begins with a narrative overview of the topic designed to place its subject within the context of specific wars, societies, and times; this introduction evaluates the significance of the leader, battle, or technology under study. Each work points to key archival and document collections as well as printed primary and secondary sources. Citations are numbered, allowing easy access via the index(es). Individual volumes may present discussion of their citations in styles ranging from bibliographical essays to individually annotated entries and some titles provide chronologies and suitable appendix(es).

It is my hope as editor that these bibliographies of battles and leaders will enable broad audiences to select and work with the best items available within literature and to benefit from the wisdom of some of today's leading military scholars.

Myron J. Smith, Jr., Series Adviser
Tusculum College
Greeneville, Tennessee

Preface

This book, a volume in the Bibliographies of Battles and Leaders series, is intended to be a reference and research guide for the student, scholar, and general reader who is interested in the life and career of Field Marshal Viscount Montgomery of Alamein (1887-1976), one of the best known and most controversial military commanders of World War II.

Part I, the heart of this bibliographical study, is an historiographical narrative that evaluates and critically reviews the literature on Field Marshal Montgomery. Assuming command of the British Eighth Army at a grim moment in the war, Montgomery led that Army to one of the great Allied victories of World War II – El Alamein. It was a turning point of Allied fortunes and "Monty" became a household name, the recipient of enormous fan mail, and three proposals of marriage! Wearing corduroy trousers, turtle-neck sweater, and black beret, Monty became an instantly recognizable Allied leader, like the corn-cob pipe-smoking General MacArthur. Montgomery was a man of strong views, unbending principles, and outspoken frankness. Needless to say, disagreements were inevitable and Monty was both loved and disliked, praised and criticized.

My aim in this bibliography has been to present and evaluate the extensive body of writing that has grown-up around the controversial Field Marshal. Any serious study of the military campaigns of World War II must invariably confront a man who both admirers and detractors would agree was a "character," an individualist. Part II of the book consists of an extensive, but selective, alphabetical listing of the significant writings that relate to the Field Marshal. Citations are cross-referenced from the historiographical narrative in Part I to the alphabetical listing in Part II and vice versa. The Index includes only those sources discussed at some length in Part I of the text.

I would like to extend my gratitude to the following individuals for their suggestions, encouragement, and assistance during the preparation of this Montgomery bibliography: My good friend Eugene Rasor, Emory, Virginia; Carlo D'Este, New Seabury, Massachusetts; Field Marshal Lord Carver, Fareham, Hampshire; my patient Greenwood editor Cynthia Harris, and Myron J. Smith, Jr., Series Advisor; warmest thanks to Janet Keener and Janet Pickel for their professional help in preparing the manuscript for publication; Kelly Hensley and the ETSU library staff; Stephen Walton and the Imperial War Museum staff; my colleagues, Professors Doug Burgess, Ronnie Day, Stephen Fritz, Emmett Essin and Margaret Wolfe. Finally, a special word of thanks to my wife, Tamara, and son, Andrew, without whose understanding this book would not have been written.

PART I

NARRATIVE AND HISTORIOGRAPHICAL SURVEY

Chapter 1

Historical Background

In the desperate summer of 1942, Hitler's Germany seemed to be on the verge of victory in both Russia and the Middle East. With the world-famous Field Marshal Erwin Rommel almost at the gates of Cairo, a relatively unknown lieutenant-general named Bernard Law Montgomery took command of what Prime Minister Winston Churchill called a "baffled and bewildered" British 8th Army that had see-sawed back and forth across the North African desert too many times. At 1400 hours on August 13th, 1942, two days earlier than authorized, Montgomery assumed command of the 8th Army and issued his famous order, "Here we will stand and fight; there will be no further withdrawal. If we can't stay here alive, then let us stay here dead." Montgomery recorded in his war diary, in typical self-confident and abrupt fashion "If changes in the high command had not been made early in August, we would have lost Egypt." His first hours in the desert, perhaps the most important in Montgomery's military career are described by his first biographer, the Australian war correspondent Alan Moorehead in his 1946 account, *Montgomery* [278]. The resulting victory at El Alamein, the foundation of Montgomery's reputation, led Winston Churchill to ring the church bells all over Britain for the first time in the war. Historian A.J.P. Taylor, in his 1965 volume, *English History 1914-1945* [376], declared that Montgomery was the best British battlefield commander since Wellington. Over two decades later, military historian John Keegan, in his book, *The Second World War*, wrote that "Montgomery's debut on the battlefield had been one of the most brilliant in the history of generalship."

With typical clarity and directness, Montgomery opened his *Memoirs*, published in 1958, with the sentence: "I was born in London, in St. Mark's Vicarage, Kennington Oval, on 17th November 1887." His birthplace is a few hundred yards from the famous Oval cricket ground. From an Anglo-Irish family, his father was the Reverend Henry Montgomery, and his mother, Maud, was a daughter of the Victorian cleric, educator, and author Frederic William Farrar. Before Bernard was two years old, the already large Montgomery family sailed for Australia, where his father had been appointed the Anglican Bishop of Tasmania. During Bernard's formative years his mother's affectionless tyranny left deep scars on his personality, and produced "the cold, merciless pursuer of professional excellence,"according to Nigel Hamilton, author of the monumental three-volume Montgomery biography [174A]. It was not until he was thirteen that the family returned to Britain. In Montgomery's own words, he arrived from Tasmania "self-sufficient, intolerant of authority and steeled to take punishment." After attending St. Paul's School in London, he passed the entrance examination to the Royal Military Academy at Sandhurst and was commissioned in 1908 into the Royal Warwickshire Regiment. The World War I experience was especially formative for Montgomery. In a letter to his mother in 1917 (Imperial War Museum, Montgomery papers 1/63 - 8/11/17), commenting on the Canadians, ("magnificent fighters"), he wrote, "They don't consider they have had a good fight unless they lose heavily; they forget that the whole art of war is to gain your objective with as little loss as possible." After the war, he devoted himself to the study of his chosen profession with the self-denial of a monk. Except for an all too short marriage to the war widow and artist, Betty Carver, Montgomery was a loner for whom the military profession took absolute priority. Tragedy struck. After ten intensely happy years of marriage his wife died from a reaction to an insect bite. Left a widower with a young son, he dedicated himself with renewed obsession to the Army. With his usual no-nonsense realism he wrote in his *Memoirs*: "In September 1939, the British Army was totally unfit to fight a first class war on the continent of Europe." Subsequently, he commanded a division, a corps, and an army, until, in August 1942, he was appointed to command of the British 8th Army in the Western desert where it had recently suffered defeat at the hands of German and Italian forces led by Field Marshal Erwin Rommel. "At a moment when history held its breath," wrote Fred Majdalany in his book, *The Battle of El Alamein: Fortress in the Sand* [242], "he [Montgomery] rallied his country's soldiers as Churchill had rallied its people." Commanded by Montgomery, British Empire soldiers won a decisive victory over Rommel's Axis forces at the Battle of El Alamein between October 23 and November 4, 1942.

From those long-departed days in the desert when "Monty" became a household name, until the present, he has been at the center of historical controversy. American John Gunther, one of the best reporters of the day, wrote in wartime book, *D Day* [173], "When you mention Monty to people, they may curse or grin." Although Montgomery commanded British, American, Canadian, Australian, Indian, South African, Polish, and other Allied soldiers in two of the turning-point battles of the war – El Alamein and Normandy – he remains the most controversial Allied commander of World War II.

Monty was not the stereotype of the model British general – a "nice chap" with charm and modesty, physically big, handsome and wearing a Sam Browne belt. On the contrary, he did not look like a general. Small and unimpressive-looking, Montgomery was 5' 7" in height and weighed about 147 pounds or 10-1/2 stone.

His high-pitched voice, small size, and odd mannerisms made him an easy target to caricature. American war correspondent Quentin Reynolds, in his book, *The Curtain Rises* [331], remarked after visiting Montgomery in Italy: "a slight figure, who should have looked rather absurd in his shorts and his jaunty black beret – but who somehow didn't."

Getting behind the surface appearance, Irish playwright George Bernard Shaw described him as "that intensely compacted hank of steel wire." Patton biographer Carlo D'Este in his book, *Bitter Victory: The Battle for Sicily, 1943* [97], observed that Monty exuded the air of authority that all great commanders seem to possess. He compensated for his lack of physical presence, except for the penetrating grey-blue eyes which fastened upon a speaker, by dominating both soldiers and public with his magnetism and professional competence.

Noel Annan remarks in his *tour de force*, *Our Age: The Generation that made Post-War Britain* [12], that while British intellectuals satirized the inefficiency of the army during World War II and its outdated training programs, they also denigrated the general who recognized the fact. Annan writes that, "They did not warm to Montgomery's personality. But Montgomery knew too well that he had no cadre of trained commanders and staff officers to draw upon, few potential army or corps commanders and not all that number fit to command divisions: such is the inevitable fate of a country with only a small professional army."

In his memoir, *The General Who Never Was* [154], Canadian Strome Galloway writes, "The most remarkable thing about General B.L. Montgomery, as we Canadians knew him in our early days together, was his lack of remoteness." Six different levels of command existed between the ordinary soldier and "Monty." Yet, observes Galloway, to the soldier the Army Commander seemed to be his own personal commander, with no one else in between: "It was this remarkable ability of Montgomery to project his personality over the heads of all his subordinate formation commanders, that made him the soldier's general."

Military historian Michael Howard (Lord Howard) explained why many British officers found Montgomery unpleasant and difficult before World War II, "For Montgomery was that rarest of creatures in the British Army, a thoroughly *professional* soldier: one who took his calling as seriously as does a surgeon, a lawyer or an engineer." [190]. In perhaps the best of the many books that marked the 50th Anniversary of World War II, *Why the Allies Won* [303], Richard Overy wrote that, "He [Montgomery] suffered fools not at all, and had little respect for rank and distinction." The New Zealand General Bernard Freyberg once remarked, "Montgomery? The British say that Montgomery is a cad. But I say that if Montgomery is a cad it's a great pity that the British Army doesn't have a few more bounders." [222]. On another occasion, however, Freyberg declared, "The little bastard!", when he over-heard Monty tactlessly break the news to Freddie de Guingand, his former chief of staff, that he would not be his Vice Chief of the Imperial General Staff. De Guingand tells the story in his short reminiscence, *From Brass Hat to Bowler Hat* [107]. Although the decision not to appoint de Guingand as Vice-CIGS was actually Alanbrooke's, the story became almost legendary as an example of Monty's ingratitude and cruelty. Eisenhower later wondered why de Guingand tolerated such behavior. In 1976, as de Guingand accompanied Montgomery's funeral process ion, he himself wondered too. He supposed the answer was: "to anyone with eyes to see and ears to listen, to anyone who had been involved with the British Army between 1919 and 1945 he was, indisputably, the greatest military field commander our nation managed to produce. He commanded men's loyalty because he was so utterly, ruthlessly professional." A former member of his TAC headquarters staff, Johnny Henderson, observed that, "The loyalty which Monty seemed to command from so many who served under him, of all ranks from General to private, was extraordinary." Henderson's views, as well as those of Kit Dawnay (his personal diarist), Bill Williams (his Chief of Intelligence – "Did I like him personally? Yes, I did")and others are found in the volume edited by T. E. B. Howarth in 1985 titled, *Monty at Close Quarters: Recollections of the Man* [193].

Monty was not an easy person to like, however, and he was all too easy to dislike. Once asked to name history's three greatest generals, he replied, "the other two were Alexander the Great and Napoleon." [362]. His egocentric personality inspired many jokes during World War II: *Eisenhower to King George VI*: "Sir, I am sorry to say so, but I am afraid Montgomery is after my job." *The King:* "You relieve me greatly. I thought he wanted mine." General David Fraser once heard Montgomery advise: "Military History? They'd better just read my campaigns. It's all they'll need." [147]. Juvenile bragging, but as Fraser notes, very much Monty! Americans have often been among his most severe critics. U.S. Army historian Martin Blumenson titled his article in the 1960 issue of publication *Armor* [34], "The Most Overrated General of World War II." American, Eric Larrabee, in his 1987 comprehensive collective portrait of the American war leadership, *Commander in Chief: Franklin Delano Roosevelt, His Lieutenants, and their War* [220], noted that "For many Americans, however, his [Monty's] 'greatness' is only another example of an inflated military reputation, of a halfway competent general mistakenly elevated to a level above his capacity, where he could no longer cope with either a mobile battlefield or the complexities of an Allied relationship." Reviewer Russell F. Weigley, noted in the *Journal of American History* [397], that Larrabee offered "one of the most judicious American interpretations of the relationship between General of the Army Dwight D. Eisenhower and Field Marshal Sir Bernard Law Montgomery."

On the other hand, Geoffrey Perret's , *There's a War to be Won: The United States Army in World War II* [315], published in 1991, falls into the Monty-bashing category. The "myth of Monty flowered mightily," declared Perret, "as the British presence in combat shrank, its pale blossoms a consolation." Montgomery is described as, "Small and mousy looking, sporting an identikit British general's mustache."

The fiftieth anniversary of the Normandy invasion witnessed and outpouring of publications on World War II, including a welcome one volume account by Nigel Hamilton, *Monty: The Battles of Field Marshal Bernard Law Montgomery* [175B].

Historian Alistair Horne offered a sympathetic study in his book, *The Lonely Leader: Monty 1944-1945* [186], which was written in cooperation with David Montgomery, the Field Marshal's son. Montgomery's contribution to Operation *Overlord* received high marks from military historian David G. Chandler in the *D-Day Encyclopedia* [73], which he edited together with retired Brigadier General James Lawton Collins, Jr.

A less than enthusiastic view of Montgomery is found in Gerhard L. Weinberg's 1994 volume, *A World at Arms: A Global History of World War II* [399]. Weinberg is the eminent historian of Hitler's foreign policy. In *The New York Times Book Review*, historian David Reynolds stated that Weinberg's global history was "a tour de force, classical diplomatic history at its best." Montgomery does not fare well in Weinberg's account, where he is labeled, along with generals Patton and MacArthur, as "essentially egomaniacs." Historian Norman Davies noted in *The New York Review of Books* [105], that while Weinberg's survey has many strengths, "He emerges as the archetypal armchair expert, ensconced in an ivory tower filled with the debris of bygone Operations rooms."

Norman Gelb's, *Ike and Monty: Generals at War* [157], drew an unflattering contrast between Eisenhower – "open and gregarious," "most," "courteous and straightforward," and Montgomery – "arrogant, conceited, boastful, abrasive, tactless and capable of gross boorishness." A similar contrast was drawn by Nancy Caldwell Sorel [362] in *The Atlantic Monthly*. In an accompanying caricature, a glaring Monty demands from a red-faced Ike that he stamp out a cigarette in their "First Encounter."

In 1994 a Normandy conference was sponsored by the Cantigny First Division Foundation and the U.S. Naval Institute. The proceedings were published in 1998 under the title, *The Greatest Thing We Have Ever Attempted: Historical Perspectives on the Normandy Campaign* [400]. The distinguished historian and biographer of Eisenhower, Stephen E. Ambrose, gave the kickoff address. His references to Montgomery were scathing: "the positive reason [for Montgomery's appointment as Allied ground force commander for *Overlord*] did not have a whole lot to do with his military abilities, such as they were." Ambrose blamed Montgomery for Allied unpreparedness to fight in the Normandy hedgerows, since he had promised to take Caen on the first day on the invasion, and failed to do so. Montgomery's claim that he had always intended for the Americans to breakout on the right flank is rejected by Ambrose with the charge, "Well, he was a liar." Historian H. P. Willmott, in his lunchtime speech, declared "it is hard to avoid the conclusion that historical portrayal and interpretation have largely followed national lines, and, in so doing, for the most part have generated more heat than light." Willmott noted later that "We may assess blame for this failure on national or personal levels, but frankly one wearies of such finger-pointing ..." He accused Ambrose of "chauvinistic claptrap." Small wonder that in the Foreword to the published proceedings, John F. Votaw commented on the "spirited exchanges" among conference participants.

Historian John Grigg argued in the anthology, *Churchill* [169], edited by

Robert Blake and William Roger Louis, "there was surely a strong case for removing him [Monty] after Arnhem." In Grigg's opinion, Montgomery was a general with a hyped-up reputation who possessed a hold over the media that made him scarcely more removable than General Douglas Haig in World War I.

Ambrose has remained a persistent Montgomery critic. Before the national Press Club in Washington, D.C., in 1997, he replied in answer to a question, "everybody knows what a supercilious little prick Montgomery was. (Laughter.) ... not a very good general, but a great trainer of troops." [6]. Ambrose served as historical consultant to the hugely successful 1998 motion picture, *Saving Private Ryan*. Over fifty years after the "crusade in Europe," and at the close of the 20th Century, the film is a fitting tribute to the citizen-soldiers of World War II. Digressing from the theme of the film, however, the script gratuitously refers to Montgomery as "over-rated," and blames him for the failure to take the town of Caen on D-Day, as called for in the *Overlord* plan.

If Montgomery became a national icon to much of the British public, it is also true that he never lacked for critics, either among his contemporaries or among later historians. Some had good cause to dislike him, while others had simply a personal axe to grind.. In 1960, appeared the brilliant and provocative book, *The Desert Generals* [16], Correlli Barnett. The young and irreverent Barnett set out to demolish the very basis of Monty's claim to fame, his victory at the Battle of El Alamein. Taking aim at what he called the "Montgomery myth," Barnett credited General Claude Auchinleck with defeating the legendary German General Erwin Rommel, at what Barnett called "first Alamein," before Monty arrived in the desert.

In 1967 there appeared the first book devoted exclusively to a debunking attack on Montgomery: *The Montgomery Legend* [382] by R. W. Thompson. Thompson's relentless criticism of Montgomery's generalship largely echoes the pro-Auchinleck stance taken by Barnett. In 1976, at the time of Monty's death , appeared Alun Chalfont's account, *Montgomery of Alamein* [70]. Chalfont was not given access to the Field Marshal's private papers; the author acknowledged his "estrangement" with Montgomery. Offering an "impressionistic" treatment of Monty's military campaigns, Chalfont applied the Field Marshal's own comment on a fellow World War II general to Monty himself: "he was a very good plain cook."

Max Hastings, a distinguished historian of World War II and a former editor of *The Daily Telegraph* acknowledged Montgomery's military competence in a 1983 book review, but added, "The British Army seemed reluctant to accept that effective commanders are often ruthlessly unlovely human beings, Montgomery not least among them." A British icon in his own right, Winston Churchill once described Monty as "a little man on the make."

In his entertaining post-war book, *I Was Monty's Double* [80], Clifton James, who, as part of the D-Day deception effort, acted as Montgomery's double, expressed his astonishment at some of the "fanciful and derogatory stories" that circulated about the Field Marshal. He noted the reaction of an ex-officer who had served under Montgomery's command: "'Monty!' he snapped, when the conversation got around to him. 'I disliked the man intensely. A swaggering braggart. He used to terrify his officers on principle.'" James asked the ex-officer if he had ever met Montgomery and he man answered no but he had heard all about him. Clifton James preferred to remember the story of the elderly lady who came up to him and declared, "Excuse me, sir, but you were Monty's Double, weren't you?" When James admitted that he was, the elderly lady laid her hand on his arm and said, "He is a wonderful man. My son was one of his soldiers. When he was killed I wrote to the General about him and he wrote back. Now he sends me a letter every Christmas. My boy would have been so proud to know this." James wrote, "I saw that Monty had brought great consolation to that old lady and that it was all done in secret."

In a 1994 review article for the American professional journal *Parameters: U.S. Army War College Quarterly* [33], Martin Blumenson asked the question, "Well, who is ever going to reconcile the contradictory interpretations, discover the truth, and present a thesis acceptable to the citizens of both nations [American and British]?" Such a person, proposed Blumenson, would need to be someone who is a military historian with an American father and a British mother or a British father and an American mother!

Reflecting on the state of Montgomery historiography, historian Raymond Callahan has observed that despite all of the writing on Monty, there is no fully satisfactory study of the man. Callahan regarded Hamilton's biography as "a sustained piece of advocacy" that weakened the author's case. Ronald Lewin's study, *Montgomery as Military Commander* [222], remains perhaps the best one volume account, although much new documentary material has become available since its publication in 1971. Lewin concluded that in spite of all his weaknesses and limitations, Montgomery has every right to be accepted as Wellington's heir. Despite concern over its undertone of hagiography, Hamilton's three volume official biography remains the point of departure for any new Montgomery study. Both Alan Moorehead's 1946 biography, *Montgomery*, and Ronald Lewin's 1971 study, *Montgomery as Military Commander* [222], remain vital sources on the Field Marshal, although much new material has become available since their publication. Lewin concluded that in spite of all his weaknesses and limitations, Montgomery has every right to be accepted as Wellington's heir. Heir to the Duke of Wellington? The best battlefield commander of World War II? The most overrated commander of World War II (Wellington himself has been accused of being overrated)? The historical debate over Montgomery's generalship will continue and it is to be hoped that historians will avoid the pitfall of merely engaging in tit for tat, replying in kind to one another's charges. One thing seems certain, the always controversial and never dull Monty refuses to follow the old soldier's adage and simply fade away.

On March 24, 1976, at the age of 89, Montgomery died at Isington Mill on the river Wey in Hampshire. He had converted the derelict mill into a house using lumber given by the grateful governments of Australia and New Zealand. A simple granite stone beneath a 250-year old yew tree marks his grave in the local churchyard at Binsted. With funds contributed by private individuals, a bronze statue of Monty by Oscar Nemon was unveiled by the Queen Mother on June 6, 1980, outside the Ministry of Defense in Whitehall. A similar statue was erected by a grateful people in Brussels, Belgium, in 1980. In 1996, On the 52nd anniversary of D-Day in 1996, a statue by Vivien Mallock was unveiled in the small Norman town of Colleville-Montgomery. The town had changed its name in 1946 in honor of the man who had commanded Allied armies in one of the decisive battles of World War II.

Chapter 2

Chronology

November 17, 1887	–	Bernard Law Montgomery born at St. Mark's Vicarage, Kennington, south London
January 30, 1907	–	Enters Royal Military College, Sandhurst
September 19, 1908	–	Commissioned 2nd Lieutenant Royal Warwickshire Regiment
October 13, 1914	–	Wounded in First Battle of Ypres. Promoted Captain and awarded the Distinguished Service Order
February 12, 1915	–	Brigade-Major 112 Infantry Brigade (later 104)
January 22, 1917	–	GSO2, Headquarters 33rd Division
July 6, 1917	–	GSO2, Headquarters IX Corps
June 3, 1918	–	Promoted Brevet-Major
July 16, 1918	–	GSO1 Headquarters 47th Division. Temporary Lieutenant-Colonel
September 5, 1918	–	Commanding Officer 17th Battalion Royal Fusiliers
March 24, 1919	–	Staff officer with the British Army of Occupation in Germany
January 22, 1920	–	Student, Staff College, Camberley. Brevet-Major

January 5, 1921	–	Brigade-Major 17 Infantry Brigade, Cork, Ireland
May 24, 1922	–	Brigade-Major 8 Infantry Brigade, Plymouth
May, 1923	–	GSO2, Headquarters 49th Division (Territorial), York
March, 1925	–	Commander A Company, 1st Battalion Royal Warwicks, Shornecliffe
January 23, 1926	–	Instructor, Staff College, Camberley, 1926-29. Lieutenant-Colonel
July 27, 1927	–	Marries Betty Carver (nee Hobart)
August 18, 1928	–	David Montgomery born
January, 1931	–	Commanding Officer 1st Battalion Royal Warwicks, Palestine and Egypt
June 29, 1934	–	Senior Instructor, Quetta Staff College, India, 1934-1937. Colonel
August 5, 1937	–	Commander 9 Infantry Brigade, Portsmouth Brigadier
October 19, 1937	–	Death of his wife
December, 1938	–	Commanding General 8th Division, Palestine. Major-General
August 28, 1939	–	Commanding General 3rd Division, England and British Expeditionary Force
July 22, 1940	–	Commanding General V Corps, England. Lieutenant-General
April 27, 1941	–	Commanding General XII Corps, England
August 13, 1942	–	Commanding General 8th Army, Egypt
November 11, 1942	–	Promoted General. Created Knight Commander of the Order of the Bath

January 3, 1944   –   Allied Ground Forces Commander and Commander-
                           in-Chief 21st Army Group

September 1, 1944   –   Promoted Field Marshal

January 1, 1946   –   Created Viscount Montgomery of Alamein

July, 1946   –   Chief of the Imperial General Staff, 1946-1948

November, 1946   –   Created Knight of the Garter

October, 1948   –   Chairman of the Western Union Chiefs of Staff
                           Committee, 1948-1951

April, 1951   –   Deputy Supreme Commander, NATO

September 18, 1958   –   Retirement. Publication of *The Memoirs*

March 24, 1976   –   His death at Isington Mill, Hampshire. Buried in the
                           local churchyard at Binsted

Chapter 3

Sources for Research on Field Marshal Montgomery

Principal Research Collections

Imperial War Museum
Lambeth Road
London SE1 6HZ
England

In 1943 Montgomery told the American war correspondent John Gunther that he had kept a war diary for years and that it would "blow off everybody's head between Alamein and London." Gunther told him how important the diary would be for a future historian. "Tell me, would I get any money for my diary?" He asked smiling. Gunther replied very deadpan: "About a hundred thousand dollars, General." He turned to "Bill" Williams his chief of Intelligence and asked: "A hundred thousand dollars? What's that?" "That's twenty-five thousand pounds, sir," answered Williams solemnly. "Well," Monty grinned, "Guess I won't die in the poor-house after all." He sold his diaries and military papers to an old and valued friend, one of his battalion commanders, Denis Hamilton (then editor of *The Sunday Times* and the Thomson Organization) in 1962. He stipulated that he would have to have absolute right of veto "on anything published in my lifetime." "After that," he added, characteristically, "you could do as you liked." The papers were presented to the IWM by Sir Denis Hamilton on behalf of the International Thomson Organization in 1982. Mr. Stephen Brooks prepared a detailed, 275-page catalog to the pre-1948 collection.

Nigel Hamilton's tape-recorded interviews that were made during the course of his research for the "official" biography of Montgomery are deposited at the IWM.

On display at the IWM is the Grant tank used by Montgomery in North Africa, Sicily, and Italy until the end of 1943. Monty's famous caravan, a captured trailer fitted out as an office with a portrait of Rommel, his famous adversary, on the bulkhead, is no longer in the IWM but may be seen at the Duxford Museum outside of Cambridge.

Public Record Office,
Ruskin Avenue,
Kew,
Richmond, Surrey, TW9 4DU
England

Unit War Diaries, Cabinet Papers, Prime Minister's Papers, Foreign Office Papers, Alexander Papers, Dempsey Papers

Liddell Hart Centre for Military Archives,
King's College London,
Strand,
London WC2R 2LS
England

Includes B. H. Liddell Hart's correspondence with Montgomery; Field Marshal Lord Alanbrooke papers (Chief of the Imperial General Staff); Major-General Sir John Kennedy papers (Director of Military Operations); General Sir Hastings Ismay papers (Churchill's military advisor); General Francis de Guingand papers (Montgomery's Chief of Staff); Chester Wilmot papers.

Churchill Archives Centre
Churchill College
Cambridge CB3 0DS
England

Winston Churchill papers; P. J. Grigg (Secretary of State for War) correspondence relating to Montgomery; Historian Ronald Lewin's papers (biographer of Montgomery, Wavell, and Rommel)

National Army Museum,
Royal Hospital Road,
Chelsea,
London SW3 4HT
England

Prior permission is required to view the papers of Field Marshal Sir Gerald Templer.

Royal Air Force Museum,
Hendon,
England

The papers of Air Chief Marshals Sir James Robb, Sir John Slessor, and Lord Tedder.

University of Southampton,
The Hartley Library,
Highfield, Southampton SO17 1BJ

The Broadlands collections include the Mountbatten Papers containing correspondence with Montgomery.

Directorate of History and Heritage,
National Archives of Canada,
Ottawa, Canada

Charles P. Stacey, who wrote the official Canadian World War II army histories, investigated the planning of Dieppe thoroughly, and the findings are deposited in the Canadian archives. Other collections include the papers of General Henry Crerar and General Guy Simonds.

Dwight D. Eisenhower Library,
Abilene, Kansas

Eisenhower's correspondence with Montgomery, de Guingand, as well as other World War II figures; Walter Bedell Smith papers (Eisenhower's chief of staff); Kay Summersby diary; diary of Harry C. Butcher (Eisenhower's naval aide).

United States Army Military History Institute
Carlisle Barracks,
Pennsylvania 17013-5008

Omar Bradley papers; Chester B. Hansen diary (Bradley's aide): Montgmery antagonized Hansen, then a major, when he said to Bradley (recorded by Hansen in the diary), "I say now do you have a major for an ADC. Simply a dog's body, you know, a whipping boy. I would not have an ADC who is more than a captain." Hansen recorded Montgomery as saying that aides were "Messenger boys, simply messenger boys"; historian Forrest C. Pogue's interviews for the official U.S. Army volume, *Supreme Command.*

Bibliographies and Guides

Colin F. Baxter, *The Normandy Campaign, 1944: A Selected Bibliography.* Greenwood Press, 1992.

Colin F. Baxter, *The War in North Africa, 1940-1943: A Selected Bibliography.* Greenwood Press, 1996.

John D. Cantwell, *The Second World War: A Guide to Documents in the Public Record Office.* London, 1993.

Peter Catterall, *British History 1945-1987: An Annotated Bibliography.* Cambridge, MS, 1991.

O. A. Cooke, *The Canadian Military Experience 1867-1983: A Bibliography.* 3rd ed. 1997.

A.G.S. Enser, *A Subject Bibliography of the Second World War: Books in English, 1939-1974.* Boulder, CO, 1985.

A.G.S. Enser, *A Subject Bibliography of the Second World War: Books in English, 1975-1983.* Boulder, CO.

Vincent J. Esposito, *The West Point Atlas of American Wars. Vol. II.* New York, 1959.

Janet Foster and Julia Sheppard, *British Archives: A Guide to Archive Resources in the United Kingdom.* New York, 1989.

Robin Higham, *A Guide to the Sources in British Military History.* Berkeley, CA, 1971.

Gerald Jordan, *British Military History: A Supplement to Robin Higham's Guide to the Sources.* New York, 1988.

Myron J. Smith, Jr. *World War II: The European and Mediterranean Theaters. An Annotated Bibliography.* New York, 1984.

Janet Ziegler, *World War II: Books in English, 1945-1965.* Stanford, CA, 1971.

Biographical Dictionaries

Lord Blake and C. S. Nicholls, eds., *The Dictionary of National Biography: 1971-1980.* The excellent, eight-page entry on Montgomery was written by E.T. Williams, his former chief intelligence officer and Oxford academic.

John Keegan, *Who Was Who in World War II.*

David Mason, *Who's Who in World War II.*

Christopher Tunney, *A Biographical Dictionary of World War II*. Dent, 1972.

Elizabeth-Anne Wheal, Stephen Pope, and James Taylor, *A Dictionary of the Second World War*. P. Bedrick Books, 1990.

Encyclopedias and Collections

Stephen Brooks, ed., *Montgomery and the Eighth Army: A Selection from the Diaries, Correspondence and other Papers of Field Marshal The Viscount Montgomery of Alamein, August 1942 to December 1943* [47]. Having spent four years cataloging the Montgomery papers at the Imperial War Museum, Brooks was well-qualified to edit this essential reference work published by the Army Records Society. Seventy-nine letters written by Montgomery are included in the volume, written in what Brooks calls "that bold, childlike script" which never varied until his health failed at the end. The documents contain Montgomery's frank and controversial opinions such as, "Auchinleck should never be employed again in any capacity." Brooks offers a helpful introduction and includes a useful bibliography.

David G. Chandler and James Lawton Collins, Jr., eds., *D-Day Encyclopedia*. [73]. The biographical entry on Montgomery is written by Chandler who observes that the British general was "either worshiped or despised by most of his contemporaries." Chandler credits Montgomery with playing "a truly vital part" in the success of Operation *Overlord*.

Robert Cowley and Geoffrey Parker, eds., *The Reader's Companion to Military History*. Houghton Mifflin, 1996. The Montgomery entry is written by Alistair Horne.

Trevor N. Dupuy, Curt Johnson, and David L. Bongard. *The Harper Encyclopedia of Military Biography*. Harper Collins, 1992. Bongard concludes that Montgomery was an able commander.

Noble Frankland, ed., *The Encyclopedia of Twentieth Century Warfare*. Orion Books, 1989. A favorable assessment of Montgomery's generalship by General Sir William Jackson.

International Military and Defense Encyclopedia. Brassey's, 1993. Harold E. Raugh, Jr., wrote that Montgomery was "a rather unimaginative but highly charismatic commander."

F. M. Leventhal, ed., *Twentieth-Century Britain: An Encyclopedia*. Garland, 1995. Karl G. Larew concludes that "no one doubted his [Montgomery's] basic competence."

Kenneth Macksey and William Woodhouse, *The Penguin Encyclopedia of Modern Warfare, 1850 to the Present Day*. Viking, 1991. The entry echoes Monty's own controversial opinion that "if he had been allowed his way by General Eisenhower, [he] might have finished World War II that autumn [of 1944] with a narrow-front advance" into Germany.

Parrish, Thomas, ed., *The Simon and Schuster Encyclopedia of World War II*. Simon and Schuster, 1978.

Memorabilia

Monty became a household name in wartime Britain although greatly surpassed in popularity by Winston Churchill. Shortage of raw materials and government restrictions did not allow the manufacture of items honoring national heroes. After the war, the Royal Doulton china company produced Monty character jugs, and his image appeared on a few other items along with that of other wartime leaders. On his death in 1976, a plate and mug in fine china were produced "In Memoriam" to him.

Chapter 4

The Making of a General

Family Background

A good place to begin in search of Montgomery are his candid and controversial *Memoirs* [268], which were published in 1958. On the very first page he makes no bones about his early years: "Certainly I can say that my own childhood was unhappy. This was due to a clash of wills between my mother and myself...There were obvious faults on both sides . . . I was the bad boy of the family... She made me afraid of her when I was a child and a young boy . . . The three outstanding human beings in my life have been my father, my wife, and my son." According to Montgomery, if his mother could not see him anywhere, she would say – "Go and find what Bernard is doing and tell him to stop it."

In 1981, Nigel Hamilton, the son of Sir Denis Hamilton who had arranged the original purchase of the Montgomery papers, published the first volume of the official biography based on that collection. In the "Author's Note," to *Monty: The Making of a General 1887-1942* [174A], Nigel Hamilton wrote, "I was twelve when I first met him, thirty-two when he died. The gift of his friendship – the manner in which he took me into his house as a second son – is not something I can ever forget; and in undertaking this biography I felt I would be repaying a debt of gratitude." At the same time, his aim was not to "whitewash or flatter." The volume is not a pious hagiography, and Hamilton does not hide Montgomery's faults. The author observes that while Montgomery liked later to see himself as heir to Marlborough and Wellington, in many ways he was "much closer to the egotistical Nelson who, had he not fallen at Trafalgar, might also have become noted for insufferable vanity and arrogant over-simplification."

Hamilton finds the key to Montgomery's character in the unhappy relationship with his mother. Married when she was still only sixteen, Maud had five children by the age of twenty-five. She coped by imposing strict, unbending rules on the family; if the children disobeyed they were almost invariably beaten with a cane.

Though Montgomery came to respect his mother, he never forgave her. Hamilton postulates that Montgomery's rebellious, mischievous behavior was the protest of an unloved, attention-seeking child. The conflict of their personalities lasted until her death in 1949. He did not attend her funeral. Above all, Hamilton sought to revive Montgomery's military reputation, portraying him as the consummate professional soldier, the master of his craft. He writes, "However unseemly Bernard Montgomery's vanity, it was matched by a veritable genius both for smelling out inefficiency and for discovering and nurturing young talent."

The Making of a General was widely reviewed at the time. Calling the biography lifeless, flat, and boring, one critic remarked, "That such a nasty little man as Montgomery should have risen to such heights is a remarkable story." General Sir John Hackett, an admitted "Monty man," thought the book too long (871 pages) and the early chapters marred by uncritical adulation. General Sir Anthony Farrar-Hockley found "the iteration and reiteration of psychological influences tedious," but he praised Hamilton for writing "quite simply the best biography of Montgomery yet to emerge and I wait with pleasurable anticipation for the second volume to appear." Military historian Jeffrey J. Clarke called the book "a first-class study" and in many ways "the meat of the tale" since it was during the time-frame of the volume that Monty's penchant for detail, order, and planning were fully developed.

More about the Field Marshal's family background is to be found in Brian Montgomery's fascinating portrait, *A Field-Marshal in the Family: A Personal Biography of Montgomery of Alamein* [272]. The author, himself a professional soldier, was the Field Marshal's youngest brother. Their mother was a formidable woman, a daughter of the famous Dean Farrar. Brian Montgomery explains her shortcomings by remarking that she was engaged at fourteen and married at sixteen, and did not have much education. The Bishop, a lovable man, was allowed five shillings a week for expenses! Bernard often told his brother, "I do not care for the Farrar blood." However, his brother thought that Bernard drew his strength of character and tenacity from their mother. He fought with her and neither gave way. On the Montgomery side of the family, the Bishop's father, Sir Robert, had played a prominent role in preserving British control of the Punjab during the Indian Mutiny. The author thought his brother possessed the same iron will, determination, and absolute conviction as seen in his grandfather two generations earlier. Monty's brother felt that a certain "streak of intolerance" became stronger in him after his wife's tragic death in 1937. He mentions Monty's legendary rudeness: instead of attending his brother's wedding reception he went to a football match instead! Invited by Lady Churchill to be a pall-bearer at the funeral of his old friend Winston Churchill in 1965, Monty declined to return home from a trip to South Africa where he had gone to recuperate following prostate surgery. He avoided funerals whenever he could; including his mother's.

In April 1976, just three weeks after the death of the Field Marshal, their appeared Lord Chalfont's (Alun Chalfont) unsympathetic study, *Montgomery of Alamein* [70]. Chalfont, a former career army officer, *Times* defense correspondent, and Foreign Secretary, caused a tempest in a teacup with his controversial psychological biography. In a review, Brian Montgomery criticized the author's "sarcasm" and "sneering or snide remarks" about his brother, but especially the innuendo that his brother had had a homosexual relationship with one of his young liaison officers. Chalfont concluded: "He was certainly not one of the great commanders."

A much more sympathetic character analysis of Montgomery is presented by Alan Moorehead in his 1946 book, *Montgomery: A Biography* [278]. The first full story of Montgomery's life, Moorehead wrote,"He has tried hard to emulate his father." To Moorehead, Montgomery most resembled not Cromwell or Stonewall Jackson but Mahatma Gandhi – "both enjoyed the genial conviction that what they said and did was absolutely right." Moorehead's book is not an analysis of Montgomery's battles.

Information on his father as well as other family matters can be found in Maud Montgomery's memorial to her husband, *Bishop Montgomery: A Memoir* [274]. Maud wrote a foreword to a tribute biography written in 1945 by Michael C. McGill and William D. Flackes, *Montgomery, Field Marshal: An Ulster Tribute* [253]. His mother wrote in the foreword: "I always say he has done so well because he is an Irishman."

Monty's widely known maternal Victorian grandfather was the subject of a biography by his son Reginald Farrar, *The Life of Frederic William Farrar* [140]. The zealous and independent-minded Dean Farrar of Canterbury was a pall-bearer at the funeral of biologist Charles Darwin, where he preached the sermon, and was instrumental in having Darwin buried in Westminster Abbey.

World War I

After spending eleven years in Tasmania, the Montgomery family returned to England in 1902; at the age of fourteen Bernard entered St. Paul's School in London (his later headquarters before the Normandy invasion) where he excelled at sports. Family holidays were spent at New Park, the family property at Moville in Ireland, which the bishop had inherited from his father. Bernard entered the Royal Military College at Sandhurst on January 30, 1907. In his *Memoirs* he remarked, "It is doubtful if many cadets were as poor as myself . . . Outside attraction being denied to me for want of money, I plunged into games and work." A perceptive essay on Montgomery by Field Marshal Lord Carver, who served under Monty in World War II, is to be found in the collection, *Churchill's Generals* [207], edited by John Keegan. Montgomery was lucky to graduate from Sandhurst. He set fire to the shirt-tails of a cadet who suffered severe burns. Montgomery was reduced in rank and held back for a term before being commissioned into the Royal Warwickshire Regiment on September 19, 1908, and joining the 1st Battalion on the North-West Frontier of India. There he took his profession seriously. It was this ambition to succeed that marked him out from his colleagues. He did not always do as he was told. When a visiting German battleship called at Bombay, Montgomery was ordered to pick a second-class football team to play the visitors.

Instead, he put every man on their first-team on the soccer field: they won something like 40 to nothing! He played to win.

Montgomery recorded in his *Memoirs*: "In August 1914, I was a full lieutenant of twenty-six. It was to take the experiences of the 1914-18 war to show me what was wrong in the Army." His battalion crossed over to France as part of the 4th Division, Montgomery commanding a platoon. Scarcely twenty-four hours after arrival at the front, they were under fire. He was severely wounded after he had led his platoon in a gallant attack on the village of Meteran, for which he was promoted captain and awarded the Distinguished Service Order (regarded as a "near miss" for a Victoria Cross), a rarity for a twenty-six year old platoon leader. He was lucky not only to survive the sniper's bullet, but because such a severe wound led to his service as a staff officer for the rest of the war. Had he returned to the front line, his chances of survival would have been small. Poorly planned, poorly executed operations that wasted of soldiers' lives appalled Montgomery. By 1917 he would write, "the whole art of war is to gain your objective with as little loss [of lives] as possible." Lord Carver, in his essay on Montgomery, observed that "The 1918 experience was especially formative."

Montgomery's later reflections on World War I can be found in his 1968 book, *A History of Warfare* [264]. In that account he wrote, "I would name Sir John Monash as the best general on the western front in Europe; he possessed real creative originality, and the war might well have been won sooner, and certainly with fewer casualties, had [Field Marshal] Haig been relieved of his command and Monash appointed to command the British armies in his place." Besides his own experience, Montgomery's views were based on the writings of Liddell-Hart, Cyril Falls, and A.J.P. Taylor.

In his book, *John Monash: A Biography* [353], author Geoffrey Serle makes it clear that David Lloyd George and Liddell-Hart used Monash's reputation as a weapon with which to bludgeon Haig and other senior British officers. Citing Norman Dixon's study, *The Psychology of Military Incompetence* [116], Serle claims that Monash possessed the qualities assigned by Dixon to Montgomery: capacity for "sheer hard work, a refusal to conform to the dead hand of military tradition, and the possession of [an] open, clear and sensitive mind," also "'the knack of creating oases of serenity around himself.'"

A very fair-minded assessment of Monash is presented by P.A. Pedersen in his article, "General Sir John Monash: Corps Commander on the Western Front," in D.M. Horner, editor, *The Commanders: Australian Military Leadership in the Twentieth Century* [188].

Biographer Nigel Hamilton, however, in *The Making of a General*, points out that Montgomery was still too young and too junior an officer in World War I to question the conduct of the British high command. Hamilton credits General Sir Herbert Plumer with leaving "the deepest and most lasting lessons of the war [on Montgomery]." In this sense, states Hamilton, Montgomery was to prove "very much a product of the 'First War' school – though hardly in a pejorative sense." Plumer had shown that meticulously planned, realistic offensives, supported by enough firepower could succeed.

The best brief account of the British army in World War I is that by J.M. Bourne, *Britain and the Great War 1914-1918* [42]. See also Paddy Griffiths, *Battle Tactics of the Western Front: The British Army's Art of Attack*.

Between the Wars

By the time the 1914-18 war was over, wrote Montgomery in his *Memoirs*, "it had become very clear to me that the profession of arms was a life-study, and that few officers seemed to realize this fact. It was at this stage in my life that I decided to dedicate myself to my profession, to master its details, and to put all else aside." The first step was to attend the Staff College at Camberley, which he did in 1920. In 1921 he was posted to Cork in southern Ireland, the center of Republican unrest against British rule. During the War for Irish Republican Independence, Montgomery served as Brigade-Major of the 17th Infantry Brigade, comprising 7 battalions! His responsibilities were large; Chalfont, in his far from uncritical biography, *Montgomery of Alamein* [70], wrote that Montgomery, of Protestant northern Irish background, seems to have carried out his responsibilities in an "objective, dispassionate and efficient way." In his *Memoirs*, Montgomery declared, "In many ways this war was far worse than the Great War which had ended in 1918. It developed into a murder campaign in which, in the end, the soldiers became very skillful and more than held their own. But such a war is thoroughly bad for officers and men; it tends to lower their standards of decency and chivalry, and I was glad when it was over."

An Irish Republican account is presented by Tom Barry in his book, *Guerilla days in Ireland: A Firsthand account of the Black and Tan war (1919-1921)* [18]. Robert Kee's *The Green Flag: A history of Irish nationalism* [206] is an unsentimental and dispassionate work; Carlton Younger, in his book, *Ireland's Civil War* [411], observed that "As always, the bitter truth was that neither side had much to be proud of."

Then, in January 1926 Montgomery received an assignment much more to his liking. He was sent back to Camberley as an instructor. Also on the staff was Alan Brooke, the future Chief of the Imperial General Staff during World War II. Many of their students would be commanders during the war. For three years Montgomery settled down to the enjoyable business of telling them exactly how he believed battles should be fought.

Montgomery had presented a number of his ideas earlier in a remarkable series of articles in *The Antelope* (the regimental magazine of the Royal Warwickshire Regiment). On Montgomery's regiment, see Marcus Cunliffe, *History of the Royal Warwickshire Regiment 1919-1955* [95]. In his book, *Montgomery: A Biography* [278], Alan Moorehead commented: "He was entering the period of his life which was to end in his becoming one of the most notable pamphleteers ever produced by the British Army." In addition to Moorehead's biography, Montgomery's tactical views are described in the works of Alun Chalfont, *Montgomery of Alamein* [70], Ronald Lewin, *Montgomery as Military Commander* [222], and Nigel Hamilton,

The Making of a General [174A]. He rejected the notion that victory in battle was a matter of brute force. Instead, he emphasized the importance of the individual soldier. Morale was everything and the soldier must be made to feel that he was part of a team carrying out an intelligent plan that was bound to succeed. To Montgomery a battle was as precise and technical an act as building a house, and no one should go into action until he was absolutely certain he was going to prevail.

Though always a *reformer*, he was not radical or revolutionary in his military thinking. That Monty was a pragmatist is argued by Alistair Horne with David Montgomery in their book, *The Lonely Leader: Monty 1944-1945* [186]. He was not an apostle of modern armored warfare in the sense that Liddell Hart, "Bony" Fuller, and Martel were tank enthusiasts. Liddell Hart's comments on Monty can be found in volume I of *The Memoirs of Captain Liddell Hart* [228].

The inter-war years are discussed by John Keegan in the volume, *A Guide to the Sources in British Military History*, edited by Robin Higham. In the 1920s few army officers had grasped the need for new ideas, new equipment and new techniques. Montgomery was one of them. For most, the end of the war meant a return to "real soldiering" that is, regimental life with its "horsey, paternalistic officer class."

An essential source on the period is Brian Bond's, *British Military Policy between the Two World Wars*. According to the author, Montgomery was perhaps the "most ardent of all the officers of the 1920s who were determined to correct the faults of leadership they had recently witnessed in France."

Now suddenly at the age of 38 Montgomery decided that marriage was a necessary and desirable thing. Previously he had told his amused skeptical colleagues: "Marriage is not a good thing for officers. You cannot be both a good soldier *and* a good husband." He married Betty Carver, a widow with two small boys, in the summer of 1927. Friends described her as "a charming eccentric with a tremendous vitality and zest for life." She was an amateur painter and sculptor, and lived in a colony of artists and writers near Chiswick. The marriage opened new horizons to the monastic, dogmatic soldier, and was intensely happy. In 1928 their son David was born.

From mid-1935 to early 1937, Montgomery, then a Colonel, was a senior instructor at the Army Staff College, Quetta, India. Michael Carver observed in his essay on Montgomery in *Churchill's Generals* [207], edited by John Keegan, that "He excelled as an instructor, analysing the problem with remorseless logic, simplifying and explaining it with terse clarity and mastery of detail." Montgomery's teaching technique at Quetta is described by E.K.G. Sixsmith, *British Generalship in the Twentieth Century* [358].

In 1937, Montgomery was posted to Portsmouth to command the 9th Brigade. Tragedy struck when his wife died from an insect bite. The marriage had lasted just ten years. He was not yet fifty. He said shortly, "My married life was absolute bliss. The death of my wife was a shattering blow from which I recovered with great difficulty, and very slowly."

Montgomery, now more dedicated to this profession than ever. Biographer Alun Chalfont noted in *Montgomery of Alamein* [70] that the 9th Infantry Brigade became the "star" brigade of the British army. Monty's men made no great show on parade but excelled at maneuvers on Salisbury Plain. General (later Field Marshal) Wavell reported: "Brigadier Montgomery is one of the cleverest brains we have in the higher ranks, an excellent trainer of troops and an enthusiast in all he does . . . He has some of the defects of the enthusiast, in an occasional impatience and intolerance when things cannot be done as quickly as he would like, or when he meets brains less quick and clear than his own."

Montgomery's attitude toward authority was displayed in the famous Portsmouth football ground affair. Ignoring army regulations and procedure, he rented War Office land, the army football field, to a promoter for use as a fairground over the August Bank Holiday. Montgomery spent the one thousand pound rental payment that he received on his garrison welfare services. The War Office was infuriated at this violation of Army Regulations and his career was in serious trouble. He was fortunate indeed to be saved by Wavell who recognized the value of an unorthodox individualist. In his *Memoirs*, Montgomery remarked that for a while he was "dicky on the perch."

In October 1938, Montgomery was ordered to Palestine to take command of the 8th Infantry Division. Wavell commented upon the new major-general: "He will do extremely well." By the time of Montgomery's arrival, Palestine was in a state of half-war as Arabs revolted against Jewish immigration into the British Mandate. Richard O'Connor commanded the 7th Division in the south. Chalfont wrote in *Montgomery of Alamein* [70], "By the time the Arab revolt died down in the spring of 1939 Montgomery had his part of Palestine very much under control."

In the meantime, Montgomery had been told that he had been selected to command the 3rd Infantry Division (the old Iron Division of World War I), one of the few units which was anywhere near combat ready in the event of war. In his book, *Wavell in the Middle East, 1939-1941: A Study in Generalship* [326], Harold E. Raugh, Jr., observes that Montgomery was unwanted by many senior commanders; it was Wavell's influence which secured from him command of the 3rd Division which he commanded brilliantly in France in 1940.

Suddenly, in May, he became seriously ill in Palestine. On the voyage back to Britain, however, he made a remarkable recovery. In August, Alan Brooke, appointed to command the II Corps in the British Expeditionary Force, pushed to have Montgomery immediately assume command of the 3rd Division. Brooke had been a fellow instructor at Camberley Staff College in the 1920s. He needed the energy and drive that he knew Montgomery would bring to the training of a relatively raw division. Montgomery took command of the 3rd Infantry Division just six days before the outbreak of World War II.

Hitler's War Begins

Before the fighting began, there occurred in November another one of those incidents that nearly ruined Montgomery's career. The Venereal Disease incident is described in his brother's account, *A Field-Marshal in the Family* [272]. Brian

Montgomery prints the entire order which his brother issued to deal with the problem of V.D. among the troops. Montgomery's frank instructions caused an outcry from the senior chaplains of both the Church of England and the Roman Catholic Church (in his book, *Montgomery as Military Commander* [222], military historian Ronald Lewin observed that "all Hell broke loose"), and Lord Gort, the Commander-in-Chief of the British Expeditionary Force, favored withdrawal of the order by Montgomery. Taking a pragmatic view, Montgomery felt that V.D. should be prevented by rapid medical attention after intercourse. His order made several useful points about prophylactics: "My view is that if a man wants to have a woman, let him do so by all means: but he must use his common sense and the necessary precautions against infection – otherwise he becomes a casualty by his own neglect, and this is helping the enemy . . . We must face up to the problem, be perfectly frank about it, and do all we can to help the soldier in this very difficult matter." Montgomery's enlightened and pragmatic approach to the problem of venereal disease was the opposite of the "authoritarian attitude" declares Norman Dixon in his book, *On the Psychology of Military Incompetence* [116]. In his 1976 book, Dixon posited a close link between military incompetence and the authoritarian personality, which might be defined as the opposite of the individualistic, tolerant, democratic, unprejudiced and egalitarian.

Montgomery was saved from being sent home – and not for the last time – by General Alan Brooke, II Corps Commander and later Chief of the Imperial General Staff until 1946. Brooke's wartime diaries were edited by Arthur Bryant for his book, *The Turn of the Tide* [49]. Brooke, who knew Montgomery well from the days when they were both instructors at Camberley, wrote in his diary: "I never ceased to thank Heaven that I saved Monty at this danger point in his career." Brooke called Montgomery a "trainer of genius." In his superb 1982 biography, *Alanbrooke* [144], General Sir David Fraser observes that after the campaign of 1939-40, Brooke viewed Montgomery as "having no peer" as a soldier of swift understanding, total calm in crisis, and iron will. Montgomery's own opinion of Brooke is found in, *A Field-Marshal in the Family* [272], where Brian Montgomery reports being told by his brother that "Both as a commander and staff officer Brooke was by far the greatest soldier of the war."

Montgomery's dramatic impact on the 3rd Division is described vividly in the 1995 account, *Monty's Iron Sides: From the Normandy Beaches to Bremen with the 3rd Division* [110], by Patrick Delaforce.

In April 1940, still not happy with the Division's existing leadership, Montgomery wrote to his corps commander, Alan Brooke, that front line commanders must possess "initiative, energy and 'drive'." As Delaforce comments, "The famous Monty purges had started!"

A young officer's impression of his newly arrived divisional commander can be found in the delightful account, Lord Carrington, *Reflect on Things Past: The Memoirs of Lord Carrington*. Carrington notes, "He began to instill into us what he was later to do for most of the army–a long-overdue professionalism."

Other useful sources include: Norman Scarfe, *Assault Division: A History of the 3rd Division from the Invasion of Normandy to the Surrender of Germany* [350];

Robin McNish, *Iron Division 1809-1977* [254]; Sir John Smyth, *"Bolo" Whistler* [361]; on Monty's former Regiment, "my Regiment," see Marcus Cunliffe, *History Royal Warwickshire Regiment* [95].

Dunkirk

An eye-witness account of the retreat to Dunkirk is presented by General Sir Brian Horrocks, who fought most of his battles in World War II under Montgomery, in his post-war memoir, *A Full Life* [189]. Horrocks saw Montgomery every day, sometimes several times a day, and he was "always the same; confident, almost cocky you might say, cheerful and apparently quite fresh. He was convinced that he was the best divisional commander in the British army and that we were the best division." During the retreat, with his supply situation precarious, Montgomery drove a herd of cattle on the hoof as food for the troops!

With the British army forced to evacuate from Dunkirk, on May 29 Brooke was ordered to hand over command of II Corps and return home. He handed over command to Montgomery on the beaches, with tears streaming down his cheeks. In his *Memoirs*, Montgomery remarks , "This surprised me as I was the junior major-general in the corps."

As the Dunkirk evacuation continued, Lord Gort nominated the commander of the 1 corps to coordinate the final stages of the withdrawal. In *Montgomery of Alamein* [70], Alun Chalfont writes, "Montgomery, with all the assurance of a corps commander of twenty-four hours' standing, told the commander-in-chief that this was a mistake." Montgomery recommended General Harold Alexander of the 1st Division. In his *Memoirs*, Montgomery remarks, "I knew Gort very well; so I spoke very plainly and insisted that his was the right course to take." Gort agreed and Alexander conducted the evacuation with great skill. Military historian Ronald Lewin described the episode in his outstanding 1971 study, *Montgomery as Military Commander* [222]. Although Lewin was not an uncritical admirer of Montgomery, he stated that, "There can be little doubt that to Montgomery's act of intelligent effrontery a good many men owe, if not their lives, then at least salvation from years in a German prison camp." In his book, *On the Psychology of Military Incompetence* [116], Norman Dixon cites the episode as an example of personal risk-taking for the sake of larger issues. On several occasions, Dixon states that Montgomery risked his own career by sacrificing popularity with those on whom promotion might depend, for the sake of what he felt was right militarily.

At dawn on June 1, Montgomery himself was evacuated from Dunkirk and landed at Dover. The Dunkirk evacuation has been the subject of several studies. In his outstanding account, *The Nine Days of Dunkirk* [115], published in 1959, author David Divine notes that Brooke's share in the campaign had been "wholly overstated."

Montgomery appears as practical, crystal-clear and incisive in journalist Richard Collier's, *The Sands of Dunkirk* [84].

Once back in England, Montgomery resumed command of the 3rd Division, the first of the formations to be re-equipped from the few weapons available. Montgomery's first biographer, Alan Moorehead, wrote in his 1946 account, *Montgomery: A Biography* [278], "Only two qualities counted now: one was character, and the other was professional knowledge."

The realistic Montgomery recognized only too well that Dunkirk had been a humiliating defeat. He wrote in his *Memoirs*: "I remember the disgust of many like myself when we saw British soldiers walking about in London and elsewhere with a colored embroidered flash on their sleeve with the title 'Dunkirk.' They thought they were heroes, and the civilian public thought so too. It was not understood that the British Army had suffered a crushing defeat at Dunkirk and that our island home was now in grave danger."

Montgomery's division was ordered to dig itself into defensive positions on the Sussex coast; however, his experience in France convinced him that a purely defensive attitude was fatal. He sought a mobile, counter-attack role, enlisting the support of Churchill himself, bypassing his superiors to their annoyance. It was in the summer of 1940 on the south coast near Brighton that Montgomery first met Churchill. In his *Memoirs*, Montgomery relates the famous story that when he was asked by Churchill what he would drink at dinner, he replied – water. This "astonished" Churchill. Montgomery added that he neither drank nor smoked and was 100 per cent fit; Churchill "replied in a flash, that he both drank and smoked and was 200 per cent fit."

In July 1940 Montgomery was promoted to command the 5th Corps, stationed in Dorset and Hampshire, and from that time began his real influence on the training of the army in Britain. In his *Memoirs*, he wrote: "So the ideas and the doctrine of war, and training for war, which began as far west as Dorset, gradually spread along the south of England to the mouth of the Thames." In April 1941 he was put in charge of XII Corps, which held the crucial Kent area; and in December 1941 he took over South-East Command, re-named by Montgomery, "South-Eastern Army." Montgomery's impact is described in Brian Horrocks memoir, *A Full Life* [189]: "It was as though atomic bombs were exploding all over this rural corner of Britain." Before his arrival a peace-time atmosphere had existed. Everyone seemed to expect an invasion at any moment, but nobody was doing very much about it. All this changed almost overnight: "deadwood" (inefficient and lazy officers) were removed, wives and families were packed off home, and regardless of age or rank, every officer was ordered to carry out two cross-country runs weekly. Horrocks relates that Montgomery's senior medical officer protested against the no-exception rule and mentioned a senior staff officer: "'Colonel X must not run, sir. If he runs he will probably die.'" Montgomery replied, "'Let him die. Much better to die now rather than in the midst of battle when it might be awkward to find a replacement.'" The colonel in question did run and he did not die.

The 5th Corps was trained by Montgomery to be an all-weather combat formation – "in rain, snow, ice, mud, fair weather or foul, at any hour of the day or night – we must be able to do our stuff better than the Germans." There were constant training exercises followed by Montgomery's famous conferences where he played the role of teacher. Horrocks describes the scene: on the stage were large maps and diagrams, while the walls were covered with "No smoking" signs. Suddenly the audience would be called to attention, as Montgomery wearing battle-dress advanced to the center of the stage: "'Sit down, gentlemen,'" he would say in a sharp, nasal voice. "'Thirty seconds for coughing – then no more coughing at all.'" Perhaps for as long as two hours he would keep the listeners spell-bound as he described all the major points of the exercise.

Michael Carver's essay on Montgomery in, *Churchill's Generals* [207], makes the point that while he may have been unrealistic in thinking than an infantry division with hardly any tanks could conduct a mobile counter-attack, Montgomery must be credited with being among the first to recognize, when he was transferred to command XII Corps in May 1941, that the threat of invasion had passed and that it was more important to instil offensive spirit into the army and to prepare to attack. He dismissed any idea of a scorched-earth policy. In Montgomery's view, "There is no need for 'scorching-earth' whatever. We are not going to retreat. We will attack." In his *Memoirs*, Montgomery declared, "My whole soul revolted against allowing troops to get into trenches and become 'Maginot-minded.'"

The new wind of change brought in by Montgomery is described by Brian Urquhart in his 1987 memoir, *A Life in Peace and War* [390]. Urquhart, who would later become a bitter critic of Montgomery over Operation *Market-Garden*, was an eyewitness to one of Montgomery's conferences. When the war seemed endless and unwinnable, writes Urquhart, Montgomery made a "tremendous impression. Whatever else he may have been, Montgomery was a genius at morale-building and training, and we desperately needed both."

It was during this time that he first met General Claude Auchinleck, his immediate superior. In his *Memoirs*, Montgomery noted, "I cannot recall that we ever agreed on anything." Brian Montgomery, in his book, *A Field-Marshal in the Family*, tells the story of Auchinleck's order, during the invasion crisis after Dunkirk, that no soldier was to be parted from his weapon, at any time. Montgomery regarded the order as completely impractical, asking: "But what happens when a soldier goes to bathe in the sea, or when he is with his girl friend in the dark in the back row of the cinema? What does he do with his rifle then?" Once again he risked his career by giving orders that no one in V Corps was to obey the order. An "appalling row" occurred with Auchinleck's headquarters, and Montgomery was lucky that Auchinleck returned to India as Commander-in-Chief at that moment.

Historians have tended to blame Montgomery for the breakdown in relations between the two men: Ronald Lewin, in his account, *Montgomery as Military Commander* [222], observed that Montgomery was warm and considerate towards those of whom he approved, and "icy in his contemptuous disregard of those he rejected." In Lewin's opinion, "Throughout the war, and afterwards, Montgomery's conduct in respect of 'the Auk' was unpardonable." Alun Chalfont, in *Montgomery of Alamein* [70], faults Montgomery for withholding from Auchinleck – "in a most unprofessional way" – the whole-hearted support he had earlier given Brooke. In Chalfont's view, "it seems clear that only in the grave wartime situation could he [Montgomery] have reached the pinnacle of his profession . . . Presumably his insubordination was ignored in 1940 because his ability was outstanding."

"As for the men," wrote Alan Moorehead in *Montgomery: A Biography* [278], "the majority liked a colorful and eccentric leader. They liked the absence of brass-hattery and pomposity in Montgomery. They appreciated the fact that the bulk of their work went, not into useless ceremonial parades, but into very definite exercises in the trade of war. Deliberately Montgomery cultivated their friendship." To the men he was already "Monty."

An amusing account of an "attack" on Montgomery's headquarters – to test its defenses – is related in Michael Calvert's book, *Fighting Mad* [60].

In command of the South-Eastern Army, Lieutenant-General Montgomery was now an important and increasingly well-known officer in the British Army.

The Dieppe Raid

The most controversial event with which Montgomery was associated during his time as commander of the South Eastern Army was the raid on the French port of Dieppe. Charges of cover-ups and blunders abound. In the August 19, 1942 raid on Dieppe, Operation *Jubilee*, the 2nd Canadian Division suffered a casualty rate of 68 per cent, with over 900 men killed in a single day. Colonel C. P. Stacey, author of the *Official History of the Canadian Army in the Second World War* [367], wrote, "At Dieppe, from a force of fewer than 5,000 men engaged for only nine hours, the Canadian Army lost more prisoners than in the whole eleven months of the later campaign in North West Europe, or the twenty months during which the Canadians fought in Italy." It was Canada's greatest tragedy of World War II. As commander of the South Eastern Army, Montgomery was given a place in the chain of command; as far as the army was concerned, the final decision as to whether the raid was to be launched or not rested with him. Because of bad weather conditions in July, Montgomery had said "no" to the original operation, and recommended cancellation of the raid and that it should not be revived. Had Montgomery still been in command of the South Eastern Army in August, whether he could have overridden pressures to carry out Operation *Jubilee* (including the demand for a "Second Front Now" to help the Russians) is a matter of speculation. Montgomery was basically opposed to the raid. See Dominick Graham, *The Price of Command: A Biography of General Guy Simonds* [164].

Historian Brereton Greenhous of the Canadian Directorate of History and Heritage in Ottawa has described the Dieppe raid as a "rat's nest" for historians. The literature on the raid is extensive and all too often polemical. Canadians, understandably, continue to have particularly strong feelings about the raid. Lord Louis Mountbatten, head of Combined Operations with overall responsibility for the Dieppe raid, has been the main target for Canadian criticism. In his memoir, *Ruling Passions* [122], British journalist Tom Driberg refers to the dinner party episode where Canadian-born newspaper baron, Lord Beaverbrook hurled the accusation at Mountbatten – "You murdered my Canadians in order to wreck my Second Front campaign."

Military historian Ronald Lewin noted in his 1971 study, *Montgomery as Military Commander* [222], "There are Canadians who – pardonably – lay the catastrophe at his [Montgomery's] door." He further remarks that Montgomery had not helped matters by the inaccurate account which he provided in his *Memoirs* [268]. In his *Memoirs*, Montgomery faults the revived plan (after July 7) for two critical mistakes: the use of commandos instead of paratroops, and the elimination of the preliminary air bombardment. He wrote, "I should not myself have agreed to either of these changes." Montgomery observed that while lessons were learned from the operation, "I believe that we could have got the information and experience we needed without losing so many magnificent Canadian soldiers."

On the other hand, in his book, *The Watery Maze: The Story of Combined Operations* [141], Brigadier Sir Bernard Fergusson pointed out that Montgomery was in the chair and presided at the meeting on June 5 when the preliminary air bombardment was canceled.

An essential source on Montgomery during this time is the memoir of Goronwy Rees, *A Bundle of Sensations: Sketches in Autobiography* [327]. Rees was selected by Montgomery to be his liaison officer to Combined Operations Headquarters – "That's Admiral Mountbatten's show" – which was planning the Dieppe raid. Rees recalled how other officers sympathized with him when they heard he was being posted to Montgomery's staff – "He's a bit of a terror, you know . . . Very keen on physical fitness, and all that. Makes all his staff officers do a five-mile run once a week."

When Rees once remarked on the confusion and excitement at Combined Operations Headquarters, Montgomery said reflectively: "Yes, Admiral – [Mountbatten], Admiral – [Mountbatten], A very gallant sailor. A very gallant sailor. Had three ships sunk under him. *Three* ships sunk under him. (Pause). Doesn't know how to fight a battle." Judging from Rees book, Montgomery was never really interested in the project and did not like have responsibility without authority. His primary concern was with raising a new army in South-Eastern Command.

In his biography, *Monty: The Making of a General 1887-1942* [174A], Nigel Hamilton blames Mountbatten for the disaster; however, he concludes that the Dieppe plan "bears too many of the critical fingerprints of the Commander South Eastern Army for Bernard Montgomery to be completely exonerated." In Hamilton's view, the fatal flaw was the lack of naval support fire, a failure he traces to Mountbatten – "Like a spoilt child he toyed with men's lives with an indifference to casualties that can only be explained by his insatiable, even psychopathic ambition." Instead of accepting the raid's cancellation on July 7 as final – because of bad weather – Hamilton charges that Mountbatten, driven by "hunger for power and prestige," pushed to re-mount the raid on August 19. Montgomery, on the other hand, concerned that security may have been breached, was adamant that it should be canceled "for all time." Montgomery's total opposition to revival of the raid led to his exclusion from the new chain of command altogether!

The Mountbatten side of the Dieppe affair is presented by Philip Ziegler in his highly acclaimed biography, *Mountbatten* [412]. Ziegler took issue with Nigel

Hamilton's "strikingly intemperate attack on Mountbatten." In varying degrees, Mountbatten, Captain John Hughes-Hallett (on the Combined Operations staff), and General Henry Crerar of the Canadian I Corps, would later blame Montgomery for the disaster.

In 1989 appeared the controversial and provocative account, *Unauthorized Action: Mountbatten and the Dieppe Raid* [395] by the Canadian scholar Brian Loring Villa. Reviewer Hew Strachan noted in the *Times Literary Supplement* that the author showed, "excessive predilection for conspiracy theory when the arguments for cock-up may be less complex but more convincing." Villa places blame for the disaster squarely on the shoulders of the late Lord Louis Mountbatten. He concludes that Mountbatten approved the Dieppe raid on his own initiative, after the July 7 cancellation, without the authorization of the Chiefs of Staff or Churchill. On the question of cancellation of the preliminary bombing, Professor Villa states that the abandonment of the bombing has always been blamed by Mountbatten and his defenders on Montgomery. In defense of the bombing decision, Villa remarks that Montgomery and the other commanders felt that the proposed bombing was not large enough to be effective. A massive bombing effort on Dieppe had been ruled out since Bomber Command's highest priority was the attack on Germany. A night-bombing attack on Dieppe, with less than maximum forces, would probably not have been effective against the German defenses. Canadian historian Brereton Greenhous thinks that bombing would have made no effective impact on German defenses.

Professor Villa criticizes Ziegler in his article, "Mountbatten, the British Chiefs of Staff, and Approval of the Dieppe Raid," in *The Journal of Military History* [394]. Ziegler's rebuttal, in the same issue, contends, "If Mountbatten had indeed laid on the operation without the prime minister's authority, Churchill's fury would have been terrible and must have left some mark – on Mountbatten at least!"

Villa's *Unauthorized Action* served as the basis for the 1993 Canadian television four-hour min-series, *Dieppe* [114]. Although Mountbatten is portrayed as the main villain of the fiasco, the docu-drama does challenge conventional wisdom that Canadians were innocent colonials duped by the British; the script points out that Canadian commanders insisted on an all-Canadian operation. As Villa remarks in *Unauthorized Action*, after two years of inaction, the Canadian military leadership "threw heart and soul into securing the lead in raiding activities." The same point, that the Canadians had been "kicking their heels for so long," is brought out in Jacques Mordal's 1962 book, *Dieppe: The Dawn of Decision* [281]. Mordal remarks that Montgomery had never shown anything but "lukewarm enthusiasm" for the raid. In 1963 appeared *Dieppe: The Shame and the Glory* [339], by Terence Robertson, a British journalist. Robertson selected Mountbatten and Montgomery as the principal culprits, blaming Montgomery for adoption of the frontal attack strategy, although it is doubtful that flank attacks on Dieppe would have been any more successful. The author accepted the Establishment view that the lessons learned were well worth the Glory.

In his entry for the *Dictionary of National Biography* [113], Brigadier E. T. "Bill" Williams, the Oxford don who became Montgomery's Intelligence chief, remarked that Montgomery was inclined to be reticent "on this score [his involvement in the Dieppe raid]" in his later years. Montgomery burned all his own papers relating to the raid.

Other sources include W.A.B. Douglas and B. Greenhous, "Canada and the Second World War: The State of Clio's Art," in *Military Affairs* [121]; Lord Lovat, *March Past* [231]; Lucian Truscott, *Command Missions* [387]; Strome Galloway, *The General Who Never Was* [154]. Canadian Galloway remembered that by 1942 the war had become a real bore – "fed-up, browned-off" – for Canadian troops in England. Eric Maguire's, *Dieppe, August 19* [241], is a short, lucid account that points out that most of the lessons of Dieppe could have been learned in a cheaper way; Brigadier General Denis Whitaker and Shelagh Whitaker, *Dieppe: Tragedy to Triumph* [402], which blames Churchill for the tactical failure of the raid. Grim photographs of the carnage on Dieppe beach are found in R.W. Thompson's article, "Massacre at Dieppe," in Purnell's *History of the Second World War* [380].

In John P. Campbell's 1995 book, *Dieppe Revisited: A Documentary Investigation* [61], which is based on the reading of wartime German records, he asks the question, "Another book about Dieppe?" He knew, however, that the long-running controversy over the parentage, purpose, and planning of the Dieppe raid continues.

Chapter 5

El Alamein to Tunis

> I was leaving England to exercise high command in the field.
> The work and experience of many years were about to be put to
> the test.
>
> Montgomery, *Memoirs*

The Montgomery-Auchinleck Controversy

At about 7 a.m. in the morning of August 8, 1942, while Montgomery was shaving in London, he received a telephone call from the War Office. On the previous day he had been ordered to take command of the British 1st Army, and begin working under Eisenhower on the plans for Operation *Torch*, the landing in French North Africa planned for November. But the new telephone call canceled those orders; to quote from Montgomery's own *Memoirs* [268] – "I was to hold myself ready to proceed to Egypt at once to take command of the Eighth Army in the desert." General "Strafer" Gott, who had been selected to command the Eighth Army, had been killed, and Montgomery was appointed to take his place. His immediate superior (and former student at Camberley) would be General Harold Alexander, the newly appointed Commander-in-Chief, Middle East. Alun Chalfont observed in *Montgomery of Alamein* [70] that the War Office phone call "changed Montgomery's entire career and possibly even the course of the war as well."

After a summer of defeats, capped by the surrender of Tobruk in June and a four-hundred mile retreat, the British Eighth Army, made-up primarily of troops from Britain, Australia, India, New Zealand, and South Africa, uneasily awaited Field Marshal Erwin Rommel's next attack. The Suez Canal and the Middle East itself seemed wide open to Axis conquest.

Prime Minister Winston Churchill's first choice as commander of the Eighth Army had been General Gott, see his volume, *The Hinge of Fate* [275]. It was

General Alan Brooke, the Chief of the Imperial General Staff, who "was very anxious to place Monty in command of the Eighth Army." Brooke's views are to be found both in his diary edited by Arthur Bryant, *The Turn of the Tide* [49], and in David Fraser's excellent biography, *Alanbrooke* [144]. Brooke wrote that he "pressed for Monty to replace Gott. Had some difficulty; PM. rather in favor of [General H.M. "Jumbo"] Wilson." Brooke regarded Montgomery as the best tactical commander in the British Army: "I never interfere with Monty in tactical matters," Brooke once said to a colleague, "he's generally right", but then with a twinkle, "and he doesn't let you forget it!" With the assistance of Field Marshal Jan Smuts, however, Brooke prevailed and Montgomery took command in the Western Desert. On August 19, Brooke visited Montgomery's desert headquarters, confiding to his diary: "He is in tremendous form, delighted at being out here, and gave me a wonderful feeling of relief at having got him out here."

In the introduction to *Churchill's Generals* [207], John Keegan observes that Montgomery may not have conformed to the Churchillian military ideal, which was personified by the handsome, gracious, and physically courageous, Alexander – a man with panache. Yet, as Keegan notes, in some strange way the two personalities of Churchill and Montgomery were to mesh by antithesis. In Keegan's view, no more creative tension existed in Churchill's war leadership than that between himself and Montgomery.

A balanced view of Alexander is to be found in Brian Holden Reid contribution to Keegan's, *Churchill's Generals*[207]. Reid comments that Alexander was "perhaps the last of the great British amateur generals."

Montgomery's first few hours and days in the desert are graphically described in his *Memoirs* [268]. Initially titled, *The Sparks Fly Upward*, the memoirs caused an uproar on both sides of the Atlantic, and no statement caused more outrage than Montgomery's claim that Auchinleck had intended to withdraw from the El Alamein position.

Soon after his arrival in Cairo, on August 12, 1942, Montgomery was taken straight to see Auchinleck. In his *Memoirs* Montgomery records that, "Auchinleck took me into his map-room and shut the door; we were alone." According to Montgomery's account, Auchinleck's plan of operations were based on the fact that "at all costs the Eighth Army was to be preserved 'in being' and must not be destroyed in battle. If Rommel attacked in strength, as was expected soon, the Eighth Army would fall back on the Delta; if Cairo and the Delta could not be held, the army would retreat southwards up the Nile, and another possibility was a withdrawal to Palestine. Plans were being made to move the Eighth Army H.Q. back up the Nile. . . I listened in amazement to this exposition of his plans... I was not to take command till the 15th August . . . "

Stung by the allegation that he had intended to withdraw from El Alamein, Auckinleck threatened legal action. In later editions of his memoirs, Montgomery, under duress, softened somewhat his criticism of Auchinleck. Auchinleck is defended by Philip Warner's essay in *Churchill's Generals* [207]. In the same volume, Michael Carver concludes that "it [Montgomery's allegation] was not far off the mark."

Did Montgomery misinterpret Auchinleck's pessimism? In his volume, *Monty: The Making of a General* [174A], Nigel Hamilton wrote that Montgomery had "the caricaturist's gift for over-simplification and exaggeration for effect." The "Auk" never denied having informed Montgomery about his contingency plans for withdrawal if Rommel was successful. But he completely denied that withdrawal to the Nile was uppermost in his mind. Hamilton thinks that Montgomery "may well have exaggerated" Auchinleck's pessimism, but he was definitely not inventing the preparations for a possible withdrawal. Hamilton sees "distinct parallels" between Montgomery's arrival in Egypt in 1942 to his assumption of command of Auchinleck's 5th Corps in 1940: in both cases he wanted to restore aggressive morale.

General Sir Brian Horrocks, in his memoir, *A Full Life* [189], attempted "to ferret out the truth" regarding the withdrawal controversy. Horrocks, who had been a corps commander at the time, writes "There is no doubt that Monty really believed this [Auchinleck's intention to withdraw] to be so, yet Field-Marshal Auchinleck has flatly denied that he ever said anything of the sort." Horrocks believed that Auchinleck wanted to return to the offensive as soon as possible. On the other hand, headquarters staff in Cairo continued to work on contingency plans should a further withdrawal become necessary. Horrocks writes, "There is no doubt that at this period defeatism was prevalent in the rear and particularly in Cairo." In Horrocks view, it is understandable that Montgomery should have concluded that a further withdrawal by the 8th Army was contemplated. Montgomery could also see that too many troops were being kept in Cairo as part of Auchinleck's reserve. There were endless rumors of withdrawal in Cairo. Author Olivia Manning in her essay, "The Flap," published in Purnell's *History of the Second World War* [246], describes the atmosphere in Cairo in August 1942 as one of "incipient panic."

Montgomery's accusation that Auchinleck intended to withdraw from El Alamein is denounced by his brother in, *A Field-Marshal in the Family* [272], calling the charge "most unfair and wholly unjustified." A former officer in the Indian Army, Brian Montgomery describes Auchinleck as a "very friendly and charming person, always ready to listen to anyone else's opinion." The best biography of Auchinleck remains John Connell's 1959 account, *Auchinleck* [87]. A perceptive assessment of the Auk is that by Correlli Barnett in Michael Carver's 1976 volume, *The War Lords: Military Commanders of the Twentieth Century* [64]. Auchinleck died in Marrakech, Morocco, on March 23, 1981. Field-Marshal Michael Carver, a veteran of El Alamein and a military historian in his own right, commented in a review for the *Times Literary Supplement*, that there had been too much bitter partisanship between the Montgomery-Auchinleck camps. Carver blamed Montgomery for much of the misunderstanding.

The day after his controversial meeting with Auchinleck in Cairo, Montgomery left for British Eighth Army Headquarters in the desert where he found the atmosphere "dismal and dreary . . . It was clear to me that the situation was quite unreal and, in fact, dangerous. I decided at once to take action." (*The Memoirs*). Montgomery's sudden seizure of command of the 8th Army two days early is criticized by both Ronald Lewin – "an act probably without parallel in the annals of the British Army" – and Alun Chalfont – a sign of Montgomery's "animus [toward the "Auk"]."

A particularly important source for assessing Montgomery's impact on the 8th Army is the memoir by Francis de Guingand, *Operation Victory* [109]. Before his selection by Montgomery as his new chief of staff, de Guingand had served in the same position under Auchinleck and liked him very much.

De Guingand attended the evening meeting of August 13 where the new commander of the 8th Army addressed his entire staff. Montgomery had already issued his famous "no withdrawal" order. Remembering the Greek words at Thermopylae, "Go, tell the Spartans, thou that passeth by, That here, obedient to their laws, we lie," Montgomery declared that the 8th Army would, if necessary, do the same at El Alamein: "Here we will stand and fight; their will be no further withdrawal. If we can't stay here alive, then let us stay here dead." He told the assembled officers that all transport must be sent back to the rear. There would be no withdrawal! De Guingand described the impact of Montgomery's address as "electric." In his own memoirs, Montgomery observed that "One could have heard a pin drop if such a thing was possible in the sand of the desert!" There was to be no more uncertainty about anything. "But," wrote Montgomery, "the old hands thought that my knees were very white!" The desert veterans did indeed wonder what the new, white-kneed general from England know about desert warfare. The reaction of seasoned veterans to Montgomery's words was "oh we've heard it all before." They had been back and forth across the desert many times in what they called "the Benghazi stakes."

At the end of a full day Montgomery went to bed "with an insubordinate smile," he noted in his memoirs – "I was issuing orders to an Army which someone else reckoned he commanded! [referring to Auchinleck]."

For the views of Dominion commanders, who welcomed the arrival of Montgomery, see D. M. Horner's, *High Command: Australia and Allied Strategy 1939-1945*. An extremely frank memoir is that by New Zealander H. K. Kippenberger, *Infantry Brigadier* [216]. General Bernard Freyberg, who commanded the 2nd New Zealand Division, later commented that the appointment of Montgomery and Alexander marked the end of his three unhappiest years in the desert. On his first visit to the New Zealanders, Montgomery said to General Freyberg: "I notice your soldiers don't salute." Freyberg replied: "Wave to them, sir, and they'll wave back." Monty did so. Freyberg is the subject of an essay by Dan Davin in, *The War Lords* [64]. The famed Australian commander, General Leslie Morshead of the 9th Australian Division, is the subject of J. H. Moore's, *Morshead – A Biography of Lieutenant-General Sir Leslie Morshead* [275]. Official national histories which contain references to Montgomery include New Zealand's R. J. Taylor, *Kiwis in the Desert: The North African Campaign, 1940-1943* [377], and J. L. Scoullar, *Battle for Egypt* [351]; Barton Maughan, *Tobruk and El Alamein: Australia in the War of 1939-1945* [251]; India's official history by P. C. Bharucha, *The North African Campaign, 1940-1943* [27]; General I. S. O. Playfair, the author of the British official history, *The Mediterranean and the Middle East* [317] was not a fan of Montgomery's. Neither was war correspondent,

Alexander Clifford, author of, *Three against Rommel: The Campaigns of Wavell, Auchinleck and Alexander* [79]. The absence of Montgomery's name in the title indicates Clifford's partisanship.

In 1985, General Charles Richardson published his memoir, *Flashback: A Soldier's Story* [335]. In 1942, Richardson was a young officer on the 8th Army planning staff. He doubts that the Auk could have turned the tide: "We youngsters felt that the removal of Auchinleck was essential."

In his delightful book, *Out of Step: Memoirs of a Field Marshal* [67], Michael Carver has many favorable things to say about Auchinleck as a person, but expresses less confidence in his ability as an armored commander. He is especially critical of Dorman-Smith's influence over Auchinleck. Also important is Michael Carver's study, *Harding of Petherton* [66]. John Harding (a future Field Marshal) was one of the young new commanders appointed by Montgomery, in his case the 7th Armored Division, the "Desert Rats."

Alam Halfa

The day after his arrival at the front, Montgomery toured the area and, as he relates in his memoirs, at once recognized that "the key to the whole Alamein position was the Alam Halfa Ridge." Several miles behind the Alamein line, it was undefended because there were no troops available.

Once thought likely to undermine Montgomery's military reputation more than that of any other Allied commander, the revelation in the 1970s that the Allies had broken the German military codes sent by the Enigma machine – the best kept secret of World War II – has not done so. Instead, the decoded German messages, called *Ultra* by the Allies, have illuminated both Montgomery's strengths and his weaknesses. In his landmark 1989 study, *Ultra and Mediterranean Strategy* [25], Ralph Bennett comments that Montgomery "appreciated at once that the Alam Halfa ridge was of vital importance, but was virtually undefended." Within hours Montgomery asked for and got the 44th Division from Alexander to garrison the ridge.

Like Montgomery, Rommel had previously spotted that Alam Halfa was the key to the El Alamein position and, two days after Montgomery's decision, Rommel informed Berlin that he planned to attack in the British southern flank, that is toward Alam Halfa ridge. Rommel's message was intercepted, and *Ultra* confirmed that Montgomery's decision had been the right one. The Battle of Alam Halfa at the end of September was Montgomery's first victory and halted Rommel's attempt to reach the Nile. In his memoir, *A Full Life* [189], General Brian Horrocks makes the point that while Rommel was leading his troops in person against the strongly-held British positions on the Alam Halfa ridge, Montgomery was already planning for the Battle of El Alamein. That was the difference between the two commanders, observes Horrocks. He further comments that

A German perspective on Monty's conduct of the battle is provided by General F. W. von Mellenthin's memoir, *Panzer Battles: A Study of the Employment of*

Armor in the Second World War [256]. Von Mellenthin served as Rommel's Intelligence Officer.

Besides illuminating the critical nature of Montgomery's decision to fortify Alam Halfa ridge before Rommel's attack, Bennett's book, *Ultra and Mediterranean Strategy* resolved some long-disputed points in the Montgomery-Auchinleck debate. The most articulate exponent of the Auchinleck position was Correlli Barnett whose brilliant account, *The Desert Generals* [16], set off a firestorm of controversy with its publication in 1960. In the 1981 preface to the second edition, Barnett acknowledged that his harsh criticisms of Montgomery were made at a time "when the Montgomery myth held almost unchallenged sway." In *The Desert Generals*, Barnett argued that Auchinleck had actually defeated Rommel in July 1942, at what he termed "first Alamein." Thus "first Alamein" was "the *true* turning-point" in the Desert War, not Montgomery's later battle.

Barnett relied heavily on the views of Auchinleck's disgruntled deputy chief of staff, Eric "Chink" Dorman-Smith, later O'Gowan. His exaggerated claims for "first Alamein" were expressed in an article, "1ˢᵗ Alamein: The Battle that Saved Cairo," in Purnell's, *History of the Second World War* [119].

Canadian historian John Ferris, in his important review essay, "Ralph Bennett and the Study of Ultra," in the journal, *Intelligence and National Security* [142], stated that Bennett's *Ultra and Mediterranean Strategy* "nails shut the coffin which encloses the earthly remains of *The Desert Generals*, R.I.P." After studying the Ultra decrypts of German signals, Bennett concludes that the evidence does not support the claim of a "first Alamein" victory. Rather it supports the view that Rommel's forces simply "ran out of steam," and that "first Alamein" was no more than a "temporary check."

Besides resolving the controversy over the July battles, Bennett put another contentious issue to rest. F. H. Hinsley, the official historian of British Intelligence in World War II, declared in his volume, *British Intelligence in the Second World War: Its Influence on Strategy and Operations, Vol. II* [184], that "No basic change was made to Eighth Army's plans following the change of commander." Bennett states flatly that the official historian "mischievously mishandles evidence" when he implies that Montgomery simply took over his predecessor's plan of operations. Personal bias, often in reaction to Monty's own overweening self-confidence has marred much of the literature, including the official histories.

After Alam Halfa, Montgomery wasted no time reorganizing, reequipping, and retraining the 8ᵗʰ Army. Under pressure from Prime Minister Churchill to attack Rommel, Montgomery was adamant that he would only attack when ready and not before. He got his way.

The Battle of El Alamein (October 23-November 4, 1942)

A vast literature has grown up around the Battle of El Alamein in which British Empire forces consisting of British, Australian, New Zealand, Indian, South African troops, together with some French and Greek units, decisively defeated

Rommel's German-Italian Army. Montgomery's official campaign narrative, *El Alamein to the Sangro River* [266], published in 1948, presented a chronological account of the battle. The El Alamein line was one of the few times in the desert war where outflanking the enemy was impossible: Rommel's heavily mined and fortified defensive line ran from the Mediterranean coast some 45 miles down to the edge of the impassable Qattara depression, with no open flank.

Some critics have claimed that the battle itself should never have been fought in the first place. In *The Desert Generals* [16], Correlli Barnett argued that El Alamein was "an unnecessary battle," since the Allied landings in Operation *Torch* would have forced Rommel to retreat anyway. In his not uncritical study of the Field Marshal, *Montgomery as Military Commander* [222], British military historian Ronald Lewin asked rhetorically: Would Churchill have calmly accepted inaction on the part of the 8th Army? Were the American supplied tanks not to be used? Would Hitler and Mussolini have permitted Rommel to withdraw at El Alamein?

On the night of October 23 a mighty artillery barrage opened the Battle of Alamein. After a weeks' hard fighting and ten thousand casualties – the figure Montgomery had predicted before the battle – the offensive seemed to stall and Prime Minister Churchill became anxious. The events are described in Brooke's diary, *The Turn of the Tide* [49] edited by Arthur Bryant. Summoned into Churchill's presence, Brooke met a "storm of reproach." "What," Churchill asked, "was *my* Monty doing now, allowing the battle to peter out. (Monty was always my [Brooke's] Monty when he was out of favor.). Had we not got a single general who could even win one single battle?" Keeping his own doubts to himself, Brooke calmed Churchill down and prevented any interference in the conduct of the battle.

After ten days of ferocious combat, the result was a complete Allied victory and Churchill was able to order that the church bells be rung throughout Britain. To quote from Ronald Lewin's, *Montgomery as Military Commander*, "On balance, Montgomery has received more praise than blame for his conduct of Alamein."

Michael Carver, who served under Monty for so much of the war, observes in his contribution to Keegan's work, *Churchill's Generals* [207]: "The battle had not followed Montgomery's 'master-plan'; but he had won it by his thorough preparation, his determination, his clear-headed realism and the flexibility with which he applied it, as well as by his considerable superiority in resources of all kinds, including in the air." Carver correctly notes that Montgomery had frequently changed his point of attack, switching his attacks "now here, now there" to avoid individual units being pushed to the point of destruction. Instead of claiming credit for such tactical flexibility, Montgomery always insisted that everything had gone according to plan. Short of infantry, he further displayed a willingness to sacrifice tanks (if not tank crews) which were replaceable rather than infantry. Carver, who fought in the battle, authored the standard account, *El Alamein* [65].

In his book, *The Causes of Wars and Other Essays* [191], historian Michael Howard (Lord Howard), rejected the notion that Montgomery "could not miss" at El Alamein since he possessed numerical and material superiority. Howard acknowledged that Montgomery had "enormous advantages," but there had been too many defeats – Dunkirk, Singapore, Burma, Greece, Crete, and then the humiliating surrender of Tobruk – to speak of a foregone conclusion. Rommel had come to seem invincible. A "Rommel myth" had grown up among many in the British 8th Army, observed Brian Horrocks in his memoir, *A Full Life* [189]. In just three months Montgomery had conveyed a new spirit of confidence to both cynical old desert veterans and untried newcomers. Lewin calls it an "extraordinary *tour de force*."

To author John Ellis, however, El Alamein was "never much in doubt." In his 1990 study, *Brute Force: Allied Strategy and Tactics in the Second World War* [129], Ellis argues that Allied victory in World War II was the inevitable consequence of their industrial superiority and that public relations officers and a press hungry for heroes only made generals like Montgomery "seem like great commanders." The author's interpretation is not new, but his argument is forcefully presented. Reviewer Carlo D'Este noted in *The Journal of Military History* [101] that Ellis relies too heavily on hindsight and that he overlooks the all-important qualities of generalship that inspires men to fight in a place like El Alamein. Montgomery's debut on the battlefield, writes military historian John Keegan in *The Second World War* [210], was one of the most brilliant in the history of generalship. Australian journalist Alan Moorehead notes in his biography, *Montgomery* [278], "To the whole Army now he was known simply as 'Monty.'" He was instantly recognizable by his Australian bush hat covered in badges which he had started to wear after Alam Halfa. He adopted the famous black beret when the Australian hat kept blowing off his head while riding in a tank during the Battle of Alamein. After stopping a few times to pick up the Australian hat, the tank driver suggested that Montgomery wear his beret: "Tell him to try this on. And if he wears it we'll get there a lot quicker." From this point on the black beret with two badges, a general's badge and the Royal Tank Corps insignia, became the sign by which his soldiers recognized the General and they waved and shouted to him – and he waved and shouted back. Officially asked twice to discard the beret as inappropriate to a general's dignity, Monty flatly refused. "I don't give two hoots what anyone says," he declared. "This beret is worth two divisions."

Morehead's *Montgomery* contains an excellent description of Montgomery's Army staff. He notes that Montgomery had "no truck at all" with the "old school tie" system. Pure merit was the only way of getting onto and staying a member of his staff.

And what of Rommel after El Alamein? In November he wished "I were just a newspaper vendor in Berlin." Important sources on Rommel that contain material relating to Montgomery include, *The Rommel Papers* [225] edited by B. H. Liddell Hart; the official German history by Charles Burdick, *Unternehmen Sonnenblume* [53]; Desmond Young's, *Rommel: The Desert Fox* [408]; and General David Fraser's, *Knight's Cross: A Life of Field Marshal Erwin Rommel* [146].

Pursuit

Whatever criticisms have been leveled at Montgomery's generalship at El Alamein, they pale in comparison to the derision heaped on his head for the failure to prevent Rommel's escape. In *The Desert Generals* [16], Correlli Barnett thought that Montgomery's pursuit "showed all the bustling confidence of an archdeacon entering a brothel." Alun Chalfont, *Montgomery of Alamein* [70], called the pursuit "abysmal." In the words of John Ellis in *Brute Force* [129], Montgomery "waddled tortoise-like behind Rommel across North Africa." In an otherwise favorable treatment of Montgomery, General E. K. G. Sixsmith in his book, *British Generalship in the Twentieth Century* [358], regretted that the pursuit phase was the "most disappointing" phase of the El Alamein victory. On the other hand, the British themselves had escaped from Rommel's grasp on prior occasions.

The *Ultra* disclosures of the 1970s gave renewed impetus to the charge that Montgomery had missed a golden opportunity to annihilate the Axis forces at El Alamein. The official historian of British Intelligence, F. H. Hinsley expressed frustration over the failure to destroy Rommel when he was down to just 11 tanks. Historian Ralph Bennett, in *Ultra and Mediterranean Strategy* [25], claimed that *Ultra* signals "powerfully supports these criticisms" of missed opportunities. Bennett, himself a wartime code-breaker, in his essay in the volume, *Codebreakers: The Inside Story of Bletchley Park* [185], edited by F. H. Hinsley and Alan Stripp, recalls that he found Montgomery's slow pursuit of Rommel "incomprehensible." Michael Howard, in *The Causes of Wars and Other Essays* [191], remarks that such criticism is legitimate since Montgomery excelled at the set-piece battle and not pursuit. It would have been nice, declares Howard, if Rommel could have been "put in the bag" but he thinks it would have changed the war only marginally.

On to Tripoli

On January 23, 1943, three months after El Alamein and 1,400 miles to the west, Montgomery's 8th Army took the previously unattainable seaport of Tripoli. In February, Montgomery appeared on the cover of American magazine, *Time*, with the caption, "The Lord and John Bunyan were with him." [383]. The article reported that one of his prized fan mail letters was from an Atlanta Sunday school teacher, signed by all her pupils, who "pray for you every night."

Churchill flew to Tripoli from Britain in the first week of February to congratulate the 8th Army and its commander. A splendid parade was organized for the Prime Minister who was deeply moved when the troops marched past him. Churchill would later say, "In days to come when people ask you what you did in the Second World War, it will be enough to say: I marched with the Eighth Army."

After Tripoli, Montgomery headed for Tunisia where Allied forces from Operation *Torch* were already fighting. The Afrika Korps, for the last time under Rommel's eyes, attacked Montgomery at Medenine on March 6. The Battle of Medenine is described by Nigel Hamilton in his volume, *Master of the Battlefield:*

Monty's War Years 1942-1944 [175A]. Hamilton calls Medenine "the most immaculate brief defensive battle fought in World War II, the crowning laurel upon the head of the Eighth Army." Brian Horrocks, in a *Full Life* [189], regards it as a model defensive battle second only to Alam Halfa.

Rommel's state of mind in this his last battle in Africa is discussed by David Fraser in his book, *Knight's Cross: A Life of Field Marshal Erwin Rommel* [146].

Desert Victory

Soon after the Battle of Medenine, Montgomery heard news of the film *Desert Victory*: "I understand I figure in it a good deal myself!!" he boasted. Filmed by a British Army Film and Photographic Unit under the direction of David MacDonald, *Desert Victory* begins with Montgomery's victory at El Alamein and ends 1,400 miles to the west in Tripoli. The Scottish born, Hollywood trained MacDonald was a British lieutenant-colonel. Immediately after its premiere at the Odeon Theater, Leicester Square, on March 5, 1943, MacDonald flew to the United States where a copy was shown to President Roosevelt who thought the film was "about the best thing that has been done about the war on either side." *A Time* magazine reviewer considered *Desert Victory* to be a "first-rate work of art."

The film's impact on American opinion was described by Isaiah Berlin in one of his famous despatches which can be found in the volume edited by H. G. Nichols, *Washington Despatches* [296]. In April 1943 Isaiah Berlin found that British military prestige was at its height owing to the vivid personalization of Montgomery and the 8th Army. A year later *Desert Victory* won an Oscar as the best documentary of 1943.

The Imperial War Museum Film and Video Archive holds the original master print as well as other materials relating to the film's production. Sources that discuss the film include: Clive Coultass, *Images for Battles: British Film and the Second World War, 1939-1945* [91]; Ivan Butler, *The War Film* [55]; Roger Manvell, *Films and the Second World War* [247]; Jeffrey Richards and Dorothy Sheridan, editors, *Mass Observation at the Movies* [334]; Peter Rollins, "Document and Drama in *Desert Victory*," *Film and History* [341].

The End in North Africa

Montgomery's last three offensives in Africa were now to follow – at Mareth, Wadi Akarit and Enfidaville. They involved assaults on well-prepared and naturally strong defensive positions. In *Master of the Battlefield* [175A], Nigel Hamilton compared the Mareth position to a Norman castle protected by a deep moat – the Wadi Zigzaou. Hamilton faults Montgomery for "dangerous over-confidence" before the battle, a consequence of fame, adulation, and a growing sense of infallibility after Medenine. In his *Memoirs* [268], Montgomery gives the impression that the main feature of the plan was an outflanking attack to the west supported by a limited frontal attack.

Ronald Lewin's study, *Montgomery as Military Commander* [222], calls the initial attack at Mareth a "total and unmitigated failure." In his campaign study, *Crucible of Power: The Fight for Tunisia 1942-1943* [240], critic Kenneth Macksey argues that Montgomery expected to break through the Mareth line with a frontal attack, and provided for only a weak outflanking movement. When the frontal attack failed, Montgomery displayed his realism and tactical flexibility by closing down his frontal attack and reinforcing his left hook. In *Churchill's Generals* [207], Michael Carver declares that while Montgomery must be given credit for reacting quickly to the initial failure, Mareth was "not a battle of which Montgomery could be proud." A useful account is that by General Francis Tuker, *Approach to Battle* [389]. The outspoken Tuker commanded the 4th Indian Division.

The final breakthrough was preceded by an innovative low-flying air blitz devised by Air Vice-Marshal Harry Broadhurst, the new commander of the Desert Air Force. He even took Montgomery's suggestion of hanging bombs onto fighter planes!

Montgomery's relations with Broadhurst's superiors, Air Marshals Arthur Tedder and Arthur Coningham, were far less satisfactory. Both airmen opposed close ground support for the army. In his biography, *Montgomery* [278], Alan Moorehead observes that while air-ground cooperation, thanks to Broadhurst, worked well at Mareth, "the happy issue of the affair did not endear Montgomery to his opponents." Relations between Tedder and Montgomery eventually soured, and they grew to dislike each other intensely. Tedder's memoir was aptly titled, *With Prejudice: The War Memoirs of Marshal of the Air Force Lord Tedder* [378]. For Coningham, see Vincent Orange's study, *Coningham: A Biography of Air Marshal Sir Arthur Coningham* [302]. Coningham's dislike of Monty grew to the point where it was unequaled in bitterness by any of the better-known quarrels of World War II. The anti-Montgomery stance of the air marshals is reflected in John Terraine's, *A Time for Courage: The Royal Air Force in the European War, 1939-1945* [379].

Italian General Giovanni Messe commanded the Axis army facing Montgomery's 8th Army. Messe's memoir, *Come Fini La Guerra in Africa: La "Prima Armata" Italiana in Tunisia* [255], is an important personal narrative. Montgomery's last battles in Tunisia, at Wadi Akarit and Enfidaville, were as brutal as any fought in North Africa. Michael Carver, in *Churchill's General* [207], is quite blunt: the only excuse of Montgomery's launching a "hopeless frontal assault at Enfidaville" was that he was preoccupied with revising the plan for the invasion of Sicily. In his *Montgomery as Military Commander* [222], Ronald Lewin declared that it was impossible to justify "such a wonton waste by a seasoned commander except on the grounds that he is mad, ill, or otherwise preoccupied." Montgomery was not mad but he was ill and he was deeply preoccupied with thoughts of Sicily. The same point is made in Alun Chalfont's, *Montgomery of Alamein* [70], that he had to concentrate on two things at once – Enfidaville and the upcoming invasion of Sicily, Operation *Husky*. Chalfont observes that like Dieppe, when Montgomery did not give a problem his full attention he was inclined to make mistakes.

Monty's own views are found in his *Memoirs* [268] and in his wartime messages to Brooke and Alexander which are found in the volume edited for the Army Records Society by Stephen Brooks, *Montgomery and the Eighth Army* [47]. He compared the rugged country on his front to the N. W. Frontier of India and completely unsuitable for armor. Highly critical of General Kenneth Anderson, who commanded the British First Army, which together with the U.S. II Corps and French XIV Corps, was approaching Tunis from the west, Montgomery believed that Anderson was "not fit to command an Army in the field" and should be removed. In his volume, *Master of the Battlefield* [175A], Nigel Hamilton credits Monty with "Masterminding the Final Offensive" in Tunisia in that Monty proposed to Alexander that the 8th Army transfer its weight (7th Armored Division, 4th Indian Division, and 201st Guards Brigade) to First Army to assist in the final blow on Tunis.

The Flying Fortress Affair

As the Tunisian campaign came to a close, the infamous "Flying Fortress" incident occurred in April 1943. When on April 10, the 8th Army entered the town of Sfax, Montgomery sent a message to Eisenhower: "Personal. Montgomery to Eisenhower. Entered Sfax 0830 this morning. Please send Fortress." The origin of this signal was a bet which Montgomery had made with Walter Bedell Smith, Eisenhower's chief of staff, that if he entered Sfax by April 15 Eisenhower would send him a Flying Fortress for his personal use. In his *Memoirs*, Montgomery records: "Later, I got properly ticked off by Brooke, the C.I.G.S., (Chief of the Imperial General Staff) for my action in the matter." In *The Turn of the Tide* (the Alanbrooke diary) [49], edited by Arthur Bryant, Brooke wrote that he hauled Monty "over the coals" for upsetting Anglo-American relations. Monty had considered the matter great fun; Ike did not.

During the Tunisian campaign, Eisenhower had visited Montgomery and spent the night. In a letter to Brooke, which is included in the volume edited by Stephen Brooks, *Montgomery and the Eighth Army* [47]: Montgomery noted, "I liked him very much. I should say his knowledge of how to make war and fight battles is not on a very high level!!"

Eisenhower's own view of Montgomery is found in *The Papers of Dwight David Eisenhower* [71], edited by Alfred D. Chandler, Jr., and Stephen E. Ambrose. In a confidential letter to George C. Marshall, Eisenhower described him as an "able tactician and organized" and "very conceited." Unfortunately, neither man really understood the other and their misunderstandings would grow.

Chapter 6

Sicily to the Sangro

> Planning so far has been based on assumption that opposition
> will be slight and that [Sicily] will be captured relatively easily.
> Never was there a greater error. Germans and also Italians are
> fighting desperately now in Tunisia and will do so in [Sicily].

Montgomery to Alexander, April 24, 1943

Return to England

On May 17 1943, five days after the Axis surrender in North Africa,
Montgomery flew back to England in his Flying Fortress. At Northolt airport near
London he was "mobbed" – wrote Nigel Hamilton, in his volume *Master of the
Battlefield* [175A], the first real indication that he had become a national hero. In
the street the crowds fought literally to touch his uniform – the man who had
brought victory to Britain's army after four years of war and defeat. When he went
to see the play *Arsenic and Old Lace*, the audience stood and cheered the
conquering hero.

Montgomery noted in his *Memoirs* [268] that "One thing made me feel lonely."
He did not receive an invitation to attend a Thanksgiving Service at St. Paul's
Cathedral to mark the end of the war in Africa. It was explained to him *after the
service* that it was desired to keep his presence in Britain a secret. Yet, to his
"delighted surprise," wherever he went he was followed by crowds. The incident
made him realize that if he was "pretty popular with a lot of people, I was not too
popular in some circles." Alan Moorehead, in his biography *Montgomery* [278],
noted that "The genuine opposition came almost entirely from the top and from
Whitehall and the West End of London." He was an upstart, vulgarly flamboyant,
a "film-star commander." Was not Alexander the actual brain behind the success?

The Invasion of Sicily

From the spring of 1943 until the end of the year, Montgomery was mainly engaged in fighting the Sicilian and Italian campaigns. It was a period of argument and dissension. Historian Ronald Lewin, in his excellent study *Montgomery as Military Commander* [222], cites an interview with General Miles Dempsey, British corps commander and later commander of the Second Army from Normandy to Germany. Shortly before his death, Dempsey told Lewin that in his opinion the part Montgomery played in making the final plan for *Husky* was his "finest hour." Alone among the senior Allied commanders, Montgomery had the courage to refuse to carry out a bad plan and to insist that it be carried out correctly. Without his intervention, the Allied landings in Sicily might have suffered a near-disaster as occurred later at Salerno and Anzio in Italy.

The original plan for Operation *Husky* called for dispersed landings on Sicily in the hope that if some failed, others would succeed. Montgomery's battles with the planners and commanders – "far more exhausting than my battles against the Germans" – can be read in his own words in Stephen Brooks's volume, *Montgomery and the Eighth Army* [47]. On March 13, 1943, Montgomery signaled to Alexander, "In my opinion the operation [*Husky*] planned in London breaks every common sense rule of practical battle fighting and is completely theoretical. It has no hope of success and should be completely recast." To Alan Brooke, he wrote, "There is a lack of 'Grip'. The *Husky* planning is in a hopeless mess. We have made such a mess of it so many times in this war that it makes me quite angry to see us drifting the same way now. I should have thought we had learnt our lesson – after nearly 4 years of war. But apparently not."

An important account of the campaign is the 1962 book by Hugh Pond, *Sicily* [322]. Critical of the original plan for *Husky*, Pond declared, "the most extraordinary hodge-podge plan was concocted." The author served in Sicily as a major in the British army. The reviewer for the *Times Literary Supplement* called Pond's account, "spirited but uneven." The review appeared under the title, "Botched Campaign."

A brief account is that by Captain S. W. C. Pack, *Operation HUSKY: The Allied Invasion of Sicily* [305]. The account is too heavily tilted to the naval side.

The most complete and balanced analysis of the Sicilian campaign is that by Carlo D'Este, *Bitter Victory: The Battle for Sicily, 1943* [97], published in 1988. Basing his views on thorough research, D'Este strongly defends Montgomery from the charge that his motivation for wanting to change the *Husky* plan was self-advancement. D'Este argues that the evidence suggests the opposite: what Montgomery did in the face of powerful opposition and potential ruin was an act of courage. He correctly exposed the chaos in planning and the absence of firm leadership at the top. Montgomery's motivation was based on military grounds and not megalomania, writes D'Este.

Montgomery's strongest opponents were the British air and naval commanders for *Husky*, Air Marshal Arthur Tedder and Admiral Andrew Cunningham. Both Tedder and Cunningham favored the concept of dispersed landings. D'Este observes that honest differences of opinion were now combined in a blood feud. Not long afterwards Cunningham ordered that Montgomery's name was not to be mentioned in his presence. On the other hand, Nigel Hamilton, in *Master of the Battlefield* [175A], includes an entry from Montgomery's diary in which he which he commented that Cunningham "has not much brains, and is out of his depth when planning a big-scale operation."

Air Marshal Tedder began to spread the word that Monty "thinks of himself as Napoleon," as Tedder remarked over lunch with General George Patton who was to command the U.S. 7th Army in Sicily. An essential source is the volume edited by Martin Blumenson, *The Patton Papers, 1940-1945* [38]. By May 9, however, Patton observed that he did not "wholly trust" Tedder who seemed more intent in creating an independent air force "than in winning the war," and that he [Patton] was completely reconciled to Montgomery's plan for the invasion.

On the subject of air power, Carlo D'Este notes that Montgomery thoroughly understood the need for close air-ground cooperation, and he insisted that his protege, the young Air Vice Marshal Broadhurst, should command the whole air support operation, instead of a more senior Air Marshal at Malta. In a message to Alan Brooke, printed in *Montgomery and the Eighth Army* [47], edited by Stephen Brooks, Montgomery wrote, "They propose in fact to split up this fighting machine [Eighth Army and the Desert Air Force] which I have spent months in creating, and introduce new personalities and untried methods." Tedder refused to relent and Broadhurst, who in 1944 was to find himself again caught between Tedder and Montgomery, now had a foretaste of that later bitter conflict between the two men. In his *Memoirs* [268], Monty complained that Broadhurst, who had worked so well with the 8th Army in the desert, "sat virtually unemployed in Tripoli; he did not come into the picture until we were firmly on shore and his squadrons could be moved to Sicily."

American generals Patton, Lucas and Bradley complained numerous times to Alexander and even to Eisenhower about the failure of the Air Force to provide direct ground support. The problem is mentioned by the official American naval historian Samuel Eliot Morison in his volume, *Sicily-Salerno-Anzio* [287].

In Bitter Victory, D'Este writes that after three months of rancorous debate the crisis was finally settled in one of the most unorthodox and comical encounters of the war – Montgomery's meeting with Bedell Smith, Eisenhower's Chief of Staff, in the Allied Forces Headquarters lavatory in Algiers! Not finding Bedell Smith in his office, Monty, in his own words (*The Memoirs*), eventually "ran him to ground in the lavatory" where Montgomery presented him with a new plan for the invasion of Sicily: the 8th Army and 7th U.S. Army would land side by side thus ensuring unity of effort. In the end this was the plan adopted for the invasion of Sicily.

Before formal approval of his plan, Montgomery addressed a high level conference at which he declared: "I know well that I am regarded by many people as being a tiresome person. I think this very probably true. I try hard not to be tiresome; but I have seen so many mistakes made in this war, and so many disasters happen, that I am desperately anxious to try and see that we have no more; and this often means being very tiresome." To suffer a defeat in Sicily, he noted, "would be a shattering blow to Allied morale all over the world." His verbatim remarks can be found in his *Memoirs* [268]. At the end of the Sicilian campaign, when Eisenhower came to stay with him at his headquarters overlooking the Straits of Messina, Montgomery recalled, "We had much fun that night at Taormina [his headquarters] and I remember asking Ike, to his great amusement, if he had ever been told that the final plan for Sicily had been put forward in an Algerian lavatory!"

The 1970 film *Patton* contributed enormously to the popular misconception of Montgomery's role in the invasion of Sicily As Carlo D'Este observes in *Bitter Victory* [97], the British general is portrayed in the film as a pompous figure wearing a paisley scarf who outlines his plan on the mirror of the Algerian lavatory, adding credibility to the false image of him as a buffoon determined to usurp Patton's role in *Husky*.

A favorable contemporary view of Montgomery by an American war correspondent is that by Quentin Reynolds in *The Curtain Rises* [331].

"I Should Run *Husky*."

If Montgomery's motive in pushing to alter the original *Husky* plan was based on sound military grounds rather than megalomania, he soon displayed his remarkable inability to understand that this was no longer a British war but now an Allied coalition effort. Biographer Nigel Hamilton, in his volume *Master of the Battlefield* [175A], declares that it is "a sad tale because Monty was so often correct ... from the purely military standpoint, but so rarely from that of coalition war." In his diary, Montgomery wrote, "I should run *Husky*." Convinced that the upcoming battle in Sicily should be under one Army commander, Montgomery suggested to Alexander, his immediate boss, that the American 7th Corps be placed under his command and that 8th Army headquarters handle the "whole operation of the land battle." If Alexander had "stamped firmly" on this "arrogant and ill-considered suggestion," Hamilton surmises that "Monty's blinkered approach to coalition command might have been stopped at the outset." Although the 7th Army was not placed under his command, Montgomery believed that he could conquer Sicily without American support.

The Battle for Sicily

In *Master of the Battlefield* [175A], Nigel Hamilton remarks that the invasion of Sicily was a forerunner of that larger cross-Channel invasion in 1944. As later in Northwest Europe, so in the first few days after landing in Sicily, Monty appears to have been made "heady by success." On July 13 he boasted that, "I shall be in Catania tonight." Not until twenty-three days later, however, after a long and costly battle, did 8th Army troops enter the deserted streets of that vital port.

Monty's confidence that the British 8th Army could win the Sicilian campaign single-handed, set the stage for the famous rivalry between Patton and Montgomery, although it is doubtful the British commander was aware of such a rivalry at this point. Montgomery was confident that, given the continued luck the Allies had enjoyed in landing virtually unopposed, there was now a chance that the campaign could be won in a matter of days. To carry his offensive northward, Montgomery requested that Alexander give him Route 124 while the "American Army hold defensively" facing west. The only problem was that Route 124 lay inside the American zone, and was intended for General Omar Bradley's 2 Corps. Alexander instructed Bradley to hand the road over to Montgomery who was attempting to repeat his Battle of Mareth left hook maneuver by attacking the enemy in the rear.

Far from being the ponderous, cautious general beloved by his critics, Hamilton argues convincingly in *Master of the Battlefield* [175A], that Monty's mistakes in Sicily stemmed from his "rash and impetuous desire to finish off the campaign before the enemy had a chance to react cohesively." The parallel with the earlier Battle of Mareth was "eerie," observes Hamilton. Once again Montgomery was trying to break through the enemy's main defensive position on a one-brigade front, against determined enemy resistance. "For once," writes Hamilton, "Monty had let down his army by his overambitiousness and his lack of ruthless adherence to his own rule of concentration in strength." He committed the same mistake, declares Hamilton, for which he had condemned General Anderson in Tunisia – "the 'partridge-like drive' he had himself mocked so contemptuously."

Carlo D'Este, in *Bitter Victory* [97], agrees with Hamilton's criticism of Monty, noting that by splitting his forces the British commander had stretched the 8th Army to a "dangerously thin limit." The Germans savagely resisted all attempts to break through their defenses. Lacking sufficient transport, the British 8th Army veterans had to march long distances and fight in the intense summer heat of a Sicilian summer. Malaria was another serious problem the troops had to face. In his well-written book, *The Campaign in Italy* [230], published in 1951, Eric Linklater described the terrain in Sicily as "superbly created for defense." Monty's offensive eagerness could not overcome these obstacles.

In his *Memoirs* [268], Montgomery relates the story of a British soldier in Sicily who was completely naked driving a truck and wearing a silk top hat! As the truck passed Monty, the driver leaned out of the window and took off his hat with a sweeping and gallant gesture. Montgomery reported that "I just roared with laughter." Although Montgomery was not overly concerned about dress so long as soldiers fought well, he felt obliged to issue the only order he ever issued about dress in the 8th Army; it read – "Top hats will not be worn in the Eighth Army."

In his attempt to win the Sicilian campaign quickly, before the enemy could bring more divisions over from Italy, Montgomery naively failed to consider the American reaction to the idea of simply protecting the left flank of the British 8th Army.

The Route 124 incident (the Vizzini-Caltagirone road) is described in General Omar Bradley's memoir, *A Soldier's Story* [43]. Bradley relates the story found in many sources that after the Sicilian campaign was over Patton visited Montgomery, and during their conversation Patton complained about the unfairness of Alexander's Route 124 directive. Monty looked at Patton with amusement and said, "George, let me give you some advice. If you get an order from Army Group that you don't like, why just ignore it. That's what I do." The depth of American bitterness over Route 124 was expressed by the U.S. Army historians who wrote the official volume of the campaign: Albert N. Garland and Howard M. Smyth, *Sicily and the Surrender of Italy* [155]. Garland and Smyth wrote, "For all practical purposes, Seventh Army could have stayed on the beaches; its brilliant assault achievements . . . completely nullified . . ."

In his biography, *Patton: A Genius for War* [101], published in 1995, Carlo D'Este noted that General Omar Bradley never forgave Montgomery for relegating his corps as a defensive shield for the 8th Army, even though, declared D'Este, the "real culprit" was Alexander. In his earlier account, *Bitter Victory* [97], D'Este made the point that Alexander was blind to the fact that the American army had made enormous strides since the previous February at Kasserine Pass. In the opinion of D'Este, Alexander's reputation has been "vastly overrated."

No less critical is Nigel Hamilton in *Master of the Battlefield* who uses such terms as "feeble,""virtual shambles" and "disgrace," in describing Alexander's conduct of the Sicilian campaign. Hamilton indicts Alexander for doing nothing to prepare either himself or his two prima donna army commanders, Montgomery and Patton, to fight the campaign in Sicily.

As it was, Montgomery's left hook using Highway 124 failed, as did his subsequent bold attempt to use parachute troops to seize the Primosole bridge, which carried the main road from Augusta to Catania. The battle for Ponte Primosole was the toughest of the whole campaign. Monty's separate thrusts had been stopped; German soldiers fought with courage and determination, as did their democratic counterparts.

In his 1971 study, *Montgomery as Military Commander* [222], Ronald Lewin observed that the Sicilian campaign brought Monty few laurels, though it was mainly due to him that it was "launched on the right foot." He rejected the "ususal criticism" of Montgomery's "caution" – because he did not make a headlong assault on the Mount Etna defenses – "This is nonsense," remarked Lewin.

General Eisenhower's opinion can be found in his memoir, *Crusade in Europe* [126]. Eisenhower remarks that at the time of the campaign "again there cropped up criticisms of Montgomery's 'caution,' which I had first heard among pressmen and airmen when he was conducting his long pursuit of Rommel across the desert. Criticism is easy – an unsuccessful attack brings cries of 'butcher' just as every pause brings wails of 'timidity' . . . Those critics of Montgomery who assert that he sometimes failed to attain the maximum must at least admit that he never once sustained a major defeat. In this particular instance I went over all details carefully . . . I believed then, and believe now, that a headlong attack against the Mount Etna position, with the resources available in the middle of July, would have been defeated."

Patton and the "Race" to Messina

In his book, *Bitter Victory* [97], Carlo D'Este makes clear that Montgomery had not only fully grasped the futility of his offensives to break through on the 8th Army front, but had arrived at the "cold realization that it was vital he and Patton cooperate." At Montgomery's invitation Patton flew to Syracuse on July 25 to discuss a common strategy for the final phase of the Sicily campaign. They quickly got down to business around Montgomery's staff car where a map of Sicily was spread across the hood. To Patton's amazement, Montgomery not only proposed that the U.S. 7th Army rather than the British 8th Army capture Messina. He even gave Patton *carte blanche* to cross his boundary line if the situation developed favorably in the north. A shocked and incredulous Patton assumed Montgomery must have some ulterior motive, and he became obsessed with beating the British to Messina.

The 1970 film *Patton* made much of the so-called race for Messina and perpetuated the popular myth of "Old Blood and Guts." In the person of actor George C. Scott, Patton has a deep, masculine voice as befits the heroic image. In reality, Patton had the "world's most unfortunate voice, a high-pitched womanish squeak" – see the second book by Kay Summersby Morgan, *Past Forgetting: My Love Affair With Dwight D. Eisenhower* [283]. Eisenhower's driver, confidante, and alleged lover, Summersby liked Patton. In the case of Omar Bradley, the 1970 Hollywood film perpetuated his popular image as the soft-spoken, folksy "G. I. General," one with whom the average civilian can readily identify. The real Bradley was the most ruthless senior American commander in the European war.

In contrast to the largely favorable images presented of Patton and Bradley, the film's screen writers, Francis Ford Coppola and Edmund H. North, depict Montgomery as a pompous buffoon, a comic nitwit. Not satisfied with caricature, the film portrayed Montgomery as a megalomaniac who, in the words of the *Time* magazine film critic, "nourishes his ego on the bones of American troops." The *Time* reviewer noted, "One can imagine an equally distorted British interpretation mounting Monty as a knight-errant and Patton as a gorilla."

The Messina question is discussed fully in both of Carlo D'Este's highly regarded studies, *Bitter Victory* and *Patton*. In the former, D'Este writes, "One searches in vain through Montgomery's notes, letters and diary for traces of rivalry with Patton. If prestige was at stake, it lay solely in the mind of Patton." One of the foremost military historians of World War II, D'Este concludes that, "The truth is that this misunderstood and historically distorted incident [the capture of Messina] was largely a myth." At the same time he acknowledges that American commanders had good reason to distrust British intentions. Ever since the American defeat at Kasserine Pass in Tunisia, British commanders had assumed that only the British could win the important battles. D'Este argues, however, that by July 25 Monty understood that Sicily was not going to be won by a spectacular unilateral British advance to Messina. This was no longer the same cocksure Monty who had only days earlier sensed a quick victory, with the U.S. 7th Army merely guarding his left flank. Ever the realist, he now called for a "full-blooded" American effort to take Messina.

In his biography, *Patton: A Genius for War* [101], described by one reviewer as an "instant classic," D'Este observes that, "For all his outward arrogance, which so infuriated many Americans, Montgomery was first and foremost an honorable professional soldier" who abhorred senseless casualties. In Sicily, concludes D'Este, Montgomery demonstrated that "he would not jeopardize the Allied effort for the sake of personal glory."

Nigel Hamilton, in his volume, *Master of the Battlefield* [175A] quotes the comments of Monty's chief of staff, Francis de Guingand, on the so-called race for Messina – "no, none. It was all balls that, about who was going to get to Messina first. We were *delighted* when we heard that Patton had got to Messina first." As for the scene in the film *Patton*, where Montgomery is seen leading a formal British parade into Messina, only to find Patton waiting for him, de Guingand remarked acidly: "Absolute cock, in the film: Monty marching at the head of the Highlanders – all balls!" D'Este refers to the film version as "apocryphal fantasy."

In his book, *Patton* [101], D'Este remarks that, "Contrary to popular belief, Montgomery greatly admired the accomplishments of the U.S. Army in Sicily." Just as the so-called race to Messina was a myth, so too was the notion that Montgomery belittled Patton or American soldiers. In a letter to Alan Brooke on July 27, which is printed in *Montgomery and the Eighth Army* [47] edited by Stephen Brooks, Montgomery wrote, "The Americans have done splendidly on our left and are very easy to work with."

Nigel Hamilton, in his biography, *Master of the Battlefield* [175A], quotes Warwick Charlton, the editor of the 8th Army newspapers, who only remembered one occasion on which Montgomery complained about an article – an editorial Charlton had written about Patton! Charlton had written the editorial following reports that Patton had slapped two soldiers suffering from combat fatigue. Montgomery would allow nothing derogatory about Patton to be printed in 8th Army newspapers. Charlton recalled, "And I got one of only two raps from Monty – that he was very upset [with the editorial on Patton] – that he didn't think this was right, that Patton was a good man . . ."

Messina fell to troops of the U.S. 3rd Division on August 17, 1943, thirty-eight days after the first Allied landings in Sicily.

Evacuation

A disappointing climax to the Sicilian campaign was the successful escape of four German divisions across the Straits of Messina to the mainland of Italy. In his *Memoirs* [268], Montgomery commented that the campaign had an "unsatisfactory ending in that most of the German troops on the island got away across the Straits of Messina to Italy, and this when *we* had complete air and naval supremacy. This was to cause us great trouble later on when we ourselves went into Italy." The basic problem, as he noted, was the lack of coordination between the Allied land, air and sea forces. As he wrote in his war diary towards the end of the campaign, "I have tried hard to find out what the combined Navy-Air plan is in order to stop him [enemy forces] getting away; I have been unable to find out. I fear the truth of the matter is there is NO plan. The trouble is there is no higher-up grip on this campaign." In *Master of the Battlefield* [175A], biographer Nigel Hamilton is blunt: "Monty's disgust – not only at the tragi-comedy relating to the Allied plans for Italy, but also at the total failure of the Allies to stop the German evacuation of Sicily – was barely concealed."

Hugh Pond in his book, *Sicily* [322], concluded that the "biggest failure" of the entire operation was the "complete and utter failure of both the Air Forces and the Navies to prevent the crossing of the German and Italian armies to the mainland."

The Messina evacuation controversy is discussed fully by D'Este in his account, *Bitter Victory* [97]. He notes that Tedder's defense of the Allied air effort, in his memoir, *With Prejudice* [378], is "weak." In his moving tribute, *Engage the Enemy More Closely: The Royal Navy in the Second World War* [15], Correlli Barnett is critical of the normally aggressive Admiral Cunningham, the commander of Allied naval forces. The Axis did not lose a single man in the evacuation from Sicily. Canadian official historian, G. W. L. Nicholson, in *The Canadians in Italy 1943-1945* [297], declared that the German evacuation of Sicily "must be numbered among the successful retreats in the history of warfare."

Cunningham appears to have been inhibited by memories of the Dardanelles campaign in 1915 where ships were battered by coastal gun batteries. One of the better post-war memoirs is Cunningham's, *A Sailor's Odyssey* [96]. Cunningham criticized Monty for failing to make better use of his amphibious capability. However, the official British naval historian, Stephen Roskill, in his volume *The War at Sea 1939-1945,* Vol. III, Part I, [344], did not think amphibious "end runs" were practical on the rugged Catania coast.

Other important sources include the official American naval history by Samuel Eliot Morison, *Sicily-Salerno-Anzio* [287]; the official British military history by C. J. C. Molony, *The Mediterranean and Middle East*, Vol. V, [263]; S. W. C. Pack, *Cunningham* [306]; Oliver Warner, *Cunningham of Hyndhope: Admiral of the Fleet* [396].

An invaluable source is Captain Harry C. Butcher's, *My Three Years With Eisenhower* [54]. Butcher was Eisenhower's naval aide, and his warm and friendly portrait of Ike, is in sharp contrast to Ralph Ingersoll's critical view in *Top Secret* [196] that Eisenhower was a British stooge. While the warning *caveat emptor* is fully justified in the case of Butcher's diary, reviewer Quentin Reynolds was correct in noting at the time that it was "worth $5 of anybody's money." The diary reflects the growing anti-Monty sentiment within Eisenhower's Allied headquarters. A close-up portrait of Patton is found in Charles Codman's memoir, *Drive* [81]. The author was an aide-de-camp to Patton.

The Canadians

For the first time since the disastrous Dieppe Raid the year before, Canadian troops saw action in Sicily. When General Andrew McNaughton, the commander-in-chief of Canadian forces in Europe, set off for Sicily to visit the Canadian troops there, Montgomery refused to allow him to land. He not only banned McNaughton from visiting Sicily but threatened to have him arrested if he so much as set foot on the island! In his *Memoirs* [268], Montgomery defended his decision on the grounds that the 1st Canadian Division had not been in action before and he was determined that they be left alone. He spoke to General Guy Simonds, the young and inexperienced divisional commander, about McNaughton's intended visit and Simonds replied, "For God's sake keep him away." In his book, *Bitter Victory* [97], D'Este comments that Montgomery's long-standing ban on visitors was well known, and that he did not discriminate against McNaughton in the enforcement of this strict policy. Defense of Montgomery is found in General Francis de Guingand's memoirs, *Operation Victory* [109] and *Generals at War* [108]. The episode is noted in Captain Butcher's diary, *My Three Years With Eisenhower* [54]. Ike felt "disinclined to intrude in such a family matter."

The official Canadian historian, C.P. Stacey, takes the reasonable position in his book, *Arms, Men and Governments: The War Policies of Canada, 1939-1945* [366], that despite McNaughton's bad timing and stubbornness, the incident might have been resolved if Montgomery and Alexander had agreed to a short, face-saving visit. See also Stacey's, *A Date with History: Memoirs of a Canadian Historian* [365]. In his book, *Sicily* [322], Hugh Pond refers to McNaughton as "a crusty man at the best of times."

At the end of the campaign, McNaughton was allowed to visit Sicily and gained a measure of revenge when he stayed at Montgomery's headquarters in a beautiful villa at Taormina, high on the cliffs overlooking the Straits of Messina, with the Italian mainland in the distance. Alun Chalfont, in his account *Montgomery of Alamein* [70], wrote: "Surveying the luxurious headquarters, he [McNaughton] addressed his austere host in terms designed to reduce him to a condition of speechless rage – 'Not going soft, are you, Monty?'"

As for the Canadian troops themselves, in his *Memoirs* Montgomery declared, "The Canadians were magnificent in the Sicilian campaign."

The Italian Campaign

In his *Memoirs*, Montgomery wrote, "If the planning and conduct of the campaign in Sicily were bad, the preparations for the invasion of Italy, and subsequent conduct of the campaign in that country, were worse still."

Historian Ronald Lewin, in his *Montgomery as Military Commander* [222], observed that a "certain acidity" marks Monty's brief account of the Italian campaign in his *Memoirs*. Michael Carver points out in his essay in Montgomery in *Churchill's Generals* [207], edited by John Keegan, that he was not "at his best in Italy fundamentally perhaps because he did not believe in the campaign at all. He thought it a blind alley." To Montgomery, Italy seemed to lead nowhere. In December 1942, after Alamein, he had suggested to the CIGS, Alan Brooke, that they invade across the English Channel rather than move against Italy. His suggestion received a sharp rebuff from Brooke. The correspondence is printed in, *Montgomery and the Eighth Army* [47], edited by Stephen Brooks. Montgomery was constantly demanding a clear aim and plan, which the Italian campaign never could provide. Lewin observes that Montgomery's criticism of the lack of clarity and direction from above was correct from an Army commander's point of view, but the situation was far more complicated from Eisenhower's "lonely eminence."

If Monty did not believe in the Italian campaign, neither did he think his landing across the Straits of Messina, Operation *Baytown*, had any real strategic purpose. In the *Memoirs* [268], he remarked, "In my view, *Avalanche* [the landing of the 5th Army at Salerno] was a good operation to carry out; everything should have been put into it from the very beginning and all endeavors concentrated on making it a great success. This was not done." As with *Husky*, Montgomery had favored a concentrated assault. Instead the two Allied armies, General Mark Clark's 5th and Monty's 8th, were landed hundreds of miles apart, with the latter given no role except to secure the Straits of Messina.

Salerno

Montgomery has frequently been criticized for his response to the 5th Army's life and death struggle at Salerno. General Mark Clark's invasion force was very nearly driven back into sea, saved perhaps only by naval gunfire support.

His biographer, Nigel Hamilton, writes in *Master of the Battlefield* [175A], that "Monty's worst fears about Salerno were soon to be confirmed." Montgomery compared the situation to that in Tunisia earlier in the year, when Rommel had attacked at Kasserine Pass and Alexander had asked Montgomery to push forward and draw the Germans on to the 8th Army front, resulting in the great defensive victory at Medenine.

Referring to the Salerno crisis, Captain Harry Butcher recorded in his diary, *My Three Years With Eisenhower* [54], "Montgomery has a great chance to be a hero." The controversy is discussed by soldiers-turned-military historians Dominick Graham and Shelford Bidwell in their 1986 account, *Tug of War: The Battle for Italy, 1943-1945* [163]. Reviewer Dennis Showalter noted that Graham and Bidwell have written "easily the best single-volume study of the Italian campaign in any language."

The Graham and Bidwell volume surpassed the earlier studies by Eric Linklater, *The Campaign in Italy* [230], G. A. Shepperd, *The Italian Campaign 1943-45: A Political and Military Reassessment* [254], and General W. G. F. Jackson, *The Battle for Italy* [204]. Brigadier C. J. C. Molony wrote the official British account, *The Mediterranean and the Middle East*, Vol. V, [263]; Martin Blumenson wrote the official U.S. Army Greenbook volume, *Salerno to Cassino* [39]; G. W. L.

Nicholson wrote the official Canadian history, *The Canadians in Italy 1943-1945* [297]. General Mark Clark, commander of the 5th Army, wrote his memoir, *Calculated Risk* [76]. For Alan Brooke's views consult Arthur Bryant's, *Triumph in the West* [50]. Author John Strawson, in *Gentlemen in Khaki: The British Army 1890-1990* [370], declares that Monty was "never at his best in Italy." A useful account of Salerno is Eric Morris's, *Salerno: A Military Fiasco* [288]. Observations on Montgomery are found in, *The Curtain Rises* [331], by the American war correspondent, Quentin Reynolds; *Nine Rivers from Jordan* [205], by the BBC correspondent, Denis Johnstone, and the *Daily Telegraph* war correspondent, Christopher Buckley, *Road to Rome* [51]. The shortcomings of field marshal Alexander are brought out in Brian Holden Reid's essay, "The Italian Campaign, 1943-45: A Reappraisal of Allied Generalship," in *Decisive Campaigns of the Second World War* [160], edited by John Gooch. The viewpoint of German commander Albert Kesselring is found in, *The Memoirs of Field Marshal Kesselring* [214].

Graham and Bidwell declare that Montgomery had made it clear in August that he considered Operation *Baytown* misguided and the distance between the two landings dangerous. The two authors note, "One cannot help feeling that he (Monty) enjoyed being proved correct." As for the suggestion that he might have dispatched a sort of flying column to Salerno, they argue that it could only have been a small token force, a gesture, and perhaps misinterpreted. He could then have been accused of trying to steal the credit of Clark's success. Besides, declare Graham and Bidwell, such an improvisation was completely foreign to Monty's military philosophy. In their opinion the blame lies with General Alexander for encouraging in the first place the idea that the 8th Army could reach Salerno in time to do any good.

Although advance elements of the 8th Army reached Salerno on September 17 (an enterprising band of journalists from 8th Army headquarters had managed to arrive earlier at the Salerno beachhead), Graham and Bidwell observe that in Calabria the British had to advance "forward over crest and crag through as complete a belt of demolitions as hitherto seen in war." Roads were blocked and bridges destroyed every few miles. The same point is made by Colonel Dick Malone in his book, *Missing from the Record* [245]. Canadian Malone's 1946 account was largely a reply to the "lopsided" writings of Butcher and especially Ingersoll, which he claimed were uninformed and "even malicious."

Ronald Lewin, in *Montgomery as Military Commander* [222], concludes that Monty did what he could in the circumstances: "It cannot justly be maintained, as it sometimes is, that Montgomery crawled to the aid of Clark." But as Nigel Hamilton remarks, Monty proceeded to claim credit for saving the day, behaving in his "most offensive 'saviour' manner."

Before the end of September, the 8th Army had taken all the three provinces of Calabria, Lucania, and Apulia, and the vital Foggia airfield complex. From now on the 8th Army advanced along the Adriatic coast, from one river to the next, towards the River Sangro in front of the Gustav defensive line. In his usual concise and graphic style, Alan Moorehead wrote in, *Montgomery: A Biography*

[278], "It made no difference if you captured one river valley; another lay just beyond. And beyond that more mountains, more valleys, more impossibly entrenched positions." The weather grew worse week by week. By mid-December it was clear to Montgomery that it was futile to continue operations, and he closed down the offensive. The battle for the Sangro was Montgomery's last in Italy.

If Montgomery was not at his best in Italy, he was now to embark upon what Alun Chalfont, *Montgomery of Alamein* [70], called "the greatest operation of the war."

On December 24, he received instructions to return to Britain to take command of 21 Army Group preparing to open the Second Front in western Europe. He remarked in his *Memoirs*, "I was not sorry to leave the Italian theatre. I made a quiet resolve that when we opened the second front in North-West Europe we would not make the same mistakes again: so long as I had any influence in the responsible circles concerned."

On the last day of December 1943, Monty handed over his beloved 8th Army to General Oliver Leese and left Italy for Marrakech to spend the night with Churchill on his way back to Britain. He said his farewell in the opera house at Vasto, a picturesque town on the Adriatic coast. His chief of staff, Freddie de Guingand described the scene in his memoir, *Operation Victory* [109]. De Guingand found the occasion "intensely moving." In his biography, Alan Moorehead writes, "This [8th Army] was his family and these were his children. Could he not make his family a million men? Could he not embrace so many more like these? And could they not go anywhere together?"

On December 31, Montgomery took off in his Dakota airplane and flew to Marrakesh, Morocco, where Churchill was recovering from a recent illness. Montgomery describes the subsequent events in his *Memoirs* [268]. On New Year's Eve, Churchill asked Montgomery to read a copy of *Overlord*, the code name for the invasion of Normandy, and to give him his opinion of the plan. In the report that he handed to Churchill in his bed next morning, Montgomery wrote, "My first impression is that the present plan is impracticable." Not only was the size of the invasion force too small (only 3 divisions), but it committed the same mistake that was made at Salerno and Anzio: namely confining the invasion to one easily contained beachhead.

That night Montgomery left Marrakesh for Britain. Supreme Allied Commander Dwight Eisenhower refused to allow him to complete the journey home in the two-engine Dakota, and Monty transferred to an American four-engine C54. "I do not look with favor on risking your neck on a two engine transport," wrote Eisenhower, the full copy of which is found *The Papers of Dwight David Eisenhower* [71] edited by Alfred D. Chandler, Jr. "Right or wrong, genius or mere adventurer, Montgomery was too valuable to lose at this moment," wrote Alan Moorehead in his 1946 account, *Montgomery: A Biography* [278].

The appointment of Montgomery to command Allied ground forces during the Normandy campaign was by no means a forgone conclusion. Eisenhower preferred the agreeable and charming Alexander who was popular with almost everyone, including Churchill. The contemporary criticisms of Monty, ranging from "too slow," to his jeers and cruel remarks about other officers, are succinctly presented by Alan Moorehead in his 1946 biography, *Montgomery* [278]. Brooke, however, was determined that Montgomery should have the *Overlord* command. Brooke's views can be found in volume II of his diaries edited by Arthur Bryant, *Triumph in the West 1943-1946* [50].

In his fascinating and sympathetic biography, *Alanbrooke* [144], David Fraser comments that the British Chief of the Imperial General Staff regarded Montgomery as "Britain's outstanding tactical commander, and sufficiently ruthless in pursuit of victory." For the moment Montgomery was accepted as the key man who was to lead the actual assault on Hitler's Fortress Europe.

Chapter 7

The Normandy Campaign

Confidence in the high command is absolutely without parallel. Literally dozens of embarking troops talked about General Montgomery with actual hero-worship in every inflection. And, unanimously what appealed to them – beyond his friendliness, and genuineness, and lack of pomp–was the story (or, for all I know, the myth) that the General "visited every one of us outfits going over and told us he was more anxious than any of us to get this thing over and get home." This left a warm and indelible impression.

General Walter Bedell Smith to Montgomery
June 22, 1944

Preparations

Walter Bedell Smith, Eisenhower's chief-of-staff, ended his letter, which is quoted in Montgomery's *Memoirs*, with the observation that having spent his life with American soldiers, and knowing only too well their innate distrust of everything foreign, "I can appreciate far better than you what a triumph of leadership you accomplished in inspiring such feeling and confidence." After the war, in 1947, Smith told the veteran *New York Times* war correspondent Drew Middleton that he was getting tired of this "damned nit picking about Monty." He conceded that Monty had been a "difficult man to handle," but, declared Smith, "there wasn't anyone else who could have got us across the Channel and ashore in Normandy; it was his sort of battle." General Eisenhower would later echo Smith's comment, "no one else could have got us across the Channel."

Montgomery's impact on Canadian troops is vividly described by George G. Blackburn in his 1997 memoir, *Where the Hell Are the Guns? A Soldier's Eye*

View of the Anxious Years, 1939-44 [30]. His chapter titled, "Unadulterated B.S. But Monty Impressive," records Montgomery's informal inspection his unit before D-Day. Despite his "unadulterated B.S.," Monty's overall effect is "tremendously positive. Everyone cannot help but draw comfort from the cocky confidence of the man who is to lead them in the final, decisive battles across the Channel."

Retired Field Marshal Michael Carver makes the same point that Monty was able to spread his own supreme confidence to those he commanded and those who supported them or were only spectators. Carver's essay is found in the volume, *Churchill's Generals* [207], edited by John Keegan. Monty's efforts before D-Day were as important as his conduct of the battle, in the opinion of Carver. Ronald Lewin commented in his study, *Montgomery as Military Commander* [222], that Montgomery succeeded in raising the confidence of the army in itself and the public's morale. Apart from Montgomery, declared Lewin, no living Englishman in 1944—except for Churchill – was capable of such a feat. General Bradley wrote in his memoirs, *A Soldier's Story* [43], that Montgomery's appointment as Allied Ground Force Commander "came as a stimulant to us all."

In volume two of his biography, *Master of the Battlefield* [175A], Nigel Hamilton asserts that the manner in which Montgomery took command of *Overlord* must rank, together with his take-over of the 8th Army in August 1942, as his "greatest performance of the war." Hamilton emphasizes that Monty was far from being the only critic of the invasion plan developed by the planning staff under General Frederick E. Morgan (called COSSAC), but he argues that Montgomery *was* (Hamilton's italics) alone in having the courage and conviction to see that the COSSAC was abandoned and a better plan adopted.

At 9 o'clock on January 3, the morning after his arrival from Marrakesh, Montgomery convened his first *Overlord* conference in St. Paul's School, Hammersmith, where Monty had been a student, and which now served as headquarters of 21st Army Group. Montgomery had been specifically told by Eisenhower that during January when the Supreme Commander would be in the United States he was to be in control of all the planning for *Overlord*. After COSSAC representatives made a brief presentation followed by a short break, Montgomery stood up and expressed his complete disagreement with the proposed invasion plan. His approach to the problem of landing in northwest Europe is described in his *Memoirs* [268]. The first essential as he saw the situation was the fact that there were over fifty German divisions in France – of which six were panzer divisions. Brigadier Bill Williams, his Intelligence chief, calculated that they might be fighting against six enemy divisions by the evening of D-Day. In his *Memoirs* Montgomery wrote, "We could take no chances; if we failed in Normandy the war might drag on for years." To meet the German counter-attack threat, the Allied forces needed a bigger initial landing, a wider front to avoid congestion and confusion, and a much stronger rate of build up. Moorehead remarks in his biography, *Montgomery* [278], Monty's criticism of the COSSAC plan caused "something of a bombshell." Hamilton writes that the meeting at St. Paul's School "broke up in some consternation."

The story of COSSAC, which had its headquarters in Norfolk House, St.

James's Square, is described by General Frederick E. Morgan in his book, *Overture to Overlord* [284], as well as his 1961 memoir, *Peace and War* [285]. Morgan became Eisenhower's British deputy chief-of-staff at SHAEF (Supreme Headquarters Allied Expeditionary Force). Montgomery wrote in his *Memoirs* that Morgan considered Eisenhower "a god; since I had discarded many of his plans, he placed me at the other end of the celestial ladder." In *Master of the Battlefield* [175A], Hamilton remarks that Morgan pursued "what seemed like a vendetta against Montgomery."

The famous Pogue interviews with the *Overlord* planners and other Allied officers are an invaluable source of information on the preparations for D-Day and the Normandy campaign itself. The original interviews conducted by Dr. Forrest C. Pogue, an official U.S. army historian, were conducted shortly after the end of World War II, and are deposited in the U.S. Army Military History Institute at Carlisle Barracks, Pennsylvania.

As Eisenhower's representative in London, Montgomery was in a position to insist that his demands be met or that someone else command the Allied ground forces on D-Day. The new and final plan for *Overlord* called for a five-division assault, flanked by airborne landings, and a fifty-mile-wide beachhead. The Anglo-Canadian British Second Army under General Miles Dempsey, whom Monty had known for years, would be on the left and the First U.S. Army, commanded by General Omar Bradley, on the right. Immediately on Eisenhower's return from America to take up formally his post as Supreme Commander the revised outline plan was submitted to him on January 21 and approved by him.

Author Alun Chalfont, in his not uncritical account, *Montgomery of Alamein* [70], noted that Montgomery's relations with his British subordinates were, from the start, very good–surprisingly, perhaps, for someone with the reputation of firing officers within hours of taking command. Only Dempsey was specially imported. There were some removals at 21st Army Group headquarters. In his *Memoirs* [268], Montgomery mentions that into a somewhat "hidebound 'staff atmosphere'" it was vital to inject new blood." His changes, wrote Montgomery, were unpopular and "ribald remarks were made in the London clubs, to the effect that 'the Gentlemen are out and the Players are just going to bat." Chalfont remarks that Montgomery had in fact succeeded remarkably well in modifying his style to enable him to lead n already established British army in Britain without the unpleasant clashes which had marked his take-over of the 8th Army.

Even more remarkable, wrote Chalfont, was Monty's good relationship with the American commanders. Montgomery, argues Chalfont, was determined to avoid in *his* battle the clashes that had marred the Sicilian and Italian campaigns. From January to June *Overlord* planning proceeded well; and Allied solidarity became firmer.

In his *Memoirs* [268], Montgomery wrote, "Having got an agreed plan (or so I thought at the time!) I left the details to de Guingand [his chief-of-staff] and his staff and devoted my main efforts to ensuring that the weapon we were to use would be fit for battle." He wanted to see the soldiers, and more important, he wanted them to see him and try to gain their trust and confidence. He had the use of a special train, the *Rapier*, in which he toured the British Isles, visiting every formation which was to take part in the invasion of Normandy. In his book, *Montgomery* [278], Alan Moorehead states that Army Intelligence reports had made it clear that the average young officer was expecting to die in the assault, and among ordinary soldiers there was that same heavy weight of apprehension and dismal foreboding. Up and down Britain Montgomery went, talking sometimes to five or six meetings, addressing thirty thousand men in a single day–by May, well over one million soldiers. Chalfont, in his *Montgomery of Alamein* [70], writes that every unit was given exactly the talk it need, and he repeats one incident just before D-Day. He stood on his jeep and said, "Gather round." He asked one of the soldiers, "What's your most valuable possession?" The soldier replied, "It's my rifle, sir." "No, it isn't, it's your life, and I'm going to save it for you. Now listen to me . . . " Montgomery went on to say that he would never push anyone forward without full artillery and air cover, and that he would never hurry an operation just for effect. On this tough, reluctant audience the "Monty magic" worked completely, writes Chalfont.

Nor did it stop with the Allied soldiers. His interest in the morale of the home front was sparked by the Ministry of Supply, which asked him to address hard-pressed factory workers. Alan Moorehead,'s book, *Montgomery* [278], which so successfully evokes the attitudes and atmosphere of wartime Britain, captured the mood of the hour: "It was the flood -tide of Montgomery's life . . . The dread of the coming battle lay like a leaden weight on everyone's mind. Could it be anything else than an appalling 'blood bath'? There was something outrageous in this slow deliberate preparation for a massacre. The bombing of southern England went on. There were threats of rockets. Austerity followed one about like a lean and hungry dog. It sat by your table as you ate, followed you into the black streets at night and lay with you in the half-heated houses at night. The wreckage, the shabbiness and the overwhelming drabness of four years' garrison life stared one in the face all over England. When would it come? When? When?" Montgomery's extraordinary crusade, with its message of tremendous optimism, raised the spirits of a jaded and war-weary people. On February 22, at Euston Station, he addressed railway workers; on March 3, 16,000 dock workers. His theme was the same – there was a job to be done and together they would do it. He was received with great enthusiasm everywhere. But as he wrote in his *Memoirs* [268], "I sensed danger in this and knew my activities would not be viewed favorably in political circles. Nor were they." Moorehead notes in *Montgomery* [278] that in the House of Commons a cheer was raised at every mention of Alexander's name, while the House fell silent when Montgomery was mentioned. In volume II of his *Diaries and Letters: The War Years 1939-1945* [298], Member of Parliament Harold Nicolson noted that the names of Eisenhower and Alexander were warmly greeted; at the mention of Montgomery there was one isolated "Hear! Hear!" The newspapers were encouraged to "go slow" on Montgomery. He was not asked to broadcast on the B.B.C. Montgomery's growing fame is noted with distaste in the *Diaries and Letters* [298] of Harold Nicolson. King George VI disliked his manner even more than his beret. Even Churchill sent a minute to Lord

Ismay, his military assistant, stating, "It would seem to be about time that the circular sent to generals and other high commanders about making speeches should be renewed . . . There seem to have been a lot of speeches and interviews lately." In his *Memoirs* [268], Montgomery writes that, "I received an intimation that I should 'lay off' these visits [to factories] – to which I paid no attention, beyond replying that I had been asked to undertake them by certain Ministries in Whitehall."

Although Montgomery left the detailed planning to others, he did take great interest in the new weapons developed by his brother-in-law, General Percy Hobart for the 79th Division, the famous Hobart "funnies" or "Hobo's toys" – amphibious (DD) tanks, flail tanks, flame-throwing machines and other specialized armored vehicles. Their value was proved on June 6. Montgomery's openness to the new weapons is mentioned by Ronald Lewin in his book, *Montgomery as Military Commander* [222].

In his *Memoirs* [268], Montgomery relates that in February he began to sit for a portrait which he wanted for his son David in case he did not survive the war. The well-known artist, Augustus John, was commissioned for a fee of 500 pounds. During the sittings Montgomery met the famous writer George Bernard Shaw who visited the studio. The incident is described by Nigel Hamilton in *Master of the Battlefield* [175A]. Between Montgomery and Augustus John there was an instant dislike, but the general and the writer now "hit it off" completely. Shaw afterwards described Montgomery as "that intensely compacted hank of steel wire" with a gaze like a "burning-glass," which "concentrates all space into a small spot." In the end Montgomery disliked the portrait – "I don't like it – and I won't pay for it!" Neither did Bernard Shaw who told Augustus John, "You really weren't interested in the man." The artist was not unhappy since he sold the painting to someone else for much more money. A black and white copy of the oil portrait is found in Moorehead's *Montgomery* [278].

The most critical and successful deception scheme undertaken by the Allies before D-Day was Operation *Fortitude*, the attempt to convince the enemy that the main Allied landing would take place across the narrow part of the Channel near Calais under Patton.   Another deception scheme involved Clifton James, a lieutenant in the Army Education Corps and a professional actor in civilian life who bore a strong resemblance to Montgomery, and who was asked to impersonate the general. James was sent to Gibraltar and Algiers in an effort to induce the Germans to believe Montgomery had left the country, and to assume the invasion could not take place until his return. Montgomery insisted that James be awarded general's pay during the impersonation. The War Office protested but to no avail and James received a full general's pay. Clifton James described the entire humorous episode in his book, *I Was Monty's Double* [80], which in turn became a motion-picture film. There is no evidence that the Germans diverted any troops because of the imaginative scheme. In addition to Hamilton's *Master of the Battlefield* [175A], the affair is also mentioned by Jock Haswell in his account, *The Intelligence and Deception of the D-Day Landings* [181].

There were two large-scale presentations of what was to take place on and after

D-Day; one on April 7 and another on May 15. At both of these memorable meetings Montgomery gave very impressive presentations. The conferences are described in many memoirs: in his book, *The Business of War* [212], General John Kennedy, who served as Director of Military Operations, recorded that at the April 7 gathering Montgomery went over the Army plan with "great lucidity." The plan called for the Allies to reach the Seine River-Paris line in three months or D+90. A relief map of Normandy the width of a city street was spread on the floor of a large room in St. Paul's School. General Omar Bradley, in his memoir, *A Soldier's Story* [43], wrote "With rare skill, Monty traced his 21st Group plan of maneuver as he tramped about like a giant through Lilliputian France." The American forces, recalled Bradley, were to pivot on the British position like a windlass in the direction of Paris. Bradley's recollection of Montgomery's strategy is of great importance since controversy would quickly surround that strategy. In his memoirs, Bradley wrote: "During our battle for Normandy, the British and Canadian armies were to decoy the enemy reserves and draw them to their front on the extreme eastern edge of the Allied beachhead. Thus while Monty taunted the enemy at Caen, we were to make our break on the long roundabout road toward Paris. When reckoned in terms of national pride, this British decoy mission became a sacrificial one, for while we tramped around the outside flank, the British were to sit in place and pin down Germans."

On May 15, once again at St. Paul's School, there took place the great dress rehearsal for *Overlord* with the entire Allied high command present for the occasion. In his own moving account, *Crusade in Europe* [126], Eisenhower wrote, "During the whole war I attended no other conference so packed with rank as this one." The conferences are mentioned in many post-war memoirs, including: General Ismay's, *The Memoirs of General Lord Ismay* [199] – Ismay was Churchill's military assistant ("Montgomery in particular was at his best."); CIGS, Alan Brooke's diary, edited by Arthur Bryant, *Triumph in the West 1943-1946* [50], ("Monty made an excellent speech."); Secretary of State for War P.J. Grigg's memoir, *Prejudice and Judgment* [170], "Montgomery radiated entire confidence and the very strong feeling that nothing had been forgotten or left to chance." Wearing battledress, Monty emphasized the need for aggressive and bold action to push armored thrusts deep inland, and quickly on D-Day. As we shall see, Montgomery's strategy during the Battle of Normandy – what exactly he intended to do–became an issue of endless controversy that spilt gallons of ink.

One last minute difficulty that confronted Montgomery was the Prime Minister's unhappiness with what he considered to be too much ironmongery and not enough troops. Churchill was determined to discuss what he considered to be the excessive administrative "tail" with the staff of 21st Army Group. Barely a week before D-Day Churchill visited Montgomery's headquarters at Portsmouth. When Churchill arrived at Broomfield House, Montgomery led him into his study where he explained that he could not allow the Prime Minister to interrogate his staff. If the Prime Minister could not accept his word that every single vehicle was necessary–if he insisted on a change at this eleventh hour–then someone else must be found to lead the expedition. The bombshell fell quietly in the room. There is no doubt Churchill became very emotional. In 1946 Churchill threatened to sue Alan Moorehead if he wrote that he had broken down and wept. The two men remained a little longer in the room while the tension passed. Then Montgomery reminded him that the staff was waiting outside. Churchill passed down the waiting line of staff officers without speaking. Moorehead writes, "Then the old lion had his final roar. Some sly imp of genius made him say, and with dignity: 'I'm not allowed to talk to you, gentlemen.' Then he walked out. The scene was all his." At dinner, Churchill was in great form; Montgomery's famous betting book was brought out, and several wagers were laid on a variety of subjects, including when the war would end.

The dramatic face to face confrontation with Prime Minister Churchill is described in Monty's own *Memoirs* [268]; Alan Moorehead's biography *Montgomery* [278]; Nigel Hamilton's, *Master of the Battlefield* [175A]; Francis de Guingand's, *Operation Victory* [109]. A good overview of Monty's role before D-Day is Stephen Brooks article, "Montgomery and the Preparation for Overlord," in *History Today* [48].

The Battle of Normandy

D-Day, June 6, had been a stunning success for the Allies, but the landing in Normandy was only the first round of what would be a long, hard slogging match. In Normandy, Allied soldiers found themselves fighting not only first-class panzer divisions equipped with Panther and Tiger tanks, but up against some of the best armed infantry in the world who were fighting in ideal defensive terrain under leaders who were battle hardened from combat on the Russian front. At the beginning of July, two million soldiers were engaged against one another along a battlefront of less than 100 miles. As the Allies were on the offensive, their numerical advantage – thirty-four Allied divisions against twenty-six German divisions – was not overwhelming powerful.

Six weeks after D-Day, Allied troops had taken only as much ground as the *Overlord* plan had called for in the first five days! The vital road center of Caen, ten miles from the Channel and only 120 miles from Paris, was a D-Day objective of the British 2nd Army. The significance that the Germans attached to holding Caen is gained from the fact that more than a month would pass before Caen was at last captured. Eventually, the Germans would concentrate seven panzer divisions or two-thirds of their tanks in France on the twenty-mile Caen front. On the U.S 1st Army front, the port of Cherbourg was to be taken on D plus 8; instead it would not fall until D plus 28. The battlefront hardened and newspapers used the ugly word "stalemate."

What caused the temporary stalemate in Normandy? The Allied ground forces commander, Montgomery – the much admired, much detested Monty – became the center of this dispute. The agonizingly slow advance through the ideal defensive country of the *bocage* region of Normandy, small fields enclosed by thick hedges almost impenetrable to tanks, led to bitter argument among Allied commanders and the unraveling of tempers. Supreme Allied Commander Dwight Eisenhower appealed to Churchill "to persuade Monty to get on his bicycle and start moving." Ike's deputy, Air Marshal Arthur Tedder, pushed for Monty's removal. Had Montgomery failed? Since World War II, the ink has flowed freely over the written page in the literary battle between Monty's admirers and critics over his generalship in Normandy.

Others have argued that Montgomery wielded a "flawed instrument" in Normandy. In the 1997 study, *Steel Inferno: I SS Panzer Corps in Normandy* [330], retired Major General Michael Reynolds claimed that Montgomery's commanders, "at every level . . . failed him, and more importantly failed their men." The author cites the action on June 12-14 at Villers-Bocage where lead elements of the British 7th Armored Division were shattered by a single Tiger tank commanded by the famous panzer ace Michael Wittmann. Reynolds holds the view of distinguished commentators Chester Wilmot and Carlo D'Este that the withdrawal represented a missed opportunity. On the other hand, Gordon A. Harrison, author of the official U.S. Army volume, *Cross-Channel Attack* [179], remarked that the 7th Armored Division "found itself in a dangerously exposed thin salient." Perhaps, but within two months of the Villers-Bocage setback, both the divisional and corps commander were sacked by Monty.

The Battle of the Books

When Montgomery wrote his memoirs in 1958, he noted that much had been written about the campaign in northwest Europe, and, he wrote, "it will be a happy hunting ground for historians for many years to come." In his *Memoirs* [268], Monty insisted, "at the risk of being wearisome," that "I never once had cause or reason to alter my master plan [for the Battle of Normandy]," which was to draw German armor on to the front of the 2nd British army, so that Bradley's 1st American army could ultimately breakout on the western flank. He emphasized that, "There was never *at any time* any intention of making the breakout from the bridgehead on the eastern flank." Critical of Eisenhower for failing to understand his plan and for thinking that he intended to break out on the Caen front, Montgomery attributed much of the misunderstanding to General Frederick Morgan since the original COSSAC plan had called for a breakout from the Caen sector, on the eastern flank. Montgomery writes, "I had refused to accept this plan and had changed it." Now, as Eisenhower's Deputy Chief of Staff, Morgan and other "displaced strategists", in the words of Montgomery, "lost no opportunity of trying to persuade Eisenhower that I was defensively minded and that we were unlikely to breakout anywhere!"

Concluding his discussion of the Normandy campaign, Montgomery wrote in his *Memoirs*: "It was always very clear to me that Ike and I were poles apart when it came to the conduct of war."

Monty claimed that his own strategy involved "unbalancing the enemy" then committing a hard blow on a narrow front, whereas Eisenhower, he said, seemed to think everybody must attack all the time. Montgomery remembered that Bedell Smith once compared Eisenhower to a football coach who went up and down the line all the time, encouraging everyone to get on with the game. In Montgomery's opinion, such a strategy resulted in more casualties.

Montgomery's insistence that all had gone according to his master plan had never been without critics. In one of his post-war interviews, official U.S. Army historian Forrest Pogue spoke to Captain John Hughes-Hallett, an *Overlord* planner and no friend of Montgomery's (see Brian Loring Villa's, *Unauthorized Action* [395], for Hughes-Hallett's role in the Dieppe raid), who declared that "Monty's talk of his original intention to hinge on Caen is absolutely balls."

Scarcely had the war ended before the battle of the books began. In 1946, appeared Ralph Ingersoll's inflammatory account, *Top Secret* [196], which may be considered the first "revisionist" history of World War II since it emphasized Allied differences. According to the *New York Times*, *Top Secret* was written at such "a blood-bursting heat . . . that an ex-sergeant must have been needed to pour buckets of ice-water on [Ingersoll's] typewriter's smoking keys as he wrote." A controversial journalist before Pearl Harbor, editor of the New York tabloid *P.M.,* Ingersoll served on Bradley's staff during the war. In *Top Secret* [196], Ingersoll charged that Montgomery had intended to breakout on the Caen sector, had failed, and that only Bradley had saved the day for the Allies by breaking out on the western flank. He labeled Montgomery "a very bad general," while Eisenhower is pictured by the Anglophobic Ingersoll as a genial, incompetent puppet of the British. Bradley, asserted Ingersoll, was the greatest general of the war. *Top Secret* aroused anger on both sides of the Atlantic. In a letter to Montgomery, Eisenhower called Ingersoll's volume a "trashy book." In *The Yale Review*, T.C. Mendenhall II was driven to write, "Almost no other branch of human activity seems to produce so much polemical writing as the art of war." He declared that Ingersoll's presentation of strategy was "so badly handled that it is worse than useless." A reasoned response to many of Ingersoll's comments are found in the memoir of General Sir Francis de Guingand, *Operation Victory* [109]. De Guingand served as Monty's chief of staff.

The same year that Ingersoll published *Top Secret* there appeared Captain Harry Butcher's, *My Three Years with Eisenhower* [54], recounting his time as Naval Aide to Eisenhower. Although far more valuable and reliable than Ingersoll's polemic, Butcher's diary was unfavorable toward Montgomery and gave no indication that Eisenhower comprehended Montgomery's so-called master plan.

In a return salvo to Ingersoll's diatribe , and to a lesser extent Butcher's book, the Australian war correspondent for the London *Daily Express*, Alan Moorehead, authored the biography, *Montgomery* [278], in which he declared flatly that Montgomery master plan was followed "to the letter and with overwhelming success." Under that plan, wrote Moorehead, the British attracted the bulk of German armor in a slogging match around Caen, while the Americans were given the "fast-riding role" of breaking out at St. Lô. Ingersoll's references to the British were "so much sensational and irresponsible nonsense," wrote Moorehead. Referring to Butcher's account, it seemed "incredible" to Moorehead that SHAEF commanders could have had no notion of Montgomery's plan to attract German tanks to Caen so that Bradley could break out on the right flank.

Eisenhower's own war memoir, *Crusade in Europe* [126] was published in 1948. Although he attempted to avoid antagonizing Monty by largely side-stepping the divisive issue of the Normandy battle plan, Eisenhower left the distinct impression that he had expected the main Allied breakthrough to occur on the British front, and that when a stalemate developed Montgomery changed his plan so as to keep Rommel preoccupied at Caen while Bradley prepared to breakout on the western flank. In *Master of the Battlefield* [175A], Nigel Hamilton comments that Monty was "appalled" by Eisenhower's book.

Neither was Montgomery pleased with the publication in 1951 of General Omar Bradley's memoir, *A Soldier's Story* [43]. But at least in so far as the Normandy battle was concerned, Bradley's account substantiated Monty's claim to have always intended to hold the enemy on the eastern flank in order to promote an American breakout in the west. Describing Monty's full-dress rehearsal conference at St. Paul's School, on April 7, Bradley wrote that the British and Canadian forces were to decoy the enemy reserves and draw them to their front while the 1st U.S. Army would be free to advance with less opposition on their end of the line; in other words pivot on the British position like a windlass in the direction of Paris. Bradley commented, "When reckoned in terms of national pride, this British decoy mission became a sacrificial one, for while we tramped around the outside flank, the British were to sit in place and pin down Germans."

Joining the growing list of post-war memoirs was that of P. J. Grigg, the former Secretary of State for War, who authored, *Prejudice and Judgment* [170]. On the Caen controversy, Grigg observed that, "Of course" Montgomery's original idea was to breakout around Caen into the open in the first few days after D-Day – "it would be idle to deny that." Grigg was sure that Montgomery soon concluded that to breakout at Caen would cost more casualties than he could afford with his declining British manpower; consequently, Monty adjusted his tactics to serve his main purpose, namely, to use the 2nd Army as a hinge to facilitate an American breakout. It seemed idle to Grigg to argue about it since by D plus 80 the Allies had reached where they had planned to be by D plus 90, and the enemy had done what Montgomery had hoped but never believed they would do – fight a major battle on the wrong side of the Seine.

The casualty question is mentioned by C.P. Dawnay in his contribution to the volume edited by T. E. B. Howarth, *Monty at Close Quarters: Recollections of the Man* [193], published in 1985. Dawnay, who was Monty's personal diarist, mentions that Montgomery was told by the War Office before the Normandy battle that in the event of heavy casualties it would be necessary to cannibalize some combat units. He emphasizes that heavy casualties had to be avoided because Britain was running short of men.

The first general history of Allied operations in northwest Europe based on first-hand experience and study of the available sources was *The Struggle for Europe* [407] by the New Zealand war correspondent Chester Wilmot. *The Struggle for Europe*, published in 1951, remains, in the estimation of military historian John Keegan,"a revolutionary book in which are combined . . . not only strategic commentary and historical narrative, but penetrating economic and operational analysis, character portraiture, and, above all, riveting tactical description." The events Wilmot described he had often witnessed at close hand or heard about soon afterwards by direct questioning of participants. Oddly, remarks Keegan, Wilmot was a loner among his fellows, admired but not much liked, aloof and abrasive. An "extraordinary" book – he wrote only one book – at the time of his death in 1954 Wilmot was one of the best-known journalists in the world. He was killed in the crash of the original Comet jet airliner over the Mediterranean. See Keegan's, *The Battle for History: Re-fighting World War II* [209].

Wilmot asked, Did the British ever intend to breakout towards the Seine? Did Dempsey fail at Caen? Was Montgomery forced to change his plan? In Wilmot's opinion, the orders and declarations issued by Montgomery before D-Day and during the first few weeks ashore, made it clear that the British were to threaten a breakout at Caen while the Americans prepared to make the decisive effort at St. Lô. At the same time, however, Wilmot does qualify Monty's assertion that operations went "exactly as planned." In making such a claim, Wilmot points that Montgomery did himself less than justice, "for his real genius as a commander" was shown in his ability to change his day to day policy to meet the unpredictable situations that invariably occur on the battlefield. In pursuit of his main strategic purpose Montgomery never wavered, argued Wilmot, but he did modify and change the tactical means by which he sought to achieve it. He faults Montgomery for causing some of the misunderstanding: for example, before   Operation *Goodwood*, his three armored division offensive launched on July 18, Monty declared that "My whole eastern flank will burst into flames," and he said the operation "may have far-reaching results." On the day of the attack, Montgomery himself issued a special announcement that 2nd Army had broken through at Caen. In Wilmot's opinion, Montgomery made "a grave psychological mistake" in using the word "break-through," since the press concluded that this was another great El Alamein victory, and the headlines were written accordingly. Montgomery's announcement, wrote Wilmot, was "premature and indiscreet." The 2nd Army lost 450 tanks in *Goodwood*. Eisenhower was "livid" and Air Marshal Tedder, his British deputy, pushed for Montgomery's removal. If *Goodwood* failed to live up to Monty's advance billing, the offensive pulled two more panzer divisions on to the 2nd Army front. On the eve of Bradley's 1st Army attack on St. Lô, seven panzer divisions were on the 2nd Army front and two faced 1st Army. In his *Memoirs* [268], Monty declared, "As at Alamein, we had forced the enemy to commit his reserves on a wide front; we were now ready to commit ours on a narrow front, and so win the battle."

Operation *Goodwood*

As we have seen, the apparent stalemate in Normandy soon led to growing impatience and controversy. Eisenhower appealed to Churchill "to persuade Monty to get on his bicycle and start moving." Montgomery promised another big attack on the Caen front, code named *Goodwood*. He declared that "My whole eastern flank will burst into flames . . . The operation may have far-reaching results." That Eisenhower thought something spectacular was about to happen may be gathered from his response: "I would not be at all surprised to see you gaining a victory that will make some of the 'old classics' look like a skirmish between patrols." Preceded by the heaviest "carpet" bombing of the war, Montgomery launched the most massive tank attack in the Normandy battle: three British armored divisions got off to a good start until stopped by nearly two hundred antitank guns, 272 Nebelwerfers (the multibarreled mortars called "Moaning Minnies" by Allied soldiers), and armored counterattacks. The attack cost Monty more than 400 tanks; heavy losses had been inflicted on the Germans, but 2nd Army had suffered as well. When he called off the attack on July 19, in the words of Nigel Hamilton (*Master of the Battlefield*), "the roof began to fall about Monty's ears."

Montgomery did blame himself – "partly" – in his *Memoirs* [268] (in *The Lonely Leader* [186] Alistair Horne calls it "an extraordinarily rare *mea culpa)* for spreading illusions about the breakout: "This was partly my own fault, for I was too exultant at the Press conference I gave during the *Goodwood* battle. I realize that now – in fact, I realized it pretty quickly afterwards. Basically the trouble was this – both Bradley and I agreed that we could not possibly tell the Press the true strategy which formed the basis of all our plans [to draw enemy reserves to the eastern flank]. As Bradley said, 'we must grin and bear it.' It became increasingly difficult to grin."

Monty's *Memoirs*, however, do not tell the whole story. The press conference was not the only reason for misunderstanding. Montgomery undoubtedly hoped for greater things from *Goodwood*. In Arthur Bryant's volume, *Triumph in the West* [50], he includes a letter from Montgomery to Brooke before the attack: "The possibilities are immense: with 700 tanks loosed to the southeast of Caen and armored cars operating far ahead anything may happen." To Winston Churchill he had written, "Am determined to loose the armored divisions tomorrow if in any way possible . . . " The message is quoted in *Triumph and Tragedy* [75], the final volume in Churchill's six-volume history, *The Second World War*. Although highly personal and selective, Churchill's epic story of the war he did so much to win remains required reading for students of World War II.

When Montgomery called off the attack and expressed his satisfaction with *Goodwood's* results, there occurred an outburst of criticism at SHAEF (Supreme Headquarters Allied Expeditionary Force) over his seeming failure to press home the attack. Ike was "livid" and considered *Goodwood* a failure. Tedder, who had long been critical of Montgomery's direction of the campaign, was so angry he wanted Monty sacked. The episode is judiciously discussed by Canadian C. P. Stacey in the official Canadian history, *The Victory Campaign: The Operations in*

North-West Europe 1944-1945 [367]. Colonel Stacey observed that the misunderstandings regarding Montgomery's plans were understandable given his communications to Eisenhower before the battle, which indicated that *Goodwood* was a breakthrough operation.

Tedder's campaign to get Montgomery sacked is described in Captain Butcher's diary, *My Three Years With Eisenhower* [54]. Butcher refers to Tedder's current favorite subject the "sacking of Monty." Montgomery was also in trouble with Churchill over the former's "no visitors" policy at his headquarters in Normandy. The problem is described by Alistair Horne in *The Lonely Leader: Monty 1944-1945* [186]. Horne states that Brooke realized that his protégé Monty was in "the gravest danger of his whole career" and flew off to Normandy to warn him. According to the Brooke diaries, at his prompting, Monty wrote to Churchill inviting him to "come over here whenever you like." Horne comments that Monty "still remained in great peril" since on July 20 *Goodwood* had been called off. Did Monty really know what he was doing?

Churchill's meeting with Montgomery is reconstructed in Alan Moorehead's, *Montgomery: A Biography* [278]: "Setbacks? What setbacks? The battle was going excellently to plan," reported a self-confident and optimistic Montgomery. *Ultra* decrypts showed that *Goodwood* had left the enemy facing Bradley, where the *Cobra* attack was soon to take place, seriously under strength. Montgomery sent Churchill off with a bottle of cognac "as a peace offering." Horne remarks: "Thus Monty was saved to fight another day by that tempestuous volatility of Winston Churchill's which oscillated between love and hate."

Convinced by Montgomery's encouraging news, Churchill passed on what had been said to Eisenhower who grumbled to Butcher that Monty had "obviously sold Winston 'a bill of goods'."

Eisenhower told a fuming Tedder that, Churchill was satisfied with Monty's explanation of events, and added wisely that "there's nothing so wrong a good victory won't cure."

In his excellent 1993 study, *The Price of Command: A Biography of General Guy Simmonds* [164], Dominick Graham argues that the Normandy battle did not go according to plan tactically and Montgomery had to make changes to keep the initiative. His failure to take Caen in the first rush changed the tactical shape of the campaign. Rather than inflict heavy casualties on attacking Germans, as originally intended, the British and Canadians had to attack all through July to hold elite German panzer divisions on their front. Graham remarks, "Montgomery might have taken more trouble to explain what he was attempting."

Often highly critical of Montgomery, Stephen Ambrose in his book, *Citizen Soldiers: The U.S. Army from the Normandy Beaches to the Bulge to the Surrender of Germany June 7, 1944-May 7, 1945* [7], defends Monty against the charge of excessive caution, at least in the case of Operation *Goodwood* Having walked over the Normandy battlefield many times with Colonel Hans von Luck of the 21st Panzer Division, who was in the thick of the action, Ambrose declares: "Further, it wasn't fair to charge Monty with excessive caution or a refusal to make a full commitment, at least at *Goodwood*." The tanks were inadequately supported by infantry, comments Ambrose. The same point, lack of infantry support, is made by John Strawson in his survey, *Gentlemen in Khaki: The British Army 1890-1990* [370]. In Operation *Goodwood*, claims Strawson, Montgomery "allowed himself the luxury of an adventurous fling."

If *Goodwood* failed to achieve a breakout, the attack pulled German armored reserves toward the 2nd Army front just as Bradley was preparing for the *Cobra* breakout in the west. In his volume, *The Victory Campaign* [367], C. P. Stacey cites the German reaction to *Goodwood*, which gave them "a very bad fright and drove them to desperate expedients to meet it." The Germans concentrated their armor on the eastern flank fearing a breakout in the direction of Paris. The stage was set for the breakout on the opposite flank which was actually Montgomery's policy, declared Stacey. By the end of July the German forces containing the Allied bridgehead were stretched to breaking point. Hard-hitting General Lawton "Lightning Joe" Collins, a Montgomery favorite, with his VII Corps broke out of the infamous hedgerow country on July 27. On August 1, Patton's 3rd Army was unleashed to begin its fast-paced outflanking of the German army.

The Battle of Normandy can be said to have ended on August 19 with the closing of the Falaise Gap in which remnants of the German armies had been trapped. Since the beginning of the war Montgomery had climbed steadily upwards, gaining in popularity and enjoying confidence in high places, but as Alun Chalfont observed in his biography, *Montgomery of Alamein* [70]: "The Battle of Normandy had dispersed much of that confidence, and he was at last paying the price for his inability to communicate with his equals and most of his superiors.

Tedder's views are found in his memoir, *With Prejudice: The War Memoirs of Marshal of the Royal Air Force Lord Tedder* [378], and the 1952 biography by Roderic Owen, *Tedder* [304]. Essential accounts containing references to Montgomery include: Stephen E. Ambrose, *The Supreme Commander: The War Years of General Dwight D. Eisenhower* [9]; Alfred D. Chandler, Jr., *The Papers of Dwight David Eisenhower. Vol. III. The War Years* [71]; Martin Blumenson, editor, *The Patton Papers, 1940-1945* [38]; B. H. Liddell Hart, editor, *The Rommel Papers* [225]; Francis de Guingand (Monty's chief of staff), *Operation Victory* [109]; Arthur Harris (chief of British Bomber Command), *Bomber Offensive* [177].

A fresh reappraisal of Monty's role in the Normandy battle was presented by Carlo D'Este in his well-received 1983 book, *Decision in Normandy* [98]; the ever-provocative David Irving, dwells excessively on the personal clashes between Allied commanders in his book, *The War Between the Generals* [198]; Stephen T. Powers's article in *The Journal of Military History* [323], titled, "The Battle of Normandy: The Lingering Controversy," examines the 1980s literature, focusing on the areas of "maximum disagreement."

Official Histories

In 1946 appeared Montgomery's volume, *Normandy to the Baltic* [269], which was prepared by members of his staff from official files and personal papers. In form it is an official dispatch describing military operations rather than a personal memoir.

The official British history, written by Major L. F. Ellis, *Victory in the West: The Battle of Normandy* [130], appeared in 1962. The author takes the middle ground over whether Montgomery dawdled at Caen or set a sticky trap for German armor there. The Canadian official history, *The Victory Campaign* [367] by C. P. Stacey, is an outstanding account of the operations of the 1st Canadian Army. Stacey accepts Montgomery's claim that he always intended to attract the enemy's strength to the British front; however, the Canadian historian believes that Monty's claim that everything "went according to plan" was a "considerable exaggeration." For some reason, notes Stacey, generals are reluctant to admit that they have made changes or adjustments to fit the new circumstances of a campaign.

The story of the Supreme Allied Command in the European Theater of Operations during World War II was told impressively by Dr. Forrest C. Pogue in the official U.S. Army "green book" volume, The Supreme Command [320], first published in 1954. General Orlando Ward wrote in his foreword: "This is a history of coalition warfare." In addition to official documents and memoirs, Pogue interviewed nearly a hundred Allied military and political leaders in preparing to write *The Supreme Command*. The result is a monument to the wartime Anglo-American alliance. His account of "The Battle for Caen" is objective and he includes the reaction of the press.

The official U.S. Army operational history of the Normandy campaign, *Breakout and Pursuit* [35], by Martin Blumenson, appeared in 1961. In Blumenson's opinion, the "Failure to secure Caen by July 1 was the greatest single disappointment of the invasion." He argued that the debate over Montgomery's intentions were interesting but irrelevant since the Germans massed their power opposite the British without regard for Monty's original intentions. Blumenson's then dislike of Montgomery appeared in sharper focus in the article, "The Most Overrated General of World War II," that appeared in the journal *Armor* [34]. He wrote, "He is, I think, vastly over-rated, the most over-rated general of World War II." At that time, in 1962, Blumenson regarded Montgomery as merely "competent, adequate. He was not great . . . " He is less critical of Montgomery in his 1971 essay, "Some Reflections on the Immediate Post-Assault Strategy," which appeared in the Eisenhower Foundation book, *D-Day: The Normandy Invasion in Retrospect* [127].

The Ongoing Debate over Normandy

Montgomery's strategy in Normandy was vigorously defended by the former head of his operations and planning staff, Major General David Belchem in his book, *Victory in Normandy* [23]. Belchem was an advocate until his death in 1981 for the "all went according to plan" school of thought.

Richard Lamb's 1983 book, *Montgomery in Europe, 1943-1945: Success or Failure?* [218], is generally favorable, but not uncritical toward its subject. Lamb used official documents in the Public Record Office that had been opened to historians under the thirty-year rule (documents open after thirty years). Lamb accepted Montgomery's overall plan for the Normandy campaign.

On the 50th Anniversary of D-Day in 1994 appeared the *D-Day Encyclopedia* [73], edited by David G. Chandler and James Lawton Collins, Jr. In his insightful essay on Montgomery, Chandler observed that the strategy for the breakout from Normandy remained a "contentious issue, but on balance it would appear that Montgomery's claim is correct, that from the first his overall intention was to use the Caen area as a magnet to attract the redoubtable German armor to the eastern end of the bridgehead, and thus facilitate the American First Army's breakout farther to the west."

A contrary view can be found in Russell F. Weigley's book, *Eisenhower's Lieutenants: The Campaign of France and Germany 1944-1945* [398]. Weigley, the foremost historian of the American army in World War II, expressed scepticism about Montgomery's claims. In Weigley's opinion, Montgomery hoped to reserve the breakout role for the British 2nd Army in part because he doubted the Americans had the combat experience and capacity to perform that role.

Montgomery's role in the Battle of Normandy receives passing mention in Michael D. Doubler's prize-winning book, *Closing with the Enemy: How GI's Fought the War in Europe 1944-1945* [120]. Doubler holds to the view that Montgomery planned to breakout with the British 2nd Army, while Bradley's American 1st Army protected the southern flank.

A short persuasive defense of Montgomery's Normandy campaign is presented by Michael Carver in the 1991 essay that appeared in *Churchill's Generals* [207], edited by John Keegan. "At no time was it ever suggested, as his critics then and since have claimed," wrote Carver, "that Dempsey would attempt to break out towards the Seine while Bradley was still involved in clearing the Cotentin peninsula." He had certainly hoped to take Caen and Falaise early on, but when he did not he was not going to wreck his army to do so. Montgomery did not shrink from accepting casualties, wrote Carver, but he would not press attacks that were getting nowhere. With his supply of infantry dwindling, but possessing a surplus of tanks at that stage, Montgomery had to keep up pressure on the 2nd Army front if the German panzer divisions were not to be transferred to Bradley's front and frustrate his basic strategy. Regarding the "hysteria" among Eisenhower's frustrated staff and senior air force officers in England that followed Operation *Goodwood*, Carver believes that Montgomery must bear some of the blame for the hysteria since he had unduly raised their expectations, partly in order to persuade the senior airmen, Tedder and Harris, to support it with the latter's heavy bombers." In Carver's opinion, Montgomery's strategy had worked, although it had taken longer and cost more than he had anticipated. Carver adds that the Germans had been forced by Hitler to play into Montgomery's hands. By forbidding any withdrawal and fighting the battle forward, including the near fatal counter-attack towards Mortain, Hitler insured that the Battle of Normandy decided the Battle of France.

A "Flawed Instrument"?

While Montgomery's generalship has been the primary object for critical attention in the Normandy campaign, in the 1980s a number of historians blamed the supposedly inferior combat performance of the Allied soldier compared to the superiority of the German soldier for what they regard as the lack of sufficient progress on the battlefield. Most notably, in his provocative account, *Overlord: D-Day and the Battle of Normandy* [180], author Max Hastings concluded that the democratic soldier of the West was found wanting in Normandy. Unlike Pericles, who said of the democratic soldiers of ancient Athens, "Take these men, then, as your examples," Hastings and other critics held up the German soldier for emulation. British military writer and thinker B. H. Liddell Hart had earlier condemned the Allied performance in Normandy, calling it "disturbing and depressing."

In his 1990 revisionist book, *Brute Force: Allied Strategy and Tactics in the Second World War* [129] John Ellis claimed that any comparison between the democratic armies and the German army could only be what he terms, "invidious." Ellis argues that the Allies won only because of their material superiority, and that most Allied generals were incompetent, including and prominently Montgomery.

The argument that Montgomery wielded a badly flawed weapon in Normandy was a major theme of Alistair Horne's book, with David Montgomery (the Field Marshal's only son), *The Lonely Leader: Monty 1944-1945* [186], published on the 50th Anniversary of D-Day in 1994. In contrast to Montgomery's weak instrument, Horne describes the enemy soldiers as "Rommel's 'Trojans.'" A particularly fascinating aspect of the book are the descriptions of Montgomery's Tactical Headquarters from Normandy to Germany, which Horne and David Montgomery visited in 1992. In these camps close to the front line, Montgomery lived with a small team of dedicated young liaison officers who each day visited the forward units, bringing back firsthand information. In his review of *The Lonely Leader*, Richard Lamb observed that in his tiny mess Montgomery was isolated like a bachelor housemaster with his pupils. His liaison officers were an "impressive lot," remarks Lamb.

In his 1994 book, *The Making of Strategy: Rulers, States, and War* [292], military historian Williamson Murray made the claim that Montgomery's conduct in the buildup to Normandy and his conduct of the battle itself, was his "finest hour,"especially considering, in Murray's opinion, the relative weakness of the British army. Murray presents an even-handed view of Montgomery's role in the Normandy campaign in his insightful article, "Overlord", that appeared in the 1994 issue if *MHQ: The Quarterly Journal of Military History* [291], commemorating the 50th Anniversary of D-Day. On the Normandy campaign, Murray concludes,

"It was not pretty, but it served its purpose."

The British army is the subject of John Strawson's book, *Gentlemen in Khaki: The British Army 1890-1990* [370]. He considers Normandy to have been "perhaps the most important battle fought by the British Army in the whole Second World War, and certainly Montgomery's *chef d'oeuvre.*" Perhaps, but already in August 1944 there were signs that different perceptions existed; a strong faction at SHAEF headquarters, British as well as American, never admitted Montgomery's skill in the Battle of Normandy, in fact they believed that he had mishandled it. Criticism of Montgomery's generalship could be detected in the *New York Times* which largely credited Patton, Eisenhower, and Bradley for the Normandy victory, and commented that "only dash and daring – and speed – can assure the victory in Europe promised by General Eisenhower for this year." The *Times* wondered why Eisenhower had not superseded Monty already as Allied ground force commander.

Nigel Hamilton

In 1983 there appeared the second volume of Nigel Hamilton's monumental biography, *Master of the Battlefield: Monty's War Years, 1942-1944* [175A]. Among the most authoritative reviewers of *Monty's War Years* was General David Fraser whose essay appeared in the *London Review of Books* [147]. Formerly Commandant of the Royal College of Defense Studies, General Fraser is the author of biographies of Alanbrooke and Rommel, and a study of the British army in World War II, *And We Shall Shock Them* [145]Fraser noted that there were and are two extreme opinions about Montgomery, as well as "as large number of intermediate positions." At one end of the scale, he places those who merely regard Montgomery as competent, while at the other extreme are those who view him as the only "master of the battlefield." Hamilton, in Fraser's view, is "uncompromisingly at the latter end of the spectrum of opinion." Fraser declared that he stood – "albeit with some strong reservations – nearer what may be called the Hamilton position than its opposite."

On the question of Montgomery's "master plan," Hamilton defends Monty against the charge that he failed at Caen, declaring that it was never part of General Dempsey's original brief to breakout towards the Seine, but to pull German armor on to the 2nd Army front so as to make it easier for the 1st Army to expand on the western flank. At the same time, Hamilton agreed with Monty's own chief of Intelligence, Brigadier Sir Edgar T. "Bill" Williams, that to say that everything went according to plan – as Monty insisted – was absolutely "nonsense." Things did not go according to plan: Caen was not taken on the first day, and the deep armored thrusts – "staking out claims" – did not occur.

Hamilton cited Montgomery's private conversation to Chester Wilmot after the war that he might have taken Caen if he had been willing to incur heavy casualties just for the sake of gaining ground, which he was not. They were doing their job anyway by holding the bulk of German armor on the British sector of the front. The British army was a wasting asset. The War Office had told him that it could only guarantee replacements for the first few months. Taking Caen, he told Wilmot, might have helped his immediate reputation but "it would have crippled the British Army."

Montgomery's need to seem infallible, to insist that no enemy, no event, moved or occurred except by his will, did less than justice to his own generalship. At El Alamein, Mareth, Sicily, and Normandy, he showed his ability to adjust his ideas with speed when things did not go according to plan. Fraser believed that Hamilton's account enabled the reader to see and hear Montgomery. Although physically small and unimpressive, declared Hamilton, "this captain of men imparted an aura of clarity and conviction which infused all who served under him." In the opinion of Fraser, "That is fair. That is Right. That was Monty."

Carlo D'Este

On the eve of the Fortieth Anniversary of D-Day, joining the works of Hamilton and Lamb, there appeared the highly acclaimed study, *Decision in Normandy* [98], by Carlo D'Este. New York *Times* military correspondent Drew Middleton, who in 1944 was a war correspondent attached to Allied headquarters, called *Decision in Normandy* "the best-researched, best-reasoned, best-written account of that campaign." D'Este's book was also well-received in Britain where the reviewer for *The Economist* commented that D'Este "is surprisingly pro-Montgomery for a work by a retired American lieutenant-colonel." General John Strawson declared that D'Este's writing was a "model of clarity and elegance . . . a brilliant book." In the *London Review of Books* [147], General David Fraser rated *Decision in Normandy* an "excellent book," which examined Monty's role in Normandy with "impressive objectivity." It is critical of his bombast and of much else, noted Fraser: but it is warm in praise where the author believes praise due, and it warmly defends Monty against the more absurd and offensive charges leveled against his generalship.

D'Este argues convincingly that between Monty's actual plans and later boasting "a great gulf lay." D'Este contends that in his original plan Montgomery retained flexibility so that he could threaten to breakout on either flank. Only *after* the failure to take Caen, in D'Este's view, did Monty emphasize 2nd Army's *defensive* role in acting as a magnet for German armor. Failure to take Caen soon after D-Day, declares D'Este, was not just a "local setback," but a major failure. The author, however, is no Montgomery-basher. Although he argues that Montgomery's original plan failed, as it had at Alamein and on other battlefields, D'Este is a strong advocate of the view that Monty changed his plans to meet the new circumstances. Refusing to be shaken by initial setbacks, D'Este claims that Monty showed far greater flexibility on the battlefield than he would ever admit to at the time, a stubbornness (psychological compulsion) on his part that led to serious misunderstandings with Eisenhower, and would later arouse the hostility of many historians.

Since *Decision in Normandy*, the retired lieutenant-colonel has written four other major works on World War II, three of which touch directly on Montgomery's generalship: *Bitter Victory: The Battle for Sicily, 1943*, *World War II in the Mediterranean, 1942-1945*, *Fatal Decision: Anzio and the Battle for Rome*, and *Patton: A Genius For War*. His works offer a remarkable combination of outstanding narrative and judicious analysis, free of national bias, an especially rare find in World War II works touching on Montgomery.

Monty and the Air Marshals

In their excellent study, *Fire-Power: British Army Weapons and Theories of War 1904-1945* [29] Shelford Bidwell and Dominick Graham asserted that the vexed question of air support for the army had been settled by the end of 1943. In his 1946 biography, *Montgomery* [278], Alan Moorehead wrote, "The cooperation between the Army and the Air Force, starting here in the desert, was to continue to expand until the end of the war in Germany." Remarkably, however, going into the climactic invasion of Europe, there was a serious lack of air-ground cooperation that plagued the Normandy campaign into the summer of 1944.

Among the most bitter and dangerous controversies in Normandy was that between Montgomery and Air Marshals Arthur Tedder, Deputy Supreme Commander under Eisenhower, and Arthur "Mary" Coningham, commander of the 2nd Tactical Air Force. If the pipe-smoking, scholarly Tedder disliked Montgomery, Coningham loathed him: interviewer Forrest Pogue commented that Coningham was "the bitterest critic of Monty that I have heard speak." Coningham once burst out to a newspaper correspondent, "it's always 'Monty's Army,' 'Monty's Victory,' 'Monty Strikes Again.' You never say 'Coningham's Air Force'." Both Tedder and his protégé Coningham shared similar views on the correct use of air power which did not include close air support for the army or the use of heavy bombers as a battlefield weapon.

The literature on the dispute continues to be rancorous: historian Michael Pugh, in a review for the *New Zealand Journal of History* [325] of Vincent Orange's study, *Coningham: A Biography of Air Marshal Sir Arthur Coningham* [302], referred to Montgomery's "abysmal performance in France and northern Europe," and the rift "which Montgomery tried to solve in his usual malicious fashion by having Coningham removed." The Air Marshal's views are forcefully presented in Vincent Orange's biography.

In January 1944, when the names of the *Overlord* commanders were released to the press, a newspaper reporter remarked, "Of all the appointments for the high staff positions, Coningham's will be one of the most popular. It means that the old highly-successful Montgomery-Coningham partnership [of the desert] is to be maintained in our greatest operations of the war." The writer rejoiced that this "pair of friends," as he supposed them to be, were together again. Nothing could have been further from the truth. The behind-the-scenes conflicts are discussed by Air

Commander E. J. Kingston-McCloughry in his book, *The Direction of War: A Critique of the Political Direction and High Command in War* [215]. Kingston-McCloughry , who was chief planner to Air Marshal Trafford Leigh-Mallory, remarked that Coningham was the "last airman" Montgomery wanted as a colleague.

The critical importance that Montgomery attached to air support for ground operations is discussed by Nigel Hamilton in *Master of the Battlefield* [175A]. According to Hamilton, "It was not for want of trying on Monty's behalf, "that direct air support in Normandy did not reach its full potential. He cites the damning comment of American Colonel C.H. Bonesteel to Forrest Pogue: "The U.S. Air Corps-RAF was a house divided. The air side stank beyond belief."

The daily meeting of the Allied Air Commanders–sometimes called "the morning prayers of the air barons" – took place in the underground operations room at Bentley Priory, Stanmore, outside of London. The official records of their meetings are in the Public Record Office at Kew. In his autobiography, *From Apes to Warlords* [413], Professor Solly Zuckerman   describes the meetings in fascinating detail. The Air Commanders' meetings were chaired by Air Chief Marshal Trafford Leigh-Mallory, who in theory at least was air commander for *Overlord.* For personal and professional reasons, however, Tedder and Coningham were hostile toward Leigh-Mallory who was the odd man out in an Allied air command devoted to bomber mythology. After an unpromising start, in which Monty referred to Leigh-Mallory as "a gutless bugger" because he refused to drop an airborne division in the Caen area, relations between them warmed considerably when he realized that Leigh-Mallory was genuinely committed to helping the ground forces in Normandy.

Another eyewitness account to the meetings of the "Air Barons" is that by Charles Richardson entitled, *Flashback A Soldier's Story* [335]. Richardson was Montgomery's Chief of Plans Officer and he was transferred to Leigh-Mallory as a personal liaison officer, an indication of the high priority that Montgomery attached to army/air cooperation. *Flashback* appeared in 1985. According to Richardson, the atmosphere was tense at the June 14 meeting where Coningham bluntly announced that the situation before Caen was critical. His view was supported by Tedder who spoke of a "dangerous crisis." At the same meeting he reported what he termed, "Some queer calls for support had reached him from the Army, such as observation posts and mortar positions." Coningham did not regard them as "worthwhile targets." The next day Coningham declared that "The Army plan has failed." Richardson comments that this "unnecessary panic, perhaps artificially created by those who had no faith in Monty," had one useful result in that Leigh-Mallory visited Montgomery and offered to provide heavy bomber support. W. A. Jacobs noted in his essay, "The Battle for France, 1944," in Benjamin F. Cooling's volume, *Case Studies in the Development of Close Air Support* [90], that Leigh-Mallory was probably the most passionate believer in using all the resources of the Allied air forces to support the Allied armies. This attitude isolated him from virtually all of his senior colleagues in the Anglo-American air forces.

Before conferring with Coningham, however, about the proposed use of heavy bombers to support the army, Leigh-Mallory sent a planning team to Normandy to prepare for the bombing attack. Coningham and Tedder flew to France to break-up the meeting. The extraordinary scene is described by both Kingston-McCloughry and Solly Zuckerman who witnessed the affair. Both Tedder and Coningham viewed Montgomery's call for bomber support as a sign of a lack of fighting spirit on the part of the troops and incompetence on the part of their commander. Only one week after D-Day, with battle still raging, Tedder declared that, "The tactical phase was finishing, and that we must look further afield for our targets." A wide gulf separated Montgomery, determined to save the lives of his soldiers with whatever weapons were available, and the airmen Tedder and Coningham who insisted that their primary function was to destroy the enemy air force and strategic targets. Leigh-Mallory, however, did not abandon the idea of using the heavy bombers to support the army. He recorded in his diary, which is quoted by Nigel Hamilton in *Master of the Battlefield* [175A], that "The policy of double-dealing [by Tedder and Coningham], the effect of which as been to deny the Army what it wanted in the field, has failed."

Tedder's side of the controversy can be found in his memoirs, *With Prejudice: The War Memoirs of Marshal of the Royal Air Force Lord Tedder* [378]. The reviewer for *Newsweek* magazine commented: "His memoirs do not pulse with crunch and heartbreak of the field commander's losses and victories, but are the calm, often piqued, modulations of the imperturbable staff commander."

Severely critical of Montgomery's generalship in Normandy, all Tedder could see was an enormous effort by the ground and air forces resulting in little territorial gain. He agreed with Coningham's criticism of what he called Montgomery's "dilatory methods." He remarked, "I agreed with Coningham that the Army did not seem prepared to fight its own battles." Tedder's hostility toward Montgomery came to a head during Operation *Goodwood* when he urged that Eisenhower remove the British general from command of the Allied ground forces.

The Tedder-Coningham criticism of the army and Montgomery are repeated in John Terraine's 1985 book, *A Time For Courage: The Royal Air Force in the European War, 1939-1945* [379]. Terraine uses words like "specious," "ridiculous," and "absurd" in describing Montgomery's actions.

In his study, *Overlord: D-Day and the Battle of Normandy* [180], Max Hastings remarked that the issue is whether an earlier and wholehearted commitment by the air forces to direct support for the armies might have given more effective, perhaps decisive, support for the ground offensives. Hastings claims that if it had not been for the efforts of Coningham's subordinate, Air Vice-Marshal Harry Broadhurst, commander 83rd Group RAF, the British tactical air team would have been nonexistent in Normandy.

Other sources containing information on Montgomery and air power include: the official history by Denis Richards and H. St. George Saunders, *Royal Air Force, 1939-1945* [332]; Denis Richards, *Portal of Hungerford* [333]; Carlo D'Este, *Decision in Normandy* [98]; Charles Carrington, *Soldier at Bomber Command* [63]; Sir John Kennedy, *The Business of War* [212]; Thomas Alexander

Hughes, *Overlord: General Pete Quesada and the Triumph of Tactical Air Power in World War II* [194]. While focusing on Quesada, the American equivalent of Harry Broadhurst and a champion of close air support, Hughes's study is a valuable contribution to the literature on air power in World War II.

The Falaise Gap

One of the most debated aspects of the Normandy campaign would be the Allied attempt to surround or envelope the two German armies that began to retreat from Normandy in August 1944. Montgomery would be blamed by his critics for allowing thousands of Germans troops to escape by failing to cut off their escape route through the Falaise gap. Initially, the Allies had intended to carry out the so-called long envelopment strategy that called for Patton's armored forces to sweep eastwards and then north towards Paris, catching the enemy in a double envelopment. In the wake of the failed German counter-attack at Mortain, however, General Omar Bradley proposed a "short [left] hook" in place of the wide envelopment to trap the Germans between the Allies. The objective of Bradley's American forces was Argentan, some twelve miles inside the British boundary of operations.

Although Montgomery favored a wide envelopment to cut off the German armies in Normandy, he agreed to Bradley's short hook. In his biography, *Master of the Battlefield* [175A], Nigel Hamilton comments that Montgomery never seems "to have rued his decision." On August 4, Montgomery ordered the 1st Canadian Army under General H. D. G. Crerar to attack "*as early as possible*" in the direction of Falaise. This was Operation *Totalize*, which is described candidly by the official Canadian historian Colonel C. P. Stacey in his volume on the 1st Canadian Army, The Victory Campaign: The Operations in North-West Europe 1944-1945 [367]. Stacey speculates that the "long delayed" capture of Falaise by the inexperienced Canadians was a missed opportunity that "might even, conceivably, have enabled us to end the war some months sooner than was actually the case."

With the Canadians only half the way to Falaise, Patton foresaw that they could not close the gap quickly. On the night of August 12 he directed his advance troops to capture Argentan and then push carefully toward Falaise. What happened next would lead to seemingly endless "what ifs" and much post-war controversy. On August 13, Bradley countermanded Patton's order: "Nothing doing," Bradley told an angry Patton, who begged, saying half in jest: "We now have elements in Argentan. Shall we continue and drive the British into the sea for another Dunkirk?" Why Bradley did not allow Patton to try to close the gap and seal the Falaise pocket later became, to quote Martin Blumenson's, *Breakout and Pursuit* [35], the subject of "considerable polemic."

In *The Victory Campaign* [367], Colonel Stacey did not lose his temper over Patton's "crack" to Bradley about another Dunkirk, noting generously that while Patton undoubtedly had his failings, he had the instincts of a great battlefield commander, and he knew an opportunity when he saw one.

Patton's own views can be found in his account, *War As I Knew It* [310], and in *The Patton Papers 1940-1945* [38], edited by Martin Blumenson. In his diary entry for August 13, Patton wrote: "I am sure that this halt [Bradley's order to stop] is a great mistake, as I am certain that the British will not close on Falaise." A few days later he wrote, "I believe that the order . . . emanated from the 21st Army Group [Montgomery's command] . . . " Although Patton mistakenly blamed Montgomery for the stop order, the myth that Montgomery was behind Bradley's Argentan decision has proven among the most long-lived of World War II legends.

In his 1946 account,, *Top Secret* [196], Ralph Ingersoll blamed Montgomery for the decision to halt Patton's drive on Argentan. Nearly four decades later, in 1981, appeared the Montgomery-bashing book, *Patton's Gap: An Account of the Battle of Normandy 1944* [340], by Richard Rohmer. The author insisted that Montgomery gave the order that stopped Patton from closing the Falaise gap. Author Max Hastings, in his study, *Overlord: D-Day and the Battle of Normandy* [180], comments in a footnote: "For an extreme and extraordinary example of fanciful thinking about the failure wholly to destroy the German army at Falaise, see Richard Rohmer, *Patton's Gap.*" The same criticism could apply to the article, "Imperfect Victory at Falaise," by Flint Whitlock in *World War II* [405] magazine.

Bradley fully and frankly accepted responsibility for the halt decision in his memoir, *A Soldier's Story* [43]. Even in his much later autobiography written in collaboration with author Clay Blair, *A General's Life* [44], Bradley insisted , "Montgomery had no part in the decision." In *A Soldier's Story*, Bradley wrote, "In halting Patton at Argentan, however, I did not consult with Montgomery. The decision to stop Patton was mine alone; it never went beyond my CP [Command Post]." Bradley defended and justified his decision not to go beyond Argentan on August 13 largely on the grounds that German forces were stampeding out of the gap and might have trampled Patton's blocking force in their rush to escape encirclement. "I much preferred a solid shoulder at Argentan," declared Bradley, "to the possibility of broken neck at Falaise." On the other hand, he strongly implied that it was a mistake not to close the Falaise gap at that time, and he blamed Montgomery for the missed opportunity. Montgomery, charged Bradley, squeezed the enemy out of the pocket like one squeezed a tube of toothpaste instead of "capping the leak at Falaise."

Important questions were raised about Bradley's halt order by Russell F. Weigley, the leading historian of the American army in World War II, in his 1981 *tour de force*, *Eisenhower's Lieutenants: The Campaign of France and Germany 1944-1945* [398]. In a work highly praised by reviewer Forrest Pogue as "a fresh look at old controversies," Weigley declared that Bradley knew from *Ultra* intelligence that the bulk of German forces were still fighting within the Falaise pocket when he issued the halt order to Patton. The Germans had not yet decided to flee the pocket. Weigley asks the question, "Yet if Bradley believed that the Germans could get away so readily, then it is also questionable whether he should have attempted the short envelopment at all." Bradley compounded his error, declares Weigley, by concluding, again erroneously, that most of the enemy had escaped from the pocket, and as a consequence he abruptly reverted to the long envelopment which weakened Patton's forces around Argentan. Although Weigley agrees with Bradley that Montgomery should have reinforced the Canadians when they bogged down on the drive to Falaise, he remarks, "If failing to close the gap was a blunder, the fault was also Bradley's ... "

A scathing indictment of Bradley's indecisive generalship at the end of the Normandy campaign is presented in Martin Blumenson's 1994 study, *The Battle of the Generals: The Untold Story of the Falaise Pocket – The Campaign That Should Have Won World War II* [37]. According to Blumenson the Allied commanders "let the chance for an overwhelming victory slip through their fingers." What should have been a finely tuned and well-oiled maneuver to close the Falaise gap was, in Blumenson's opinion, "inept and bungled." As for Bradley's account of the stop order to Patton on August 13, Blumenson writes, "The explanation is dishonest and anti-British." The Germans were not fleeing eastward to escape encirclement on that date, notes Blumenson. In his earlier account, *Breakout and Pursuit* [35], Blumenson had remarked that Bradley's memory was "faulty by several days." The editor of the Patton Papers concludes, "No wonder Patton dreamed of being the Supreme Commander." After stopping Patton at Argentan, Bradley had sent Patton on a wider encirclement, only to stop him again as he moved eastwards; at this point Patton wrote in his diary, "I wish I were Supreme Commander." Although no admirer of Montgomery, Blumenson concedes that Patton and Montgomery would have produced a "perfectly matched team" that might have trapped the Germans west of the Seine through a wide envelopment, and brought about a much earlier end of the war in Europe.

The Falaise gap controversy is discussed by Carlo D'Este in his acclaimed biography, *Patton: A Genius For War* [100]. He observes that Patton did not live to participate in the post-war controversies and therefore never knew that he and Montgomery had been in complete agreement over how the Normandy campaign should be ended – both had preferred the long envelopment to cut the Germans off at the Seine. D'Este concludes, "He [Bradley] created the Falaise gap and, ultimately, he failed to close it." In D'Este's opinion, Bradley bore grudges longer and with more vehemence than Patton, and he never forgave Montgomery for trespassing on the II Corp boundary in Sicily. In Normandy, Bradley made no effort to find an accommodation over the Falaise gap.

D'Este's essay, "Falaise: The Trap Not Sprung," in the excellent publication, *MHQ: The Quarterly Journal of Military History* [99], is an even-handed discussion of the much debated subject. He sagely concludes that "The Argentan-Falaise gap was simply never the great tactical blunder that some armchair strategists have claimed. What, in retrospect, seems self-evident was, at the time, part of the inevitable fog of battle." If many German generals escaped to live and fight another day, the Battle of Normandy deservedly ranks with Stalingrad and North Africa as a crushing defeat of the *Wehrmacht*.

James Lucas and James Barker authored the 1978 study, *The Battle of Normandy: The Falaise Gap* [232], which draws heavily on German sources. In defense of Montgomery and Bradley, the authors claimed that no one on the Allied side was able to estimate the number of German troops in the Falaise pocket with any degree of accuracy.

Montgomery did not discuss the Falaise pocket issue in his *Memoirs* [268]. The short envelopment was not his idea. He simply states that, "The final victory [in Normandy] was definite, complete, and decisive." More ink is spent on the incident of the rampaging pig in his Tactical Headquarters, and the ludicrous charge by one of his own staff officers that Montgomery condoned looting! A useful glimpse of Montgomery at this time is found in General Sir John Kennedy's memoir, *The Business of War* [212]. Kennedy, Director of Military Operations at the War Office, visited Monty's Tactical HQ on August 17 and recorded that Montgomery, in shirt and corduroy trousers, looked "fit and cheerful." Kennedy noted, "Monty took his usual line that all had been done according to plan, and that he was very satisfied." Kennedy talks about Monty's famous leather-bound betting book.

Other important accounts include: Alistair Horne with David Montgomery, *The Lonely Leader: Monty 1944-1945* [186]; Martin Blumenson, "General Bradley's Decision at Argentan (13 August 1944)," in Kent Roberts Greenfield, editor, *Command Decisions* [166]; David Mason, *Breakout: Drive to the Seine* [250]; Eddy Florentin, *The Battle of the Falaise Gap* [143], translated by Mervyn Savill; Chester Wilmot, *The Struggle for Europe* [407]. Wilmot thought the Canadians should have closed the gap and prevented the escape of the German troops; Ronald Lewin, *Ultra Goes to War: The First Account of World War II's Greatest Secret Based on Official Documents* [224].

Chapter 8

From the Seine to the Baltic

> The proper development of allied strategy north of the Seine will
> become one of the great controversies of military history. At the
> time, I was, and I remain, of the opinion that in September 1944
> we failed to exploit fully the German disorganization consequent
> on their crushing defeat in the Battle of Normandy in August.
>   Montgomery, *Memoirs*

Single-thrust versus Broad-front strategy

In the spring 1994 issue of *MHQ: The Journal of Military History*, which was
devoted to the 50th Anniversary of D-Day, editor Robert Cowley posed several
pertinent questions concerning the conduct of the Normandy campaign. "Then,"
he asked, "there is the greatest question of all: Could the Western powers have
ended the war early in the fall of 1944?" At issue is the long-standing controversy
between the single thrust strategy proposed by Montgomery and the broad front
approach that was taken by Eisenhower. The question would be one of the most
passionately debated issues of World War II.

Montgomery's Proposal

History seemed to be repeating itself in 1944. In his study, *Eisenhower's
Lieutenants: The Campaign of France and Germany 1944-1945* [398], military
historian Russell Weigley wrote that the events of 1918 were very much in
everyone's mind in the late summer of 1944. After their overwhelming defeat in
Normandy, the German armies appeared to be in worse shape than they had been
when the Kaiser's regime collapsed in World War I. Half a million German

soldiers had been either killed, wounded, or taken prisoner of war. Ten thousand enemy dead were found in the Falaise pocket alone. The Allied victory ranked with Stalingrad and North Africa in its decisiveness.

The time lost before Caen had been more than made up; Paris was liberated on August 25, Brussels on September 3, Antwerp the following day. Not surprisingly, a widespread feeling existed that Nazi Germany would collapse before the onset of winter.

Montgomery shared this spirit of optimism but with an important qualification: "It was my view," he wrote in his *Memoirs* [268], "that the end of the war in Europe was most certainly 'within reach.' But what was now needed were quick decisions, and above all a plan." What he proposed, in its "simplest terms," was "the German 'Schlieffen Plan' of 1914 in reverse, except that it would be executed against a shattered and disorganized enemy." Now, in late August, Montgomery believed the moment had come to end the war with one bold and concentrated blow. His single thrust plan called for: "1. After crossing the Seine, 12 and 21 Army Groups [Bradley's 12th Army Group and his own 21st Army Group] should keep together as a solid mass of some forty divisions [about a million men] which would be so strong that it need fear nothing. This force would move north-eastwards [toward the Ruhr, the heartland of Germany's war economy]." Montgomery's 21st Army Group would be on the western flank, to clear the channel coast, while Bradley's 12th Army Group formed the eastern flank, with its right flank on the Ardennes.

On August 23, Montgomery presented his plan to Eisenhower who had flown over to his tactical headquarters accompanied by his chief of staff, Walter Bedell Smith, who Monty had not seen since D-Day in June. The meeting did not begin well when Montgomery asked if he could see Eisenhower alone "as I wanted his decision on certain vital matters of principle; these we must discuss alone, and his Chief of Staff could come in later." They talked alone for one hour.

The meeting is described in many accounts including Stephen Ambrose's, *The Supreme Commander: The War Years of General Dwight D. Eisenhower* [9]. According to Ambrose, "Montgomery then tried his best to be tactful, but he had already set Eisenhower on edge by locking Smith out and he now made matters worse by proceeding to give him a lecture, as if he were patronizing a student at a staff college."

In his *Memoirs*, Montgomery wrote, "I said that he must decide where the main effort would be made and we must then be so strong in the area that we could be certain of decisive results quickly." He warned Eisenhower "that if he adopted a broad front strategy, with the whole line advancing and everyone fighting all the time, the advance would inevitably peter out, the Germans would be given time to recover, and the war would go on all through the winter and well into 1945."

Monty further advised the Supreme Commander that he "should not descend into the land battle" and that "The Supreme Commander must sit on a very lofty perch . . . Someone must run the land battle for him." As planned earlier, Eisenhower was to assume direct operational control of the Allied armies on September 1; Montgomery would revert to a position of equality with Bradley as an army group commander– 21st Army Group.

Montgomery's bold plan for ending the war quickly while the German army in the West was in disarray meant confining Patton's 3rd Army to a defensive role of flank protection during the advance of the British 21st Army Group and the left wing of Bradley's 12th Army Group to the Ruhr. Eisenhower's reaction was that, even if it was militarily desirable (which he did not admit), it was politically impossible to stop Patton in full cry. "The American public," said Eisenhower, "would never stand for it; and public opinion wins war." To which Montgomery replied, "Victories win wars. Give people victory and they won't care who won it."

In his *Memoirs,* Monty admitted: " Possibly I went a bit far in urging on him my own plan, and did not give sufficient weight to the heavy political burden he bore. To adopt my plan he must stop the man with the ball: Patton, and his Third American Army . . . I never cease to marvel at his patience and forbearance with me on that occasion."

So strongly did Montgomery feel about the need for unified control of the armies that he told Eisenhower that, "if public opinion in America was involved, he should let Bradley control the battle and I would gladly serve under him." Eisenhower immediately declared that he had no intention of doing "anything of the sort."

"But my arguments were of no avail," wrote Montgomery. The broad front strategy was to be adopted and 12th Army Group, while thrusting forward on its left to support 21st Army Group, was to direct its main effort eastwards towards Metz and the Saar." "And so," he continued, "we all got ready to cross the Seine and go our different ways":

> Optimism was in the air, the whips were got out, and the Supreme Commander urged everyone on all along the front. Everyone was to be fighting all the time. . . All my military training told me we could not get away with it, and then we would be faced with a long winter campaign with all that that entailed for the British people.

Montgomery decided to make one more approach to Eisenhower in an effort to get "a sound plan adopted." On September 4, the day his forces captured Antwerp, he sent a message to Eisenhower at his headquarters on the Cherbourg peninsula. In Montgomery's opinion, "This was possibly a suitable place for a Supreme Commander; but it was useless [it was over 400 miles behind the front lines] for a land force commander who had to keep his finger on the pulse of his armies and give quick decisions in rapidly changing situations . . . In the early days of September he was, in fact, completely out of touch with the land battle, as far as I could see."

In his message, Montgomery declared: "1. I consider we have now reached a stage where one really powerful and full-blooded thrust towards Berlin is likely to get there and thus end the German war. 2. We have not enough maintenance resources for two full-blooded thrusts." In Montgomery's opinion the thrust likely to give the best and quickest results was the northern one via the Ruhr, rather than the other via Metz and the Saar.

Eisenhower flew to see Montgomery on September 10 – "a highly unfortunate encounter" in the words of Alistair Horne, *The Lonely Leader: Monty 1944-1945* [186]. Only a few days earlier Eisenhower had wrenched his knee. The painful injury would give him trouble for months. When he visited Montgomery, he could not leave his plane, and the conference had to take place inside it. When Eisenhower said that he had always intended to give priority to the Ruhr thrust and the northern route of advance, and that this was being done, Montgomery replied that it was "*not* being done." Eisenhower then said that by priority he did not mean "absolute priority," and that he could not in any way scale down the Saar thrust. Montgomery declared that the land battle was becoming "jerky and disjointed," and that as long as Eisenhower continued with two thrusts, neither could succeed. "It was obvious that he disagreed with my analysis," wrote Montgomery. Eisenhower repeated that they must first close to the Rhine and cross it on a wide front; "then, and only then, could we concentrate on one thrust."

According to Eisenhower biographer Stephen Ambrose, *The Supreme Commander* [9]: "As the tirade gathered in fury Eisenhower sat silent. At the first pause for breath, however, he leaned forward, put his hand on Montgomery's knee, and said, 'Steady, Monty! You can't speak to me like that. I'm your boss.' Montgomery mumbled that he was sorry." Monty did gain Ike's support for his daring plan to seize the Rhine bridges at Nijmegen and Arnhem, code named Operation *Market-Garden*. The conference ended on a happy note of agreement.

When General George C. Marshall, the American Army Chief of Staff visited his headquarters on October 8, Montgomery noted in his *Memoirs*, "I had a long talk with him, alone in my office caravan." He complained to Marshall that, "There was a lack of grip, and operational direction and control was lacking. Our operations had, in fact, become ragged and disjointed, and we had now got ourselves into a real mess." Marshall listened and said little: "It was clear that he entirely disagreed." Montgomery was correct. Marshall's reaction is found in Forrest C. Pogue, *George C. Marshall: Organizer of Victory* [319].

Convinced that a great opportunity had been lost, Montgomery wrote bitterly: "But what cannot be disputed is that when a certain strategy, right or wrong, was decided upon, it wasn't directed. We did not advance to the Rhine on a *broad* front; we advanced to the Rhine on *several* fronts, which were un-coordinated. And what was the German answer? A single and concentrated punch in the Ardennes, when we had become unbalanced and unduly extended."

Montgomery was supported in his views by General Alan Brooke, the Chief of the Imperial General Staff. Brooke's candid and sometimes caustic views–Eisenhower is described as "essentially a staff officer with little knowledge of the realities of the battlefield" – are found in the final volume of his diaries edited by Arthur Bryant, *Triumph in the West 1943-1946* [50]. Reviewer Charles Rolo noted that, "They have the flavor of an 'unauthorized' version of the events of which Churchill's great history is the authorized British version." Historian Walter Millis reproved its sometimes "waspish tone," but put it down to wartime stress and strain. Although Brooke supported Monty's single-thrust *coup de grâce* to the Ruhr in early September, soon thereafter he felt the opportunity had passed.

Then came Operation *Market-Garden*, Montgomery's ill-fated attempt to seize the Rhine bridge at Arnhem, cross the lower Rhine and outflank the German defensive barrier in the far north. By October 5, Brooke declared, "I feel that Monty's strategy for once is at fault. Instead of carrying out the advance on Arnhem he ought to have made certain of Antwerp in the first place." Montgomery would subsequently realize the mistake himself. Unwilling though he was ever to acknowledge an error, he wrote in his *Memoirs*: "I must admit a bad mistake on my part–I underestimated the difficulties of opening up the approaches to Antwerp so that we could get the free use of that port. I reckoned that the Canadian Army could do it *while* we were going for the Ruhr. I was wrong." Like everyone else after Normandy, his focus had been on crossing the Rhine.

Brooke's relations with Monty and Ike are discussed in David Fraser's first-rate account, *Alanbrooke* [144]. Monty's persistent suggestion that there should be a separate land force commander to run the land battle greatly irritated Eisenhower, and, on occasion , even Brooke who noted in his diary on November 8, "I had a talk with Montgomery before he returned to France. He still goes on harping over the system of command in France and the fact that the war is being prolonged." When Montgomery again raised the command question, Brooke replied, "Have you considered whether you are likely to be very acceptable in American eyes for this Command?" Fraser commented that while Brooke suspected a strong element of egotism in Montgomery's suggestions, he realized that it was exasperating for Monty, "a soldier of brilliant professional instincts, to see what he reckoned to be opportunities lost, lives squandered, a campaign awry."

On September 1, Eisenhower had assumed direct command of the Allied armies. Although the change of command had been agreed upon before D-Day, it still came as "an appalling shock" to Monty, according to Alistair Horne and David Montgomery, *The Lonely Leader: Monty 1944-1945* [186]. Military historian Ronald Lewin remarked in his book, *Montgomery as Military Commander* [222], "This was irksome for a man who had just won a great victory and was certain that he had the recipe for the final defeat of the Germans." At the same time Montgomery, in compensation, was made a Field Marshal: in reality, his status was equivalent to that of Bradley, under Eisenhower's Supreme Command. From this point on, Monty would command the British 21st Army Group.

In his *Memoirs*, Montgomery wrote "In the middle of all these troubles and disappointments [rejection of his single thrust plan]," he received word from Churchill that the King had approved his promotion to the rank of Field Marshal. His promotion to the highest rank in the British army did not appease Monty's sense of demotion, and his belief that a great mistake was about to be made.

Eisenhower's strategy

Eisenhower's post-war memoir, *Crusade in Europe* [126], appeared in 1948. Without referring directly to Montgomery's single thrust plan, Eisenhower wrote: "In the late summer days of 1944 it was known to us that the German still had disposable reserves within his own country. Any idea of attempting to thrust forward a small force, bridge the Rhine, and continue on into the heart of Germany was completely fantastic." Even a dozen divisions could only have been supplied temporarily, wrote Eisenhower, and the attacking force would have had to drop off units to protect its flanks and would have ended up facing "inescapable defeat."

Regarding his September 10 meeting with Monty, Eisenhower wrote: "There was still a considerable reserve in the middle of the enemy country and I knew that a pencil-like thrust into the heart of Germany such as he proposed would meet nothing but certain destruction." "This was true," he remarked, "no matter on what part of the front it might be attempted. I would not consider it."

Besides his criticism of Montgomery's single thrust strategy, Eisenhower strongly implied that his priority had always been the port of Antwerp and its approaches. All these points would be disputed by Montgomery in his own memoirs a decade later.

In 1970, *The Papers of Dwight David Eisenhower: The War Years*[71], edited by Alfred D. Chandler, Jr., and associate editor Stephen E. Ambrose, were published. The five volumes of wartime papers include almost everything vital that Eisenhower wrote during World War II.

Almost simultaneously there appeared Ambrose's biography, *The Supreme Commander: The War Years of General Dwight D. Eisenhower* [9]. In a brilliant chapter devoted to the single thrust versus broad front debate, Ambrose asked the important question, "Was his insistence on a broad front wise? Was he right or was Montgomery? Since the AEF [Allied Expeditionary Force] did not deliver the final blow in the fall of 1944, it is clear that Eisenhower's way did not work." But to say that Eisenhower's broad front approach was unsuccessful, declared Ambrose, did not mean that Montgomery's would have succeeded. Among the manifold reasons why Eisenhower rejected the single thrust, Ambrose mentions the officers at SHAEF that he saw every day to whom he looked for information and advice; "none had confidence in Montgomery."

Montgomery's unpopularity at SHAEF is supported by Noel Annan in his book, *Changing Enemies: The Defeat and Regeneration of Germany* [11]. A member of the SHAEF staff himself, Annan remarks that, "It became the mark of a good British SHAEF officer to express dismay at the behavior of Montgomery." For two such British critics of Montgomery see, General Kenneth Strong (Eisenhower's Intelligence chief), *Intelligence at the Top* [372], and General Frederick Morgan (Eisenhower's deputy chief of staff), *Peace and War: A Soldier's Life* [285].

In Ambrose's opinion, Eisenhower had fallen victim to the "victory disease," a virus which caused the patient to believe anything was possible. Since the Falaise gap, one success had followed another. Eisenhower was sure they could cross the Rhine on a wide front and seize both the Saar and the Ruhr, thus destroying Germany's capacity to wage war. According to Ambrose, Eisenhower "unconsciously" counted on a repetition of November 1918, when the Germans signed the armistice while their armies were still west of the Rhine. "Eisenhower had chosen the safe, cautious route," declares his biographer, "Under his directives no army would take heavy casualties, no general would lose his reputation, credit for the victory would be shared by all, and there was no chance of the Germans reversing the situation by surrounding and destroying an advanced force." The only trouble was that if the Germans decided to fight on it would take longer to end the war. "Time was what Montgomery wanted to save," remarked Ambrose. Every day that the war continued further drained what remained of Britain's fast declining strength. The only chance of winning the war in 1944 was to take risks, and to take them right away, in the first week of September.

In discussing the logistical and political factors that entered into Eisenhower's decision not to adopt a single thrust strategy, Ambrose cited Forrest C. Pogue's classic account, *The Supreme Command* [320]. Pogue had declared: "In hardly any respect were the Allies prepared to take advantage of the great opportunity offered them to destroy the German forces before winter . . . virtually the whole intricate military machine was geared to a slower rate of advance than that required in late August." So overwhelming had been the August victory in France that the Allies were logistically unprepared to take advantage of the great opportunity that briefly presented itself in the first week of September – a case of the German situation in 1940 in reverse.

In spite of Eisenhower's oft-repeated assertions that he made all his decisions on military grounds, Ambrose claimed that political factors were crucial in Eisenhower's decision to follow a broad front strategy. In the opinion of Ambrose, "No matter how brilliant or logical Montgomery's plan for an advance to the Ruhr was, (and a good case can be made that it was both), and no matter what Montgomery's personality was, under no circumstances would Eisenhower agree to give all the glory to the British." If the troops all been composed of one nationality, Ambrose speculated that Eisenhower might have adopted Montgomery's plan : "But as things stood Eisenhower could not make his decisions solely on military grounds. He could not halt Patton in his tracks, relegate Bradley to a minor administrative role, and in effect tell Marshall that the great army he had raised in the United States was not needed in Europe."

As for Eisenhower's ideas on military theory, Ambrose considered him to be in the Grantian tradition: "Like Grant in the Virginia Wilderness in 1864, he favored constant attack, and he became disturbed if any substantial part of his force was not gaining ground." An advocate of the direct approach, he "put his faith in the sheer smashing power of great armies."

A sympathetic portrait of Eisenhower was presented in the 1973 scholarly study by British General E. K. G. Sixsmith, *Eisenhower as Military Commander* [357]. The author takes what might be termed a middle position on the broad front strategy, observing that it was "right in the long run," but put "into effect too early." As Allied Supreme Commander, attempting to weld together different nations and services, Eisenhower, concluded Sixsmith, "did superbly."

Eisenhower's decisions were strongly defended by his grandson, David Eisenhower, in his 1986 tribute, *Eisenhower: At War 1943-1945* [125]. Reviewer Russell Weigley commented, "As a study of generalship, the book is uncritical to a fault." In spite of shortcomings, the book is a useful analysis of the Supreme Commander.

Eisenhower's side of his disputes with Monty and others is reflected in the behind-the-scenes accounts by his naval aide Captain Harry C. Butcher's account, *Three Years with Eisenhower* [54], and Kay Summersby's two books, *Eisenhower Was My Boss* [374], and *Past Forgetting: My Love Affair with Dwight D. Eisenhower* [283]. Both were part of Ike's inner circle; both disliked Montgomery. Summersby, who later claimed a secret wartime love affair with Ike, came to hate Monty with a passion, calling him "a supercilious woman-hating little martinet."

American leadership is strongly defended by Eric Larrabee in his 1987 account, *Commander in Chief: Franklin Delano Roosevelt, His Lieutenants, and their War* [220]. The well-written account echoes earlier critics of Montgomery. On the single-front issue, Larrabee declares, "Montgomery was wrong."

The twists and turns of the Montgomery-Eisenhower relationship were detailed in Norman Gelb's 1994 book, *Ike and Monty: Generals at War* [157]. The author is more critical of Montgomery.

The Historical Debate

Only six months returned from the war, where he had served on Bradley's staff, Ralph Ingersoll wrote his polemical account, *Top Secret* [196]. He labeled Eisenhower a pawn of the duplicitous British, a front-office stooge, a yes-man. According to Ingersoll, "I believe that in August 1944 a Supreme Commander . . . could have ended the war by Christmas by decisively backing either Montgomery or Bradley. But there was . . . no strong hand at the helm, no man in command." In a letter to Monty, Ike called *Top Secret* a "trashy book."

In his 1946 biography, *Montgomery* [278], the former war correspondent, Alan Moorehead, who knew both Monty and Ike, commented: "Looking back on the event it is still difficult for the non-expert to decide who was right." Moorehead thought that the extra six months on the war in 1945 acutely intensified the ensuing famine in Europe, and accelerated (through air bombing) the general down slide of civilization in the post-war years. If possible, therefore, Montgomery's thrust was well worth trying. But he noted that even among the British, Montgomery had opponents. The Russians at this time required 150 divisions to reach the Oder. Could the Allies have thrown the Germans out of the war with just thirty divisions, he asked ? In Moorehead's opinion, only the success of the July bomb plot against Hitler could have made Montgomery's single-thrust scheme "water-tight beyond all doubt."

The appearance of Chester Wilmot's, *The Struggle for Europe* [407], in 1952 was greeted by reviewer Hanson Baldwin with the acclamation, "The best history of the war in western Europe yet published." A young New Zealander who had served as a war correspondent for the BBC, Wilmot, like Moorehead, was granted access by Montgomery to his files as well as interviews, and as reviewer Drew

Middleton noted, "Inferentially, at least," Wilmot's account was a reply to the attacks on Montgomery and the British approach to war that had figured "so largely in the reminiscences of our [American] generals." Among the thousands of books written on the north-west Europe campaign, military historian John Keegan selected Wilmot's book to be on his list of the best "Fifty Books on the Second World War." If some of his judgements have been either challenged or demolished, for Keegan, Wilmot's history, "remains for me the supreme achievement of Second World War historiography."

On the fierce Eisenhower-Montgomery argument over the strategy to be pursued after Normandy, Wilmot defended Eisenhower's initial negative response to Monty's plan expressed at the August 23 meeting. It was bold enough, he noted, but it meant halting Patton and confining Third Army to the defensive role of flank protection during the advance of the Second British and First American Armies to the Ruhr. "It is not surprising [given the dash and drive that Patton had demonstrated so brilliantly since the break-out]," declared Wilmot, "that Eisenhower should have doubted at this stage whether Montgomery had the troops or the commanders to carry the northward thrust through to the Ruhr before the Germans could re-establish a coherent front."

By early September, however, Wilmot argues that Eisenhower missed a major opportunity when he allowed Bradley to reinforce the eastward drive of Patton's Third Army at the expense of General Courtney Hodges's First U.S. Army, which was supporting Montgomery's drive for the Ruhr.

Wilmot challenged the statement in the Eisenhower memoirs that, "There was still a considerable reserve in the middle of the enemy country and I knew that any pencil like thrust into the heart of Germany such as he [Montgomery] proposed would meet nothing but certain destruction." He argued that Eisenhower was influenced not by his concern about the enemy's reserves, but by his confidence that both the Ruhr and the Saar could be captured "without the unpalatable necessity of ordering either Patton or Montgomery to stop." Bradley is also censured: "In his eagerness to maintain the advance of Third Army through the Saar to Frankfurt," wrote Wilmot, "Bradley had missed the opportunity of outflanking the Siegfried Line north of Aachen or making a breach in its most vulnerable sector . . . "

Finally, Wilmot noted that, "Since the war von Rundstedt and other German generals who can speak with authority (Student, Westphal, Blumentritt, Speidel and others) have all declared that a concentrated thrust from Belgium in September must have succeeded." Field Marshal Gerd von Runstedt's views are discussed by Caleb Carr [62] in his *MHQ* article, "The Black Knight."

Wilmot was careful to add, however, that "In view of Hitler's unbroken resolve to continue the struggle even into the streets of Berlin regardless of the cost, there is reason to doubt whether the capture of the Ruhr and Rhineland alone" would have ended the war in 1944. But Wilmot was certain that the loss of these two areas would have deprived Hitler of the means of carrying out the grandiose plan already forming in his mind for a winter offensive in the West.

Unlike Wilmot, Sir Basil Liddell Hart stated categorically in his, *History of the*

Second World War, [226] "The war could easily have been ended in September 1944." Tragically, Liddell Hart died only a few months before the publication of his monumental study in 1970. In his review, Corelli Barnett wrote that it was, "A magnificent finale to a distinguished career." Many of Liddell Hart's judgments were based on his post-war interviews with senior German commanders. In support of his belief that the war could have been ended in 1944 he quoted General Günther von Blumentritt (German Chief of Staff in the West), who had tol d him, "There were no German forces behind the Rhine, and at the end of August our front was wide open." Liddell Hart's book, *The Other Side of the Hill* [229], an essential source, contains the results of his interrogation of German generals.

In his *History of the Second World War,* Liddell Hart argued that Eisenhower's broad front approach would have been a good way to strain and crack the resistance of a strong and still unbeaten enemy. But it was far less suited to the conditions after Falaise "where the enemy had already collapsed, and the issue depended on exploiting their collapse so deeply and rapidly that they would have no chance to rally." In these circumstances, he felt that Montgomery's demand for a single and concentrated thrust was far better in principle. Liddell Hart claimed that many of Montgomery's logistical difficulties were "within his own orbit"–he cited the delay in opening up the port of Antwerp.

In 1981 appeared the magisterial study of the American army by Russell Weigley, *Eisenhower's Lieutenants: The Campaigns of France and Germany 1944-1945* [398]. Reviewer Drew Middleton praised Weigley's "masterly summation" of the broad front versus single front strategy. "No one," wrote Middleton, "has treated this topic any better than Mr. Weigley." He agreed with Weigley's assessment that "American generalship by and large was competent but addicted to playing it safe." Earlier Weigley made the same charge against Monty, although in much more critical terms. In fact, Middleton's most serious criticism of the book was Weigley's allowing his distaste for Montgomery to unbalance the narrative: "Mr. Weigley's criticism of Montgomery is so incessant and insistent that this reader sometimes got the impression that the field marshal was a more obnoxious character than S. S. General Sepp Dietrich and the other Nazi bully boys who massacred prisoners at Malmédy in Belgium."

Referring to Liddell Hart's argument in favor of Montgomery's single and concentrated thrust, Weigley declared that, "The trouble with this interpretation . . . lay in the question whether 'the enemy had already collapsed.'" Facing logistical reality, Montgomery had scaled back his original forty division offensive, and Weigley did not think the sixteen or eighteen division thrust by the British 2nd Army and the American 1st Army that Monty was proposing in early September would have been strong enough to reach Berlin. Weigley considered Eisenhower justified referring to a sixteen or eighteen divisions drive on Berlin as "knife-like" or "pencil like." Weigley concluded that, "Even the emaciated version of Montgomery's 'full-blooded thrust' was beyond the capacity of Allied logistics." Did Montgomery actually intend to drive all the way to Berlin with an eighteen-division advance? In his *Memoirs* Montgomery insisted his first objective was the industrial Ruhr, followed finally by Berlin. His orders just before Operation *Market-Garden* declared: "*Our real objective, therefore, is the Ruhr.*" In his 1986 volume, *Monty: Final Years of the Field-Marshal 1944-1976* [174B], Nigel Hamilton cited Chester Wilmot's 1946 interview with Montgomery: "I knew now [the time of Eisenhower's visit on September 10 1944] that we could not hope to get much more than a bridgehead beyond the Rhine before the winter, and be nicely poised for breaking out in the New Year." He further cited Forrest Pogue's interview with Air Marshal Arthur Tedder who had attended the September 10 meeting between Eisenhower and Monty. According to Tedder (no friend of Montgomery), "Monty had no idea of going on to Berlin from here [Arnhem]. By this time he was ready to settle for a position across the Rhine."

The problems of conducting a coalition war are described by Dominick Graham and Shelford Bidwell in their controversial book, *Coalitions, Politicians, and Generals: Some Aspects of Command in Two World Wars* [162]. If scathing in their indictment of Eisenhower the military commander – "useless," "the blind leading the blind," "fig leaf strategy" – they consider him largely successful as a politician in leading the Allied coalition to victory. Graham and Bidwell view him as caught between Marshall and Bradley – both infected by the Montgomery virus, which amounted, at times, they claim, to Anglophobia.

Patton's actions during this time are discussed in Carlo D'Este's first-rate biography, *Patton: A Genius for War* [100]. On those occasions when Eisenhower allocated priority to Montgomery, Patton would rage at Monty, as well as refer to Ike as the best general the British had. At a press conference in early September, Patton declared that "if Ike stops holding Monty's hand and gives me the supplies, I'll go through the Siegfied line like shit through a goose." D'Este is doubtful that Patton's offensive could have won the war in 1944. Neither is Anthony Kemp in his study, *The Unknown Battle: Metz, 1944* [211]. Kemp argues that all the Allied strategists agreed that the prime objective was the Ruhr, and that Patton's offensive would not have fulfilled any strategic purpose. In D'Este's mind an even more serious problem would have been the inability to provide sufficient close air support for such a drive.

Patton's own views are found in his memoir, *War As I Knew It* [310], as well as volume II of *The Patton Papers* [38] edited by Martin Blumenson. In his 1994 book, *The Battle of the Generals* [37], Blumenson argue that Patton and Montgomery might have accomplished together what Bradley and Montgomery did not. Both respected each other's professionalism, and Blumenson speculates that they might have teamed up to keep Eisenhower away from the fighting. Other accounts include Hugh M. Cole, *The Lorraine Campaign* [83]; Ladislas Farago, *Patton: Ordeal and Triumph* [138]; Kent Roberts Greenfield, *The Historian and the Army* [167].

Canadian C. P. Stacey, in his country's official history, *The Victory Campaign: The Operations in North-West Europe, 1944-1945* [367], noted that Montgomery's plan for a concentrated northern thrust would probably have produced victory in 1944 if it had been possible to put the plan into practice at that moment, but he declared that Eisenhower had strong arguments on his side in favoring the conservative and prudent line rather than a bold one. Stacey concluded, "There is obviously no basis for a dogmatic statement."

Additional sources include General Sir Francis De Guingand (Monty's chief of staff), *Operation Victory* [109], and *Generals at War* [108]. His conclusion: "Eisenhower was right"; G. E. Patrick Murray examined many post-war memoirs for his study, *Eisenhower versus Montgomery: The Continuing Debate* [290]. According to Murray, the notion that a single thrust by the Western Allies could have ended the war quickly is an "ethnocentric" fallacy that ignores the far more important Eastern Front; John North, *Northwest Europe, 1944-1945: The Achievements of the 21ˢᵗ Army Group* [301]; L. F. Ellis with A.E. Warhurst, *Victory in the West*, vol. II, *The Defeat of Germany* [131]; John Ehrman, *Grand Strategy*, volumes V and VI [124]; Roland G. Ruppenthal, "Logistics and the Broad-Front Strategy," in Kent Robert Greenfield, ed., *Command Decisions* [166]; Martin van Creveld, *Supplying War: Logistics from Wallenstein to Patton* [392]; General Sir Brian Horrocks, *A Full Life* [189]; General Siegfried Westphal, *The German Army in the West* [401]; R. W. Thompson, *Montgomery the Field Marshal: The Campaign in North-West Europe 1944-45* [381]. The volume is much more favorable toward Montgomery than his earlier debunking work, *The Montgomery Legend* [382].

Operation *Market-Garden*

On September 17, 1944, Montgomery launched Operation *Market-Garden*, one of the most controversial operations of World War II. It was Monty's design and the operation failed with tragically high losses. Historian John Grigg would assert, "there was surely a strong case for removing him [Monty] after Arnhem." Montgomery, in Grigg's opinion, was a general with a hyped-up reputation who possessed a hold over the media that made him scarcely more removable than General Douglas Haig in World War I. Grigg's essay appeared in the volume, *Churchill* [31], edited by Robert Blake and William Roger Louis.

Monty's objective was to open the way to the Ruhr by seizing a bridgehead over the lower Rhine. In the largest and most ambitious airborne operation of the war, the 1ˢᵗ Allied Airborne Army (the American 82ⁿᵈ and 101ˢᵗ Airborne Divisions and the British 1ˢᵗ Airborne Division) were to seize five bridges and canals that led to the lower Rhine. The use of just such a daring deployment of airborne forces in a major strategic operation had been strongly urged by U.S. Army Air Force General Henry "Hap" Arnold and General George C. Marshall for months. Seventeen earlier airborne operations had been canceled; denied action for so long, the airborne troops were "raring to go." In his excellent account, *The Battle of Arnhem* [183], historian Christopher Hibbert quoted an airborne officer as saying, "They'd had to wait too long."

On the ground, the British Thirtieth Corps, under General Brian Horrocks, was to advance north along the narrow corridor opened by the airborne forces, and finally link up with the British 1ˢᵗ Airborne Division, at Arnhem – the place that became popularly known as "a bridge too far." The corridor consisted of a single, two-lane, raised causeway with marsh and dykes on either side. The British armor had to break through to Arnhem in forty-eight hours, before the Germans could rally to crush the 1st Airborne paratroopers. The stand of Lieutenant-Colonel John Frost's 2nd Parachute Battalion at Arnhem bridge is widely considered one of the most heroic episodes of World War II. The attempt to relieve the "Red Devils" at Arnhem bridge failed, and after a week of bitter fighting the survivors were ordered to withdraw as best they could. Of the ten thousand who landed at Arnhem, fourteen hundred were killed and over six thousand captured; only twenty-four hundred paratroopers crossed to safety in small rubber boats. Arnhem was the German army's first overt success since Normandy.

In his *Memoirs* [268], Monty insisted, "In my – prejudiced – view, if the operation had been properly backed from its inception, and given the aircraft, ground forces, and administrative resources necessary for the job – it would have succeeded *in spite of* my mistakes . . . "I remain *Market-Garden's* unrepentant advocate." Besides the supply question, Montgomery declared that the airborne forces were dropped too far away from the vital objective – the Arnhem bridge: "I take the blame for this mistake. I should have ordered Second Army and 1 Airborne Corps to arrange that at least one complete Parachute Brigade was dropped quite close to the bridge, so that it could have been captured in a matter of minutes and its defense soundly organized with time to spare. I did not do so."

As after Normandy, so again after Arnhem, Montgomery was "bitterly disappointed." It had been his second attempt to try and capture the Ruhr quickly. He acknowledged, "And here I must admit a bad mistake on my part – I underestimated the difficulties of opening up the approaches to Antwerp so that we could get the free use of that port. I reckoned that the Canadian Army could do it *while* we were going for the Ruhr. I was wrong."

Montgomery recommended Chester Wilmot's *The Struggle in Europe* [407], as probably "the best and most complete account" of *Market-Garden*. He closed the Arnhem chapter with a final quotation from *The Struggle in Europe* on the battle: "It was most unfortunate that the two major weaknesses of the Allied High Command – the British caution about casualties and the American reluctance to concentrate – should both have exerted their baneful influence on this operation, which should, and could, have been the decisive blow of the campaign in the West."

The eminent military history Russell F. Weigley noted in his thought-provoking analysis, *Eisenhower's Lieutenants* [398], that *Market-Garden* has commanded more attention than any other battle of the northwest Europe campaign save the D-Day landings and the Battle of the Bulge. In a similar vein, Nigel Hamilton, author of *Monty* [174B], remarked that "few six-day battles in history have seen so much fighting after the event, between veterans, military critics and historians."

For Eisenhower's role see his own *Crusade in Europe* [126], and more especially Stephen Ambrose's biography, *The Supreme Commander* [9]. Ambrose acknowledged that, "Even two and a half decades later it is impossible to read Eisenhower's letters and telegrams to Montgomery without a feeling of frustration because of their vagueness." He admits, for example, that "The simple question as to whether Eisenhower wanted Arnhem or Antwerp most cannot be answered." He quotes Ike as writing, " I not only approved *Market-Garden*, I insisted upon it. What we needed was a *bridgehead* over the Rhine. If that could be accomplished I was quite willing to wait on all other operations. What this action proved was that the idea of `one full blooded thrust' to Berlin was silly." His grandson, David Eisenhower, in his book, *Eisenhower: At War 1943-1945* [125], goes so far as to suggest that Eisenhower deliberately allowed Monty to undertake *Market-Garden* with inadequate resources knowing that he must fail and be placed thereafter in subordinate role.

In his account, *A Soldier's Story* [43], Omar Bradley recorded his reaction to *Market-Garden*: "Had the pious teetotaling Montgomery wobbled into SHAEF with a hangover, I could not have been more astonished than I was by the daring adventure he proposed . . . Although I never reconciled myself to the venture, I nevertheless freely concede that Monty's plan for Arnhem was one of the most imaginative of the war."

General Sir Brian Horrocks, who commanded the British Thirtieth Corps, which was charged with the thrust to link-up with the 1st Airborne Division at Arnhem, was criticized by that division's commander, General Roy Urquhart (no relation to Brian Urquhart), as well as others, with being too slow in coming to its relief. The Arnhem attack is replete with what ifs – in his *MHQ* essay, "The Failure of Market-Garden" [309], Rod Paschall wondered what might have happened if Patton and not Horrocks had commanded the XXX Corps!

In his forthright memoir, *A Full Life* [189], Horrocks wrote, "I have thought over this battle many times and wondered whether there was anything more that I could have done." He found the primary cause for their failure at Arnhem to be the "astonishing recovery made by the German armed forces after their crippling defeat in Normandy." "Was Monty correct," he asked, "in carrying out the Arnhem operation, which meant advancing sixty to seventy miles into Holland?" Would it have been better, wrote Horrocks, if Monty had turned northwest and cleared the Scheldt estuary first to open the port of Antwerp, as many of Monty's critics think he should have done? In the opinion of Horrocks, "Monty was right." They had advanced rapidly up the coastal plain while the Germans were still disorganized, and Montgomery's "eyes were focused on the big prize – to bounce a crossing over the Rhine and cut off the industrial heart of Germany, thus finishing the war in 1944. He concludes, "On the information available, Arnhem was a justifiable gamble."

By far the most popular account of Operation *Market-Garden* was Cornelius Ryan's 1974 best-seller, *A Bridge Too Far* [346]. Ryan had served as a correspondent during the war. According to Ryan, General Frederick "Boy" Browning, corps commander of the three and a half airborne divisions designated to drop on the key bridges, expressed unease and pointing to Arnhem, he asked, "How long will it take the armor to reach us?" Montgomery is supposed to have replied briskly, "Two days." Ryan reports that Browning said, "We can hold it for four . . . But sir, I think we might be going a bridge too far."

A Bridge Too Far was chosen as a Book-Of-The-Month Club selection, and became the basis for the all-star 1977 motion picture of the same name. Among the stars were Michael Caine, Sean Connery, Gene Hackman., and Anthony Hopkins as Colonel Frost. Like his earlier historical works, *The Longest Day* (dealt with D-Day) and *The Last Battle* (the fight for Berlin), Ryan used a journalistic, you-are-there technique, which in this case was based on 1,500 interviews with soldiers and civilians, including Eisenhower who spoke bitterly of Montgomery as "a man that just can't tell the truth." As *Time* magazine reviewer Melvin Maddocks noted, "Ryan does little to defend the field marshal." Ryan referred to Monty as "acrid and autocratic," "intractable," "arrogant," and "insolent." Describing *Market-Garden* as "one of the greatest miscalculations of the European war," Ryan quoted Prince Bernhard of the Netherlands as saying, "My country can never again afford the luxury of another Montgomery success (a reference to Monty's description of it as 90% successful)."

The influence of *A Bridge Too Far* can be judged from its impact on Sir Brian Urquhart who wrote in his memoir, *A Life in Peace and War* [390], "I did not fully realize until more than thirty years later, when Cornelius Ryan published his masterly account of the Arnhem battle, *A Bridge Too Far*, that 'Market-Garden' was the offspring of the ambition of Montgomery, who desperately wanted a British success to end the war." Urquhart had served as chief intelligence officer for the British Airborne Corps. He later served as Deputy Secretary General of the United Nations. In a 1996 interview made available on the Internet, Urquhart declared, "its failure [*Market-Garden*] was, I'm sorry to say, very largely an indictment of Field Marshal Montgomery."

A scholarly and well-written account of *Market-Garden* is presented in Russell F. Weigley's 1981 book, *Eisenhower's Lieutenants: The Campaign of France and Germany 1944-1945* [398]. In Weigley's opinion, Monty's plan was "refreshingly daring" in the context of cautious Anglo-American generalship, and offered "the best remaining opportunity for the Allies to win the war that autumn." With such stakes involved, wrote Weigley, "the risks were worth running . . . For it could have succeeded." In Weigley's view, the critical flaw was not in the boldness of Monty's strategic design but in the tactical execution.

A personal reminiscence of the advance on Arnhem is the 1988 memoir, *Reflecting on Things Past*, by Lord Carrington. The author served with the Guards Armored Division whose mission it was to advance up the narrow corridor and link up with the airborne divisions dropped on Arnhem and Nijmegen. Was the operation feasible, he asks? It seems to Carrington that the rate of progress planned for the ground troops was "absurdly optimistic."

In 1994, on the fiftieth anniversary of *Market-Garden*, Martin Middlebrook commemorated the battle in his book, *Arnhem 1944: The Airborne Battle, 17-26 September* [259]. Middlebrook was ready to retire after a distinguished writing career (thirteen books) when he was asked to write the Arnhem book–his self-described "literary swan-song." Reviewer Carlo D'Este lauded it as "a fitting conclusion to the career of an eminent historian." In the opinion of reviewer Sir Brian Urquhart, "This is the best book I have read on Arnhem." Urquhart observed that it was hard not to blame Eisenhower, Montgomery, and one or two generals, and planners, for the "last, and most unnecessary" British defeat of the war.

Besides interviews with fifty participants in the battle, Middlebrook used the bulging archive of Arnhem reports at the Airborne Forces Museum at Aldershot. "I am not a revisionist historian," declared Middlebrook, with dramatic disclosures about Arnhem. He is, however, highly critical of Lieutenant-General F. A. M. "Boy" Browning, the Allied airborne commander who ignored, and actually concealed, the warnings that the drop zones at Arnhem were potentially disastrous. On the other hand, high praise goes to Major-General S. F. Sosabowski, the commander of the 1st Polish Independent Parachute Brigade, who was later unjustly relieved of his command at Browning's instigation. Middlebrook is particularly critical of the air plan and RAF Air Vice Marshal L. N. Hollinghurst who decided on the dropping and landing zones, which were eight miles from the critical objective, the bridge at Arnhem, thus throwing away the airborne's most valuable asset – surprise. At the same time, Middlebrook faults both Dempsey (2nd British army) and Horrocks (Thirtieth Corps) for failing to comply with Montgomery's order that the ground attack should be "rapid and violent, without regard to what is happening on the flanks." As for Monty, who had often interfered vigorously in the handling of battles, Middlebrook noted that he was "strangely quiet now."

Volume three of Nigel Hamilton's trilogy, *Monty: Final Years of the Field-Marshal, 1944-1976* [174B], covers the Arnhem tragedy. In a chapter entitled, "A Bridge Too Far?" Hamilton questions whether General "Boy" Browning actually made the remark to Monty that Arnhem might be a "bridge too far." Hamilton thinks that it is "inherently unlikely," since Browning saw General Miles Dempsey, not Montgomery, on the day in question; furthermore, Dempsey now offered him three airborne divisions plus the Polish brigade when Browning had been preparing for the operation without the two American divisions. According to Hamilton, the decisive, almost legendary Grenadier Guardsman, General "Boy" Browning, was not the type to speculate pessimistically.

The official biographer is no Monty apologist, calling *Market-Garden* Monty's "worst mistake of the war, defying all the principles of logistic back-up, of adequate reserves, and the relentless application of superior firepower that had characterized his march of victories from 1942 onwards." In retrospect, Hamilton finds it "incredible that Monty should have allowed himself to be enticed by the idea of a unilateral British drive into Germany to the exclusion of the vital need to secure quickly the Channel ports, open Antwerp and ensure the capture of the German forces corseted between Second Army and the sea." Hamilton criticized Monty's attempt "in the months and years ahead" to shift the blame onto Eisenhower, when, declares Hamilton, "it was in truth his own doing." Montgomery's bid for the Ruhr via Arnhem, he asserts, was "nothing less than foolhardy."

How to explain *Market-Garden* when, in the words of Hamilton, it would have been best had it never been undertaken "at all." According to his official biographer, Montgomery had almost reached a state of nervous breakdown as a result of his ongoing differences with Eisenhower over command and strategy.

Hamilton does not side with "the many sympathetic historians" of Eisenhower who view him as the "'long-suffering,' forbearing Supreme Commander arbitrating between prima-donnas." Rather than vanity, egotism, or megalomania, Hamilton argues that Montgomery was motivated by a profound sense of military professionalism, which was deeply disturbed and alarmed by what he considered to be Eisenhower's potentially disastrous policy of strategic dispersal and *laissez-faire* command.

The Field Marshal himself had misgivings about *Market-Garden*, and delayed the operation from day to day. That Montgomery was driven to the "brink of distraction" in the early days of September is demonstrated by his loss of temper with Canadian General Henry Crerar. The senior Canadian officer in Europe, Crerar had arrived late on September 3 for an army commanders conference after having attended memorial parade in Dieppe to honor those Canadians who had died in the 1942 raid. In Monty's eyes, Crerar had failed to recognize the critical importance of exploiting the Allied victory in Normandy, and thus avoiding a long drawn-out winter campaign. In an emotional outburst, Monty accused the Canadian general, among other things, of disobeying orders. An outraged Crerar threatened to take the matter up with the Canadian government. Peace was restored when Montgomery wrote a letter of apology – "I am sorry I was a bit rude the other day, and somewhat out-spoken." The "tiff" is discussed in Colonel C. F. Stacey, *The Victory Campaign: The Official History of the Canadian Army in the Second World War* [367].

What made the Arnhem operation even more tragic was that Montgomery's own staff were largely against it. His chief of staff, Francis de Guingand did not support the *Market-Garden* operation, but he was in England undergoing medical treatment. He attempted to warn Monty by telephone that there were too many ifs in the plan, but he merely replied, "'You are too far way, Freddie, and don't know what's going on!' From Aldershot, linked only by phone, I could do nothing."

In their 1993 study, *Coalitions, Politicians and Generals: Some Aspects of Command in Two World Wars* [162], military historians Dominick Graham and Shelford Bidwell note that to declare *Market-Garden* a failure is to ignore its achievements. From Nijmegen the British were able thereafter to drive south-east towards the Rhine at Wesel, and the northward advance of the Thirtieth Corps helped to put a cordon around the eastern escape route of the German Fifteenth Army, still fighting against the Canadians on the Channel coast.

Other sources include Alistair Horne with David Montgomery, *The Lonely Leader: Monty 1944-1945* [186]; Richard Lamb, *Montgomery in Europe, 1943-45: Success or Failure* [218]; F. H. Hinsley, *British Intelligence in the Second World War: Its Influence on Strategy and Operations* [184]. Volume Three, Part II, concluded the series and covers the last eleven months of the European war; Milton Shulman, *Defeat in the West* [356]; Christopher Hibbert, *The Battle of Arnhem* [183], is an excellent balanced account; General Matthew B. Ridgway, *Soldier: The Memoirs of Matthew B. Ridgway* [337]; General James M. Gavin, *On to Berlin: Battles of an Airborne Commander, 1943-1946* [156]; Lewis H. Brereton, *The Brereton Diaries* [45]; R. E. Urquhart with Wilfred Greatorex, *Arnhem* [391]; J.O.E. Vandeleur, *A Soldier's Story*; Stanislaw Sosabowski, *Freely*

I Served [363]; Norman Dixon's criticism of Arnhem, *On the Psychology of Military Incompetence* [116], depends heavily on Ryan's *A Bridge Too Far*; Charles B. MacDonald, *The Decision to launch Operation Market-Garden* [235]; Peter Harclerode, *Arnhem: A Tragedy of Errors* [176].

Prelude to the Ardennes

Any hope of an early crossing of the Rhine ended with the failure of Operation *Market-Garden*.

Like everyone else, Monty had focused on crossing the Rhine river into Germany; only now did he give his undivided attention to the clearance of the Scheldt estuary, which led to the port of Antwerp. The city had been captured on September 4, but it was not until the end of November that ships were at last able to reach Antwerp itself, after a prolonged and bloody battle fought by the Canadian 1st Army against a stubborn enemy. Meanwhile things had not gone too well all along the line; Hodges' 1st Army attack on the Hürtgen Forest became a protracted bloodbath, see Edward G. Miller, *A Dark and Bloody Ground: The Hürtgen Forest and the Roer River Dams, 1944-1945* [261]. The Battle of the Hürtgen Forest was one of the worst periods of fighting in the entire war. To the south, Patton's 3rd Army was fighting the costly Battle of Metz against strong German resistance, see Anthony Kemp, *The Unknown Battle: Metz, 1944* [211]. In the thick of a particularly bitter winter the offensive in the West had reached a stalemate.

The Montgomery *Memoirs* [268] make very clear his opposition to the strategy adopted by Eisenhower during the fall and winter of 1944. He wrote that the winter war of attrition, very expensive in human life, had been forced on the Allies by "our faulty strategy after the great victory in Normandy." The strategic debate culminated in the Maastricht conference on December 7 attended by Eisenhower, Monty, Tedder, and Bradley, where Monty called for a single thrust by the 12th and 21st Army Groups north of the Ardennes with the aim of cutting off the Ruhr from the rest of Germany. He considered that one commander should be in operational control and direction of all forces north of the Ardennes: "That commander must either be myself or Bradley. I would willingly serve under Bradley." Eisenhower did not agree, remarking that their real objective was to kill Germans and it did not matter where they did it. He favored two strong thrusts, one blow being struck at the Ruhr, the other at Frankfurt, north and south of the Ardennes. In Montgomery's opinion, the result was the "unnecessary battle" of December 16,1944-January 16,1945, often called the Battle of the Bulge, which he declared, "could so easily have been avoided."

Montgomery's position is strongly defended by Nigel Hamilton, *Monty: Final Years of the Field-Marshal, 1944-1976* [174B], and Arthur Bryant, *Triumph in the West* [50]. Hamilton contends that Monty was motivated by "a profound professional conviction, based on years of clashes with his own British superiors over the decades of his apprenticeship." He was driven to exasperation by what appeared to be Eisenhower's strategy of everybody attacking everywhere with no reserves anywhere. To General Frank "Simbo" Simpson, Director of Military Operations, Monty declared, "The present situation is that were are completely stuck"; referring to Eisenhower as a battlefield commander, he told Brooke that Eisenhower was "quite useless. There must be no mistake on this point; he was completely and utterly useless." British military historian, Richard Lamb is critical of Brooke for encouraging Montgomery in his fruitless argument with Ike, see his book, *Montgomery in Europe 1943-1945: Success or Failure?* [218]. In a meeting with Eisenhower, Brooke was "brutally critical"of what he considered to be Ike's dispersal of effort which he believed would lead to failure.

The 1993 book by Dominick Graham and Shelford Bidwell, *Coalitions, Politicians & Generals: Some Aspects of Command in Two World Wars* [162], strongly criticized Eisenhower's strategy, claiming that "by failing to match their operations and goals with their logistical means, Eisenhower and Bradley, virtually bankrupted the American army that had landed in Normandy before a second wave of divisions started to arrive for the spring offensive." The authors comment: "It may be asked whether the influence of politics on Eisenhower's strategy after Normandy lengthened the war?"

On December 15 Monty wrote to Ike requesting that, "If you have no objection I would like to hop over to England on Saturday 23 December and spend Christmas with my son. I have not seen him since D-Day." On the 16th, he flew up to Eindhoven for a rare game of golf with Dai Rees, the professional golfer then serving in the British military. On the eighth hole an aircraft landed right on the fairway and taxied toward the field marshal. Montgomery was informed that the Germans had attacked in force the thinly held Ardennes, against General Courtney Hodges's U.S. 1st Army. He immediately flew back to his tactical headquarters at Zonhoven. Some 200,000 Germans had attacked 83,000 Americans. The German counteroffensive had fallen mainly on the U.S. 1st Army front that was held by VIII Corps under General Troy H. Middleton in the Ardennes, and a great "bulge" or salient was being made in the American line. On December 20 Eisenhower asked Montgomery to take command of all American forces on the northern flank of the Bulge. That afternoon he arrived at Hodges' headquarters, in the words of one aide, "like Christ come to cleanse the Temple."

In his *Memoirs*[268], Montgomery wrote: "I found the northern flank of the bulge was very disorganized. Ninth Army had two corps and three divisions; First Army had three corps and fifteen divisions. Neither Army Commander had seen Bradley or any senior member of his staff since the battle began, and they had no directive on which to work." He related the story of General Horrocks, commanding the 30 Corps, who wanted Monty to let the Germans cross the Meuse and reach Waterloo which was not far away. There, the ever aggressive Horrocks wanted to defeat them in tribute to Wellington! He recorded in his memoir, "I told Dempsey that on no account was Horrocks to allow any Germans over the river."

The Battle of the Bulge

The literature on Montgomery's role in the Battle of the Bulge runs the gamut of opinion from lavish praise to unreserved disparagement. At the time of the battle, General George Patton criticized Montgomery as a "tired little fart," (he also called the famed American cartoonist Bill Mauldin "that little son of a bitch") and blamed him for virtually every problem in the Ardennes – see Carlo D'Este's, *Patton: A Genius for War* [100]. On the other hand, Montgomery's first biographer, Alan Moorehead, told the American official Army historian Forrest Pogue after the war that he considered it Monty's "finest hour" as a battlefield commander. That view is echoed by his official biographer Nigel Hamilton in the last volume of his trilogy, *Monty* [174B], where he asserts that in the Battle of the Bulge Montgomery fought "the finest defensive battle" of the war.

Eisenhower's decision to place the United States 1st and 9th Armies under Montgomery's command made General Omar Bradley "livid," and according to the war diary kept by his military aide, Chester Hansen, he walked up and down cursing Monty. Hansen recorded that he was startled "to see Bradley like this." A glimpse of his fury and hostility toward Montgomery can be found in his memoir, published in 1951, *A Soldier's Story* [43], where he declared that the change-over in command "could be interpreted as a loss of confidence by Eisenhower in me – or more significantly in the American command." In a second book, *A General's Life: An Autobiography* [44], written in collaboration with Clay Blair, Bradley recorded that, "Never in my life had I been so enraged and so utterly exasperated." Military historian Russell F. Weigley observed in his account, *Eisenhower's Lieutenants: The Campaign of France and Germany 1944-1945* [398], that the "hurt to his [Bradley's] sensibilities . . . lingered on to permeate his every remark about the event ever afterward." In his book, *Generals of the Ardennes: American Leadership in the Battle of the Bulge* [282], J. D. Morelock comments that Bradley reacted to Montgomery's expanded command of American troops during the Ardennes crisis "with resentment, hurt pride, and pique."

An early pro-Bradley and anti-Montgomery account was the 1946 book, *Top Secret* [196], by Ralph Ingersoll, a former member of Bradley's staff. *Top Secret* was the opening gun in the post-war battle of the books. "To us in Bradley's headquarters," wrote Ingersoll, "splitting the command was an absolutely appalling thing to do." Bradley's conduct in the Battle of the Bulge is described as "magnificent . . . and on the heroic scale." Eisenhower is portrayed as a fumbling dupe of the British, while Montgomery is belittled as "a very bad general."

In sharp contrast to Ingersoll's solid was the excellent 1947 study by Robert E. Merriam, *Dark December* [257]. The author had been a combat historian attached to the 7th Armored Division and had a front row seat on the Battle of the Bulge. Reviewer Arthur Schlesinger, Jr., observed, "The book explodes a number of myths which have been winning their improper way into general belief. In so doing, it handles rather roughly a number of other experts, foremost among them, Ralph Ingersoll." Under the heading, "The British Myth," Merriam commented, "The most controversial figure in the Battle of the Bulge was Montgomery." The author rejected both the accusation that Montgomery was responsible for Eisenhower's decision to place all American forces north of the Bulge under his command, as well as the charge that he handled those forces poorly after December 20. "On both these counts, the charges are not substantiated," wrote Merriam. Nor did Montgomery contemplate withdrawal of all his forces in the Meuse River, as was claimed by Ingersoll. According to Merriam, to criticize Montgomery for not counterattacking in "the midst of the hell swirling around him is only to indicate ignorance of the situation." While noting that Monty was an egotist "hardly needs repeating," the author claimed that "the brutal criticism of Montgomery's tactics does not square up with the facts."

On the subject of "The Patton Myth," by which Merriam meant, "A great, great many people believe that the Battle of the Bulge was won by General Patton's Third Army," he argued that Hodges' 1st Army met the crisis of the German attack before Patton's involvement. The heaviest fighting around Bastogne occurred after the crisis had passed. Merriam made the fair judgment: " Patton's army performed well; his true glory was as part of a team, directed by Eisenhower, which was flexible enough to rebound from a completely surprising attack."

Montgomery's role is discussed objectively by Russell F. Weigley in his account, *Eisenhower's Lieutenants: The Campaign of France and Germany 1944-1945* [398]. While critical of Monty's arrogance, Weigley acknowledged that Montgomery "took hold on the north flank with the energy and verve that were as characteristic as his peacockery." Weigley defended Monty's tactic of giving ground the better to build up his reserves, or where the benefits of holding on would no longer match the cost. He withdrew the U.S. 7th Armored Division and the 82nd Airborne Division from their forward positions. General Robert W. Hasbrouck, commander of the 7th Armored Division, reported on December 22 that the time had come to abandon St. Vith. The defense of St. Vith had dealt a crippling delay to the German 6th SS Panzer Army's drive on Liège–as important an action as Bastogne's stand, though not as dramatic. Hasbrouck's corps commander, however, General Matthew B. Ridgway opposed withdrawal. He was decisively overruled by Montgomery. Soon a message reached Hasbrouck from Monty, "You have accomplished your mission–a mission well done. It is time to withdraw." Hasbrouck would later go so far as to say that Montgomery "saved the 7th Armored Division."

On Montgomery's order to withdraw, Hugh M. Cole, wrote in his volume, *The Ardennes: Battle of the Bulge* [82], "and here [Montgomery] showed the ability to honor the fighting man which had endeared him to the hearts of the Desert Rats in North Africa: "They can come back with all honor. They come back to the more secure positions. They put up a wonderful show." Cole, the Official U.S. Army historian of the Battle of the Bulge, had served as combat historian with the U.S. 3rd Army at the time of the Ardennes fighting. Reviewer Forrest Pogue praised Cole's work as "one of the best volumes on operations" in the army's "U.S. Army in World War II" series. Pogue noted, "In a period when the baiting of Field Marshal Montgomery by military writers is a popular indoor sport, Cole declines to make an issue out of General Eisenhower's decision to place the British commander in charge of American units north of the Bulge.

A useful source on the epic American stand at St. Vith is that by W. D. Ellis and T. J. Cunningham, Jr., *Clarke of St. Vith: The Sergeants' General* [132]. General Bruce C. Clarke, commanded Combat Command "B" of the 7th Armored Division during the critical defense of St. Vith. Montgomery paid several visits to the 7th Armored front: "General Montgomery was impressive to me," Clarke later said, "Very cool in battle." Before Montgomery's order to withdraw, Clarke said, "It looks like Custer's last stand to me."

Criticism of Montgomery is found in the account, *Troy H. Middleton: A Biography* [324], by Frank James Price. Middleton, the VIII Corps commander, remarked, "I never would have withdrawn our troops from St. Vith."

Monty looms large in the 1993 study by J. D. Morelock, *Generals of the Ardennes: American Leadership in the Battle of the Bulge* [282]. Eisenhower's decision to appoint Monty commander of all American forces north of the Bulge is strongly defended by the author who writes: "This decision, more than any other action Ike took during the battle (or, indeed during the entire war), proved his greatness as an *allied* commander." Bradley, who had judged the German offensive to be no more than a spoiling attack, in the words of Morelock, "had obstinately refused to relocate his headquarters." Any assessment of Bradley, comments Morelock, lies somewhere between Eisenhower's judgment that he was the war's "greatest battle-line commander" and Patton's view that Bradley was an "insufferably orthodox . . . nothing." Bradley did not meet with either Hodges or Simpson during the thirty-three battle. Morelock points out that while Bradley and Patton were angry at Monty's receiving command in the north, many lower level American commanders were delighted to have the British Field Marshal take charge of the confusing situation in the northern sector of the Bulge. Monty's "timely assumption of command in the north," writes Morelock, was welcomed" by Hodges, Simpson (9th U.S. Army commander), and their subordinate commanders who were fighting desperately to stop the German drive. He comments, "it cannot be denied that Montgomery brought much needed order and discipline to a confused and chaotic situation." Hodges' 1st Army headquarters was in a shambles, his staff having abandoned their command post in Spa in such panic that secret documents and classified operational maps were left scattered about. While asserting that "the Ardennes victory was Eisenhower's victory," Morelock nevertheless claims that "Eisenhower's greatest failure" was his inability to energize Montgomery into launching a timely, counterattack from the north.

The counterattack controversy is discussed by Nigel Hamilton in his volume, *Monty* [175B]. Between December 20 and 24, Montgomery visited all the Corps Commanders in his two American armies, many divisional commanders, as well as American troops. Hamilton argues that Montgomery was "not simply speaking for himself when he declared that no major American offensive was on the cards." The notion that German forces in the Bulge could have been cut-off in a replay of the Falaise Pocket is regarded as delusional and fantastic by Hamilton. Patton himself noted that, "The Germans are colder and hungrier than we are, but they fight better."

To mount an eventual counterattack, Monty wanted the most aggressive American corps commander available, General J. Lawton ("Lightning Joe") Collins. Monty much admired Collins and would not listen to any other names. Collins' stated his views with candor and directness in his memoir, *Lightning Joe: An Autobiography* [85]. In Collins' judgment, Eisenhower was right in placing Montgomery temporarily in command of all troops north of the Bulge, although he "fretted" at Monty's delay in launching a counterattack. He felt the battle witnessed what was probably the most effective Allied cooperation of the war.

Historical opinion on Monty's contribution to the successful outcome of the Battle of the Bulge remains as deeply divided as ever, and it seems to support the observation made by Alan Moorehead in his 1946 biography, *Montgomery* [278], that the Ardennes battle was "clouded by the crisis at the time and seems to have become more clouded by prejudices and emotional rivalries ever since." If John Keegan, his book, *The Second World War* [210], declares that, Montgomery's "analysis proved exactly correct", Monty-detractor Gerhard L. Weinberg, in his volume, *A World at Arms* [399], asserts that the Field Marshal was in a "complete panic" on December 25, 1944, and called for vast withdrawals of Allied troops in the south, as otherwise there could be no offensive in the north in the spring or summer of 1945. An essential source for Montgomery's own thinking during the Ardennes battle are his situation reports to the CIGS (Alanbrooke), which were sent at once to Prime Minister Winston Churchill. The War Office cut out one paragraph of his December 20 message: According to Montgomery, "They reckoned [Churchill's] sense of humor would not be up to it!!" The paragraph read "We cannot come out by Dunkirk as the Germans hold that place!!!" Copies of these messages can be found in the Montgomery papers deposited in the Imperial War Museum. His reactions to the Ardennes crisis are discussed in Nigel Hamilton's volume, *Monty* [174B]. The Allied armies faced a serious shortage of manpower during the Battle of the Bulge. Montgomery continued to emphasize the necessity of concentrating Allied forces to seize the Ruhr.

Equally hostile toward Montgomery is Stephen E. Ambrose in his 1997 book, *Citizen Soldiers* [7]. Ambrose lambasts Monty's role: "Far from directing the victory, Montgomery had gotten in everyone's way and botched the counterattack." In a similar vein, military historian Allan R. Millett, in a review of the 1994 video, "The Battle of the Bulge," for *The Journal of American History* [262], criticized what he considered to be Monty's "ill-considered decision" not to cut off the Germans at the salient's base – "It was a failure like that of the Falaise Pocket, but on a larger scale," declared Millett.

The Command Issue

In his *Memoirs* [268], Montgomery wrote, "It had taken a major crisis to do what I had been asking for ever since August [operational command of the left flank, with two American armies under his command]." In the words of Russell F. Weigley, *Eisenhower's Lieutenants* [398], Monty now resurrected "that old

Montgomery hobbyhorse, unified ground command." In a letter to Eisenhower on December 31, he included the statement, " I put this matter up to you again only because I am so anxious not to have another failure." Eisenhower's temper was stretched to the breaking point. Eisenhower had already received a telegram from General Marshall that there were to be no concessions on the issue of command, and that "there would be a terrific resentment in this country" if most American armies remained under British command. Several of Eisenhower's closest advisers at SHAEF now counseled him to force a showdown and he drafted a message to the Combined Chiefs of Staff, through Marshall, saying the chiefs would have to choose between Montgomery and himself.

An important account of the episode is that by Monty's chief of staff, Francis de Guingand, *Generals at War* [108]. Nigel Hamilton commented in his biography, *Monty: Final Years of the Field Marshal, 1944-1976* [174B], that De Guingand's recollection, published in 1960, was wrong in many respects, but post-war interviews with Bedell Smith and Eisenhower confirmed de Guingand's main memory.

Monty's chief of staff had become aware of the serious danger to him, and decided to fly immediately to SHAEF headquarters at Versailles to try and smooth the troubled waters. The generous and likeable de Guingand implored Eisenhower to delay sending the message to the CCS until he could speak to Monty in person. Eisenhower and Tedder were not inclined to agree, but Bedell Smith was on de Guingand's side. After flying back to Zonhoven in bad weather, de Guingand had the grim task of explaining the shocking situation to Monty who was still flushed with the successful role he had played in stemming the Ardennes attack. But if Eisenhower sacked him, Monty inquired of de Guingand, who could possibly take his place? De Guingand mentioned Alexander. Hamilton writes, "Monty, was, for once in his life, completely floored." Monty liked Alexander but as a general he felt that he was indecisive and ineffective. De Guingand recorded in *Generals at War*: "I felt terribly sorry for my Chief, for he now looked completely non-plussed – I don't think I had ever seen him so deflated. It was as if a cloak of loneliness had descended on him." "What shall I do, Freddie?" he asked de Guingand. In his *Memoirs*, Monty wrote that after hearing how serious it was, "I decided at once to "pipe down.'" From his pocket de Guingand pulled a piece of paper, the draft of an apology to Eisenhower. Monty swallowed his pride and sent the message, which ended: "Very distressed that my letter may have upset you and I would ask you to tear it up. Your very devoted subordinate, Monty."

In his *Memoirs* [268], Monty mentions the incident of the surprise Luftwaffe attack on Allied airfields on New Year's Day 1945 that destroyed hundreds of aircraft, including Monty's own Dakota given him by Eisenhower in 1943 in exchange for the Flying Fortress. Eisenhower immediately sent him in replacement his own brand-new Dakota, which he had just received. Montgomery was genuinely touched and wrote to Ike: "Such spontaneous kindness touches me deeply and from my heart I send you my grateful thanks."

The Press Conference

About Monty's January 7, 1945, press conference there is consensus among historians. It was a disastrous mistake. He wrote in his *Memoirs* [268], "I think now that I should never have held that Press conference. So great was the feeling against me on the part of the American generals, that whatever I said was bound to be wrong. I should therefore have said nothing." He admitted that "I should have held my tongue." "What I did *not* say," he went on, "was that, in the battle of the Ardennes, the Allies got a real 'bloody nose,' the Americans had nearly 80,000 casualties, and that it would never had happened if we had fought the campaign properly after the great victory in Normandy . . . " In was, in Montgomery's view, an "unnecessary battle."

At the time Montgomery assumed command of all Allied forces north of the Ardennes, Alan Brooke had worried that Monty would take the attitude, "I told you so." Brooke had cautioned him: "It is most important that you should not even in the slightest degree rub this undoubted fact in to anyone at SHAEF or elsewhere." In his book, *Bitter Woods* [128], John Eisenhower (the son of Ike) fairly pointed out that, "There is every reason to believe that Montgomery's press conference was given in a sincere spirit of conciliation." The British press had been critical of Eisenhower and Bradley and he wanted to set the record straight. Montgomery quoted the full text of his notes in the *Memoirs*. He praised Eisenhower and paid tribute to the fighting qualities of the American soldier at length – "I never want to fight alongside better soldiers" – but as John Eisenhower pointed out in *Bitter Woods* out the trouble was with the "tone" of the talk which gave the impression that he had personally saved the American high command from disaster. Tactlessly, he said, "The battle has been most interesting; I think possibly one of the most interesting and tricky battles I have ever handled . . . "

In his biography, *Monty* [175B], Hamilton cited his interview with Brigadier Sir Edgar Williams, Monty's Intelligence chief. After the press conference, Alan Moorehead, Monty's first biographer, said to Williams, "Oh God, why didn't you stop him? It was so awful." Williams himself called the text "innocuous," but "the presentation quite appalling."

The first reports were favorable; the *New York Times* said, "No handsomer tribute was ever paid to the American soldier than that of Field-Marshal Montgomery in the midst of combat." But the reaction of Bradley and a number of other American generals, together with their staffs, was one of anger. In his book, *Montgomery in Europe, 1943-1945: Success or Failure?* [218], Richard Lamb wrote that all the American generals were "up in arms at this tactless and not altogether truthful view of the battle." In his post-war account, *Crusade in Europe* [126], Eisenhower claimed, "This incident caused me more distress and worry than did any similar one of the war." American commanders believed that he had deliberately belittled them – and they were not slow to voice reciprocal scorn and contempt.

The episode is recorded in volume two of the diary of John Colville, *The Fringes of Power* [86]. Colville served as Churchill's wartime private secretary and his diaries contain, in the words of reviewer Drew Middleton, "shrewd observations and revealing stories" about the great figures of the war, including Montgomery. Colville recorded that Monty was "indecently exultant" over his role in the Battle of the Bulge.

Moorehead wrote in his biography, *Montgomery* [278]: "Looking back on the scene from a world at peace one might marvel that the generals could brawl so cold-bloodedly with one another at a time when so many thousands were exposing themselves to death, and dying." Military historian Carlo D'Este remarks in his study, *Patton: A Genius For War* [100], that, "The final battles of the war were as much about prestige as any fought by the Allies." Bradley and Patton were determined to prevent Montgomery from reaping the victory headlines. Bradley expressed vehement hostility toward Montgomery in the 1983 account, *A General's Life* [44], by Bradley and Clay Blair.

Who really won the Battle of the Bulge? In Montgomery's book, *Normandy to the Baltic* [269], we find the words, "The Battle of the Ardennes was won primarily by the staunch fighting qualities of the American soldier." Churchill had called it "the greatest American battle of the war." That remains the verdict of history.

Other sources include: John Toland, *Battle: The Story of the Bulge* [385];Chester Wilmot, *The Struggle for Europe* [407]; Kenneth S. Davis, *The American Experience of War 1939-1945* [106]; L. F. Ellis, *Victory in the West* [131]; Peter Elstob, *Hitler's Last Offensive* [134]; Charles B. MacDonald, *A Time for Trumpets: The Untold Story of the Battle of the Bulge* [234]; Jacques Nobécourt, *Hitler's Last Gamble* [300]; Andy Rooney, *My War* [342]. Rooney, the American syndicated columnist and "60 Minutes" commentator served with *The Stars and Stripes* during the war. The ever-candid and controversial Rooney calls Patton a "loudmouthed boor who got too many American soldiers killed for the sake of enhancing his own reputation as a swashbuckling leader in the Napoleonic style." Rooney felt that Montgomery "erred on the side of being too cautious."

In his book, *The Battle for the Ardennes*, British General John Strawson thought, "He [Monty] could claim perhaps half the credit for seeing them off [Germans] with American troops. Patton and Bradley could claim the other half."

The Final Wartime Controversies

In January, 1945, the long-awaited Soviet offensive , four million men strong, began rolling towards the Oder River, and Berlin. Montgomery's 21st Army Group, still supported by Simpson's U.S. 9th Army, prepared to break through the Siegfried Line and seize all the ground west of the Rhine. Starting on February 8 and ending on March 11, Montgomery launched Operations *Veritable* on the left, and *Grenade* on the right flank. They are described as "two admirably well-knit, almost copybook operations," by Alistair Horne with David Montgomery, *The Lonely Leader: Monty 1944-1945* [186]. It is often called the Battle of the Reichswald Forest. Fighting against fanatical enemy resistance, and mud and more mud,

General Sir Brian Horrocks called it, "the grimmest battle in which I took part," in his memoir, *A Full Life* [189]. The Canadian 1st Army suffered 15,000 casualties, the U.S. 9th Army 7,300. Ronald Lewin, *Montgomery as Military Commander* [222], referred to *Veritable* as "unmitigated hell." A critical account is that by Denis and Shelagh Whitaker, *Rhineland: The Battle to End the War* [403]. The battle is covered by Dominick Graham in his welcome study, *The Price of Command: A Biography of General Guy Simonds* [164]. From the divisional level see, Patrick Delaforce, *Monty's Iron Sides: From the Normandy Beaches to Bremen with the 3rd Division* [110]; Marcus Cunliffe, *History of the Royal Warwickshire Regiment* [95]. *Veritable* and *Grenade* had shattered nineteen German divisions which lost 90,000 men. The west bank of the Rhine was clear.

On March 7, the U.S. 1st Army captured intact the bridge at Remagen, and in his *Memoirs* Monty noted that "it loosened up the whole campaign by providing a bridgehead which could be exploited at will." His own massive crossing of the Rhine began on March 23, code-named Operation *Plunder*, with the U.S. 9th Army (still under Montgomery's command) on the right and British 2nd on the left. He crossed the great water barrier with thirty divisions from three armies. Official American army historian Charles B. MacDonald in his volume, *The Last Offensive* [236], compared Operation *Plunder* with D-Day in Normandy in terms of complexity of deception plans and in general elaboration. MacDonald declared that it "probably was the most elaborate assault river crossing operation of all time." Whether it was necessary or even justified would, in MacDonald's opinion, "forever remain conjecture." Military historian Russell F. Weigley, *Eisenhower's Lieutenants: The Campaign of France and Germany 1944-1945* [398], observed, "The elephantine aspects of Montgomery's generalship was again much in evidence" in Operation *Plunder*. Weigley noted, however, "Pachydermal preparation could on occasion be a military virtue."

Why did Montogmery cross the Rhine in such elaborate style? Biographer Ronald Lewin, *Montgomery as Military Commander* [222], thought the question was "ill-framed." He argued that the planning for the Rhine crossing occurred for many months prior to the event; no one knew in advance that the U.S. 1st Army would have the good luck to capture the Remagen bridge on March 7. Lewin wrote that Montgomery's purpose was to establish a strong presence in northern Germany; therefore, he had to ensure a formidable follow-through. In the opinion of Alistair Horne with David Montgomery, *The Lonely Leader: Monty 1944-1945* [186], the set-piece operation was to ensure the minimum of casualties in forcing Germany's great water barrier.

Once over the Rhine, Montgomery signaled Eisenhower that he was issuing orders for the British 2nd Army and Simpson's U.S. 9th Army to strike for the Elbe River, "thence by autobahn to Berlin I hope." Alistair Horne in *The Lonely Leader* [186] wrote: "Ike was, one last time, infuriated by the tone of this dispatch, as well as by Monty's ready assumption that Simpson was to continue under his command." On the night of March 28, Eisenhower informed Monty curtly that Bradley was going to aim for the Erfurt-Leipzig-Dresden line, thus swinging well south of Berlin "to join hands with the Russians," and "The mission of your army group will be to protect Bradley's northern flank." A few days later, Eisenhower declared, "You will note that in none of this do I mention Berlin. That place has become, so far as I am concerned, nothing but a geographical location, and I have never been interested in these." In the final volume of his biography, *Monty* [175B], Nigel Hamilton remarked that Ike's Berlin decision was for Monty "perhaps the biggest shock of the war." In 1944 Eisenhower had described Berlin as "the main prize." In their book, *The Lonely Leader* [186], Horne and Montgomery cite Monty's letter of "cold acceptance" to Eisenhower: "It is quite clear to me what you want. I will crack along on the northern flank one hundred per cent and will do all I can to draw the enemy forces away from the main effort being made by Bradley. Yours ever, Monty."

The Berlin question has been one of the great controversies of World War II. A severe criticism of the final wartime strategy pursued by Eisenhower and Bradley can be found in Russell F. Weigley's, *Eisenhower's Lieutenants: The Campaign of France and Germany 1944-1945* [398]. He claims that Bradley feared to emphasize Berlin as the main prize since that would continue to keep the U.S. 9th Army in Montgomery's 21st Army Group for a drive on Berlin that would award "the final, crowning laurels to the insufferable British field marshal." Weigley charges that, "in the face of strategic logic, Bradley persuaded Eisenhower to divert from the drive toward Berlin a huge slice of the American armies" – eventually some eighteen divisions, drawn from the 9th and 1st Armies best positioned to strike toward Berlin–and to turn these divisions into the "jungle of the Ruhr . . . whose strategic significance was in fact essentially nil." Eisenhower's arguments, in the opinion of Weigley, were "at least a trifle disingenuous."

Montgomery simply noted in his *Memoirs* [268], "Berlin was lost to us when we failed to make a sound operational plan in August 1944, after the victory in Normandy." His views are fully discussed by Nigel Hamilton, *Monty: Final Years of the Field-Marshal, 1944-1976* [174B]. The Official British history of the campaign by L. F. Ellis, *Victory in the West* [131], came down on the side of Eisenhower rather than Monty. Ike's controversial decisions over Berlin are defended by his biographer, Stephen E. Ambrose, *The Supreme Commander: The War Years of General Dwight D. Eisenhower* [9].

From the Rhine Montgomery drove hard to the east. In *Montgomery as Military Commander* [222], Ronald Lewin wrote, "This advance of 21 Army Group to the Elbe was not easy." There were no great battles, but the German anti-tank weapon or panzerfaust in the hands of young boys could cause delay. Victory was imminent but death still waiting round the next curve in the road. Lewin stated that "Montgomery maintained the morale of his armies to the end." In his memoirs, *Reflecting on Things Past*, Lord Carrington, a young Guards' officer in World War II, vividly described the last weeks of the war. Although the war was lost, the German soldier fought on. Carrington wrote: "Their discipline was remarkable. Their soldierly instincts, their tactical training and sense, were capable, right to the end, of teaching us a sharp lesson if we took liberties."

For critical accounts of Monty's last campaign from the Rhine to the Baltic, see John Toland, *The Last 100 Days* [386]–[General Günther] Blumentritt waged "a gentleman's battle with the British, pulling back with as little bloodshed as possible" – and Omar N. Bradley and Clay Blair, *A General's Life: An Autobiography* [44], who described the campaign as "one of the most cautious and uninspired of the war." A fervid rebuttal was offered by the popular writer Charles Whiting in his book, *The Last Battle: Montgomery's Campaign April-May 1945* [404], who wrote that Toland "gently mocked the whole campaign in the north."

A generally balanced account was the 1969 study by General Hubert Essame, *The Battle for Germany* [137]. The author took part in the battle himself as an infantry commander. He covers the period from late September 1944 through May 1945, which he called the "Battle for Germany." Essame wrote: "The more popular section of the press at the time, both British and American, tended to portray the Allied statesmen as if they were the leading actors in some gigantic play and the generals like jockeys engaged in a nightmare international steeplechase. Montgomery with his flair for personal publicity, his gift of concise and acid expression and built-in conviction that he had been selected by the Almighty to destroy Hitler and all he stood for, was the answer to the journalists' proverbial prayer. In consequence, Anglo-American clashes of opinion and personality during the campaign were exaggerated then and have been since." Essame noted that at the time of the final surrender, there were 61 American divisions (over three million men), and only 18 British and Canadian divisions.

In his *Memoirs*, Montgomery recorded that both Churchill and Eisenhower became anxious "lest I might not be able to 'head off' the Russians from getting to Denmark first. He commented, "I fear I got somewhat irritated and my replies possibly showed it!" He informed Ike that he was "very well aware" of what had to be done, but that removal of the U.S. 9th Army from his command had slowed down operations on the northern flank. In his volume, *Montgomery in Europe 1943-1945: Success or Failure?* [218], Richard Lamb declared, "These prods were timely." In the end , Montgomery's forces reached Wismar and Lübeck on the Baltic, thus sealing off the Danish peninsula "with about six hours to spare, before the Russians arrived [Monty *Memoirs*]." Lamb remarked that the last exchanges of the war between Monty and Ike showed that both commanders "to be feeling the strain of the war."

In these last days of World War II there now occurred, according to Alistair Horne with David Montgomery, *The Lonely Leader: Monty 1944-1945* [186], the "bitterest personal tragedy for Monty of the whole war" – the death of John Poston. At twenty-five, Poston was the youngest of Monty's liaison officers – in volume six of his monumental history of the Second World War, *Triumph and Tragedy* [75], Winston Churchill provided an excellent description of their function in Monty's liaison officers. They served as Montgomery's eyes and ears and were sent out each day, coming back in the evening to report on the battlefield situation. Poston who had been with him the longest, since Alamein, was the ringleader of the high-jinks at TAC, and clearly Monty's favorite, a "kind of surrogate son" write Horne and Montgomery in *The Lonely Leader*. For days he was inconsolable over the death of Poston, and would see nobody. Monty himself wrote an obituary for *The Times,* and at Poston's funeral he wept openly, "giving rise in a suspicious age to the unfounded suspicions of homosexual affections." See Alun Chalfont, *Montgomery of Alamein* [70].

Poston's death foreshadowed the end of his TAC family which had given so much happiness "to a thoroughly lonely man." Only days after Poston's burial, and the same week as the German surrender, another favorite LO, Charles Sweeny died in a car accident. He had been with Monty at Dunkirk and had only just married. In his *Memoirs*, Montgomery wrote without shame of his affection for Sweeny: "He was a delightful Irish boy and I loved him dearly." In a revealing obituary of Sweeny to *The Times*, Monty commented that, "Charles was an orphan and possibly it was that fact which drew us close together." The young daredevil LOs, with their pranks and horseplay, evoked memories of his own youth. He said that he enjoyed their company because of their "devilry." Sergeant Norman Kirby, who was in charge of TAC headquarters security, provides a close-up view of Monty's TAC "family" in his reminiscence, *1100 Miles with Monty* [217]. Other eye-witness accounts can be found in T. E. B. Howarth's, *Monty at Close Quarters: Recollections of the Man* [193].

The climactic moment came at 1830 hours on May 4, 1945, in a tent on Lüneburg Heath – 1100 miles from the Normandy beaches where it had all begun eleven months earlier – when Montgomery took the unconditional surrender of all the enemy forces in Holland, Denmark, and north-west Germany. He was persuaded to drink some champagne at dinner that night.

Chapter 9

The Post-War Years

"I Make Myself a Nuisance in Whitehall."
Montgomery, *Memoirs*

The Occupation of Germany

With Germany in ruins, the monumental task of rebuilding the shattered country was now in the hands of the occupying Allied Powers. Montgomery discusses the post-war crisis in his *Memoirs* [268]: "In the area occupied by 21 Army Group there were appalling civilian problems to be solved. Over one million civilian refugees had fled into the area before the advancing Russians. About one million German wounded were in hospitals in the area, with no medical supplies." Over one and half million German soldiers were POWs; food supplies would soon be exhausted; transport and communication services had ceased to function; industry and agriculture were largely at a stand still. It had been "a race for time", he wrote, to prevent famine and disease decimating the twenty million Germans in the British zone before winter began. True to form, Montgomery insisted that someone capable ought to be in complete charge – "appointed at once. . . But I could not get Whitehall to take any action in the matter. However, for the time being I was the boss and I decided to get on with the job in my own way."

Only in late May was Montgomery officially appointed Commander-in-Chief of the British Forces of Occupation and British Member of the Allied Control Council in Berlin. Biographer Nigel Hamilton in his volume, *Monty: Final Years of the Field-Marshal, 1944-1976* [174B], raises the issue of whether Winston Churchill would have kept Montgomery for long in those positions had he won the General Election in 1945. If Churchill had won, Hamilton declared that the Monty-Churchill relationship "would have become, without doubt, stormier and stormier." References to Monty can be found in volume two of John Colville's diary, *The Fringes of Power* [86], which covers the years 1941-1955. As Churchill's private secretary Colville was never far from the "fringes of power".

Montgomery had already disagreed with Churchill over the question of the withdrawal of Allied forces to their agreed upon boundaries. He sided with Eisenhower that to violate their pledged word to withdraw to agreed upon boundaries would wreck any possibility there might be of working in friendly cooperation with the Russians. Montgomery wrote in his *Memoirs* that "because of the Russian attitude, we should get back into our agreed zones at once." Had the western Allies captured Vienna, Prague and Berlin before the Russians, Monty argued that things might have been different. On the possibility of war with Russia, Montgomery declared: "The British people were completely fed up with war and would never have been persuaded to fight the Russians in 1945."

With characteristic drive Montgomery set about organizing the British zone of Germany. In the last volume of his biography, Hamilton records that political lack of direction forced Montgomery to become a sort of "Cromwellian dictator in Germany."

A sympathetic account of Monty's administration of British occupied Germany is found in Alan Moorehead's, *Montgomery: A Biography* [278], where he notes that Monty treated the whole affair as if it were simply another operation of war. Neutral observers, wrote Moorehead, were "almost unanimous" in agreeing that of the four zones in Germany the British was by far the best organized. His first biographer wrote, however, that "At heart Montgomery was not really interested in the Germans"– he wanted to get back to reform the post-war British army and as a result the real business of governing Germany fell more and more upon subordinates.

Lord Chalfont, often critical in his book, *Montgomery of Alamein* [70], claimed that Montgomery must receive "much of the credit" for the avoidance of famine and disease in the British zone of Germany during the winter of 1945-46. Other sources on the occupation include Lord Strang's memoir, *Home and Abroad* [368]. Strang served as Montgomery's political advisor in Germany; Noel Annan, *Changing Enemies: The Defeat and Regeneration of Germany* [11]. Annan was part of a small British intelligence staff that worked with the British occupation government; the desperate food shortage is discussed by John E. Farquharson in *The Western Allies and the Politics of Food* [139]; Arthur Hearnden, editor, *The British in Germany: Educational Reconstruction after 1945* [182]; M. E. Pelly and H. J. Yasamee, *Documents on British Policy Overseas* [313]; Konrad Adenauer, *Memoirs 1945-53* [1].

Much of Montgomery's time was inevitably taken up with the post-war celebrations of victory. He was awarded numerous honorary degrees. Seven rows of medals decorated the Field Marshal's chest, some thirty ribbons in all. For months he faced a constant round of dinners and ceremonies. One such ceremony involved receiving the freedom of the city of Newport in Wales. Unknown to Monty, the organizers had invited his mother to attend the event. In a fury, Monty declared, "I won't have her here. If she comes, I go!" He refused to speak to her and she was consigned to a distant corner of the banqueting room! It was the last time that he saw her alive. He refused to attend her funeral a few years later. In

Alistair Horne's book *The Lonely Leader: Monty 1944-1945* [186], written with David Montgomery, it is noted that "The Great Monmouth Scandal," as it came to be known within the shocked family, "was a vicious and unseemly revenge for the slights, real or imagined, of his lonely childhood." Neither did the dispersal of his wartime TAC "family," and the "bitter loneliness" that followed, bring him any closer to his son, David. The Field Marshal's relationship with his son is described as "kingly" by Nigel Hamilton in his biography, *Monty* [175B]. Monty was fortunate, in August 1945, to survive a plane crash while flying to inspect the 3rd Canadian division near Oldenburg. However, the back injury from the near fatal crash and the long strain of the war were beginning to take their toll. During January 1946 he was very ill, with a combination of pleurisy and influenza. In February he left in his special train for a recuperative holiday in Switzerland.

Lucien Trueb

In Switzerland, writes Nigel Hamilton in his biography, *Monty* [175B], "the strangest of platonic 'romances' began." Paranoically suspicious of his own family, particularly his own mother, the psychologically scarred Montgomery sought friendship and emotional outlet in the most unlikely places. He "adopted" surrogate sons over the years, the first of whom was the twelve-year-old Swiss boy, Lucien Trueb. A recuperating Montgomery met Trueb, who was vacationing with his parents, in Switzerland in February 1946. The Field Marshal wrote to the boy's parents that Lucien had a remarkable likeness to his favorite brother who had died at the age of twelve. Sometimes Monty's letters were signed "My love to you my little friend," "je vous aime beaucoup: très beaucoup." According to Hamilton, the Field Marshal was "infatuated" by the young boy and played "doting father" to him. Alistair Horne, in his book *The Lonely Leader* [186], states that neither Montgomery's son, David, nor the Trueb family inferred anything improper from what Horne calls "the bizarre friendship. If anything it displayed pitiful loneliness." Lucien's father, Dr. Trueb, wrote the chapter, "Monty's little Swiss friend," in *Monty at Close Quarters* [193], edited by T. E. B. Howarth.

In the 1946 New Year's Honors List Montgomery was raised to the peerage, taking the title of Viscount Montgomery of Alamein, of Hindhead in the county of Surrey. A few weeks later it was announced that he would succeed Brooke as CIGS, the highest post in the British army. Alan Moorehead observed his biography, that he was an obvious choice, "But – Montgomery. The diehards leapt to their guns. He would turn the whole War Office into a circus. How could you have a CIGS strutting about in a comic hat?" In Moorehead's opinion, Montgomery had "mellowed," "broadened," and "he was learning patience at last." The point is debatable. When he marched to the War Office in June 1946, where he served as CIGS until September 1948, he continued to wear the symbol of his defiant unconventionality – the black beret.

Chief of the Imperial General Staff

Montgomery had now reached the pinnacle of his profession, Chief of the Imperial General Staff (June 1946-September 1948). Field Marshal Sir Gerald Templer, who admired Montgomery as a military commander, is quoted by Nigel Hamilton in his volume, *Monty: Final Years of the Field Marshal, 1944-1976* [174B], with saying that Monty was "the worst CIGS for 50 years," neither willing nor able to cooperate with his fellow Chiefs of Staff. It must be said that he became CIGS at a very difficult time: deep cuts in the military budget as a result of Britains' dire financial condition, problems associated with decolonization of the largest empire in history, and the beginning of the Cold War between the West and the Soviet Union.

Monty recognized in his *Memoirs* [268], published in 1958, that his tenure as CIGS had been something less than an unqualified success, remarking "I made many enemies... plenty of people [were] anxious to see the back of me... my least happy theater of war. It did not provide 'my sort of battle.' I have never minded making myself an infernal nuisance if it produced the desired result. I don't know in this case whether it did – sufficiently. It is true that I managed to force agreement on certain fundamental issues [such as the eighteen months peacetime conscription and adoption of a Continental strategy – the promise of land support in any future European war], but only after terrific battles. And as a result of it all I was pretty unpopular when I left Whitehall to become an international soldier." Small wonder he called the main chapter on his time as CIGS, "I Make Myself a Nuisance in Whitehall."

British reluctance to adopt a Continental strategy is discussed by Saki Dockrill in his book, *Britain's Policy for West German Rearmament 1950-1955* [117]. The author remarks that "Field Marshal Montgomery was a lone voice in advocating in February 1948 that Britain should send two divisions to the Continent to encourage the morale of her European friends." His fellow chiefs of staff and the Prime Minister rejected the proposal.

With missionary zeal he set out to reform and modernize the British army. Biographer Nigel Hamilton, *Monty: Final Years of the Field-Marshal, 1944-1976* [174B], writes that Montgomery saw himself as the "long-awaited Messiah, coming to cleanse the British military temple." With Freddie de Guingand on his staff–de Guingand possessed warmth, wit and charm – Monty might have a been a more successful CIGS; without him Hamilton likens Montgomery to "a bull in a china shop." But Alanbrooke had nixed de Guingand's appointment and Monty was past caring. The issue is examined by Hamilton in a chapter entitled, "The Little Bastard Business."

"As CIGS, he was not a success." That is the verdict of the Alistair Horne book, *The Lonely Leader: Monty 1944-1945* [186]. However, the frequently highly critical Alun Chalfont, *Montgomery of Alamein* [70], asserts that the widely held view that Monty's tenure as CIGS was a "total disaster" is "somewhat over-simplified." He allows that some of Montgomery's work as CIGS was "useful, indeed essential." Concerned about the living conditions of soldiers, he advocated "bedrooms, not barracks."

With even-handedness, *The Times* obituary noted in 1976, "Montgomery was indeed far from being as good a CIGS as he had been a commander, but his qualities were such that they enabled him to do valuable work in spite of his inability to act as a member of a team instead of as its captain."

He despised his fellow chiefs of staff, particularly Air Marshal Tedder (who had urged his removal during the Normandy campaign). It reached the point where if Montgomery attended the Chiefs of Staff Conference, Tedder deliberately stayed away; conversely, if Tedder attended, Monty would be absent.

Emanuel Shinwell

Of the three Secretaries of State for War under who Montgomery served as CIGS, he declared that the third, Emanuel Shinwell was "the best of the three, and this is no reflection on the other two." In his excellent biography, *Manny Shinwell: An Authorized Biography* [360], Peter Slowe remarks that the idea of Montgomery working well with a Jew seemed particularly extraordinary since the one-time liberator of Belsen had ordered soldiers in Palestine to "prepare for all-out war against the fanatical Jews [referring to the Irgun and Stern Gang]".

Slowe tells the story of Shinwell borrowing twopence from Winston Churchill to phone a friend from a House of Commons phone box. "Here's fourpence ," Churchill replied. "Phone them all." The author notes that it could have applied to Monty. The were both "oddballs." Churchill and Shinwell were the only people Montgomery allowed to smoke in his presence.

The first problem Montgomery and Shinwell had to deal with together was the case of a general whose diary had been found and sent to the CIGS. It revealed the general as a highly active homosexual, and he could easily have been dismissed from the army. Shinwell and Montgomery decided on leniency. "First-class man," Monty had said; later Shinwell discovered that that was how he described nearly all his appointees, but this time he was persuaded. The general should be given a warning by Montgomery personally but the matter was to be taken no further.

In October 1948, Montgomery was appointed first chairman of the Committee of Commanders-in-Chief of the Western Union, comprising Britain, France, and the Benelux countries. Monty wanted one of his former corps commanders to succeed him as CIGS, but Prime Minister Attlee decided on General Sir William Slim, the legendary commander of the 14th Army in Burma. Monty protested to Attlee that he had already told the officer in question. Attlee for once in his life almost shouted and dismissed Monty with: "Untell him!" Attlee was so annoyed that he refused to accept phone calls from Monty or to meet him for three months. Monty noted in his *Memoirs*: "He [Attlee] must have found me an awful nuisance when he was Prime Minister and I was Chief of the Imperial General Staff. But he was very approachable and would always find time to discuss a problem when I sought his advice."

Attlee admired Montgomery and later reviewed his *Memoirs* for *The Observer*.

He commented that "even at 70 he is still something of a naughty boy." Montgomery met Attlee a few days after the review appeared and said, "You got me right and nobody else ever has." See Kenneth Harris' excellent biography Attlee [178].

Other accounts include Emanuel Shinwell's memoir, *I've Lived Through It All* [355]; Philip Ziegler, *Mountbatten* [412]; Nigel Hamilton, *Monty: Final Years of the Field-Marshal, 1944-1976* [174B]; Correlli Barnett offers a scathing indictment of post-war British policy in his book, *The Lost Victory: British Dreams, British Realities 1945-1950* [17].

Montgomery is included among the so-called "fantasists" who are blamed by the author for attempting to maintain Britain's role as a great power. Barnett also compares Sir William Beveridge, the author of the 1942 Beveridge Report and advocate of the welfare state, with Montgomery: ". . . righteousness went hand in hand with authoritarian arrogance and skill in manipulating the press to make him the Field Marshal Montgomery of social welfare."

For different views on post-war British policy see David Reynolds's study, *Britannia Overruled: British Policy & World Power in the 20th Century* [329], and Noel Annan's, *Our Age: The Generation that Made Post-War Britain* [12]. Annan calls Barnett "the Jeremiah of his generation."

On the conscription issue see the article by Frank Myers, "Conscription and the Politics of Military Strategy in the Attlee Government," in *The Journal of Strategic Studies* [293]. See also Sir George Mallaby, *Each in his Office* [244]. The author served as secretary of the Joint Planning Staff while Montgomery was CIGS; Hugh Dalton, *High Tide and After* [103]. Chancellor of the Exchequer in Attlee's Cabinet; Kenneth Young, editor, *The Diaries of Sir Robert Bruce-Lockhart* [410]; Michael Calvert, *Fighting Mad* [60]. He served on the Planning Staff of the CIGS under Montgomery.

Isington Mill

While CIGS Montgomery acquired a permanent home – his own house in Portsmouth and all its contents had been completely destroyed in a bombing raid during the war. He writes in his *Memoirs* [268], "And so, after due reconnaissance, I found what I wanted in Hampshire–an old mill on the River Wey, Isington Mill."

The dilapidated mill required major renovation and one of his friends said, "You are mad." With the scarcity of materials and labor in post-war Britain, it looked for a time as though Montgomery would be forced once more to live in the wartime caravans, in which he had lived during his campaigns from El Alamein until the war in Europe ended. It required an appeal to Prime Minister Attlee to obtain approval for the alterations to begin. Much of the wood used in the conversion of the Mill was given by the grateful governments of Australia (the flooring made from Tasmanian oak), Canada, and New Zealand. Monty wrote: "So while I had some difficulty in getting the British Government of the day even to let me spend some of my own savings on a home, all my worldly possessions having been destroyed by German bombing during the war, the Dominion Governments did their best to help me as soon as they heard of my plight." Out of ancient water-meadows he created an immaculate garden and lawn. In the museum-like house he surrounded himself with trophies and mementoes. He did not allow any flowers in the house–"they made a mess and he didn't like messes." The house and garden are described by Brian Montgomery, *A Field-Marshal in the Family* [272]. Insights can also be found in Malcolm Muggeridge's book, *Like It Was* [289]. The author was an annual visitor to Isington Mill.

Overseas Tours

During his time as CIGS Montgomery traveled extensively. His brother remarked in his account, *A Field-Marshal in the Family* [272], "It is likely that no previous CIGS had spent so much of his time out of the United Kingdom . . . " Late in 1947, he went on a month's tour of Africa and concluded that it could be used as a massive source of raw materials for a new post-war Britain – a counterbalance to the fading Empire in the East. He criticized the Colonial Office for lacking a "grand design." In 1998, the Public Record Office released Montgomery's secret 1948 report. Montgomery had dismissed the African as "a complete savage" incapable of developing the continent. In its leading article, *The Times* [384] of London declared, "What Monty Saw," with the sub-heading, "A racist verdict that Africa has done its best to prove right." In the once secret report Montgomery had urged Attlee's Labor government to adopt a "master plan" to unlock the vast wealth of the British African territories. Biographer Nigel Hamilton observed in his 1986 volume *Monty* [175B] that the paternalistic and Victorian racial attitudes of Montgomery were clearly "out of step with his time."

International Soldier

In October 1948, Montgomery took up his appointment as Military Chairman of the Western Union defense organization, known as UNIFORCE, the precursor of NATO, which was organized in April 1949. At that time Monty became Deputy Supreme Commander of NATO serving under his old chief General Eisenhower. He then served in succession under General Matthew Ridgway who in Monty's view was "not the right man" for the job (Ridgway explained his own problems with Monty in his book, *Soldier: The Memoirs of Matthew B. Ridgway* [337]), unlike General Alfred Gruenther who did "a terrific job", and General Lauris Norstad, "a very firm friend" under whom Monty gladly served. During these years, Montgomery pushed to bring West Germany into the Western Union, noting in his *Memoirs* [268] that West Germany was admitted into NATO as a full member in 1955–"over six years after I had made the approach to Mr. Bevin [British Foreign Secretary] in January 1949. It had been a long up-hill struggle."

At the same time Monty battled with the British government and Chiefs of Staff over a Continental strategy. He believed in the absolute necessity for a British ground commitment to the defense of Europe. In the *Memoirs* [268], he wrote: "[Government] Ministers would talk about the main contribution of Britain was being air and sea power. This cut no ice at all in Europe."

In their study, *The Lonely Leader: Monty 1944-1945* [186], Alistair Horne with David Montgomery, conclude that "it is generally accepted" that Monty "achieved wonders in turning NATO into a serious fighting structure." Brian Montgomery wrote in his book, *A Field-Marshal in the Family* [272], that "My brother very much enjoyed his time at NATO largely because he traveled so extensively . . . " He visited the United States frequently and reinforced the favorable impression he had made in 1946. In 1953, *Time* magazine praised his efforts in raising the quality of NATO forces: "He has done it untiringly, devotedly, brilliantly." He had served as a gadfly, a roving inspector who could say things that others could not. His "exile" in France as Deputy Supreme Commander of NATO meant that Montgomery became a comparative stranger in his own country, seen in public only on rare occasions and the popular annual Alamein Reunions held each October at the Royal Albert Hall.

The Memoirs

In volume III, *Monty: Final Years of the Field-Marshal 1944-1976* [174B], Nigel Hamilton relates the story of the occasion in the early 1950s when Montgomery threatened to resign and write his memoirs. Then Prime Minister Winston Churchill asked Field Marshal Alexander, the Minister of Defense, which was worse, to leave Monty alone or sack him and let him write his memoirs; Alexander replied without hesitation, "Far worse to sack him and let him write his memoirs!"

When, however, Montgomery stepped down as Deputy Supreme Commander of NATO in 1958, at the age of 71, and retired from the British army after fifty years of service, he was ready to publish his memoirs. In fact he had begun writing his autobiography in 1956, and by January 1957 he had finished the book. He told his former chief of staff, Francis de Guingand that the book would cause "an immense sensation." His two earlier post-war official campaign accounts, *Alamein to the Sangro* [266] and *Normandy to the Baltic* [269], had been largely non-controversial, and were ghost written by his former chief of operations, David Belchem.

Such was not to be the case with *The Memoirs*, which were first titled, "The Sparks Fly Upward." A publishing sensation (they were also serialized in the *Sunday Times* and *Life* magazine, and a BBC television program based on his career soon followed), *The Memoirs* received generally favorable reviews: In the *New Statesman* [190], Michael Howard wrote, "He is a cheerful and unashamed exhibitionist, and he confesses it throughout these *Memoirs* with disarming frankness." Nevertheless, threats of libel action were soon flying with the sparks.

Field Marshal Auchinleck threatened legal action over Monty's assertion that he had planned to retreat before El Alamein. His former Intelligence chief, Brigadier Sir Edgar "Bill" Williams acted as peacemaker between the two Field Marshals and persuaded Monty to place a note acceptable to Auchinleck in the front of all copies of the book not yet sold. The Auk was satisfied and wrote to Williams, "If I may [say] so, I think you have achieved a miracle!" Montgomery's opinion of Auchinleck had not changed, however; When his former chief of staff de Guingand proposed to invite both the Field Marshals to dinner, Monty rejected the idea, replying to de Guingand: "So pipe down – please. I note you say the Auk admires *me*. But I don't admire him – and never have from the day I first served under him in the Southern Command after Dunkirk. That experience was enough for me." The reaction to *The Memoirs* are discussed by Francis de Guingand in his book, *From Brass Hat to Bowler Hat* [107]; Nigel Hamilton offers a detailed account in the final volume of *Monty* [175B].

De Guingand pointed that Montgomery had never really forgiven Eisenhower for the references to Monty in his book, *Crusade in Europe* [126], published three years after the war. In his *Memoirs*, Montgomery wrote that Eisenhower was not a great soldier in the "true sense of the word . . . But he was a great Supreme Commander – a military statesman." He was "a very great human being" who had "the power of drawing the hearts of men towards him as a magnet attracts the bits of metal." "I can never adequately express," declared the Field Marshal, "what I owe to his personal kindness and forbearance." Such words of praise, however, could not make up for Monty's judgement regarding Eisenhower's lack of generalship, or his belief that Eisenhower had "mishandled" and prolonged the war. Only months before publication of *The Memoirs* Monty had stayed with Ike in the White House!

Eisenhower's reaction to *The Memoirs* are discussed by Stephen E. Ambrose in his book, *Eisenhower 1890-1952* [8]. Eisenhower, now President, was "absolutely incensed . . . No one had ever made him so furious – not de Gaulle, not McCarthy, not Khrushchev." The President considered holding a ten-day seminar at Camp David to refute Monty's criticisms. It marked the end of their friendship. Nigel Hamilton concludes that "once again Monty had no one to blame but himself."

The Last Years

In the years after 1958 Monty remained very active; travel included visits to China, the Soviet Union, Egypt, and many other countries – "telling leaders like Mao Zedong, Khrushchev and Nasser how to run their affairs," is how Alistair Horne describes the visits in his book, *The Lonely Leader: Monty 1944-1945* [186]. His writings included, *The Path to Leadership* [270], published in 1961. Monty never comes closer to a real definition of leadership than a catalogue of virtues – his book, *Three Continents* [271], was published in 1962. In 1968, appeared *A History of Warfare* [264]. The earlier sections were written by his research assistants but from 1914 onwards, the book is very much in his own words. For insights by members of the research team see Anthony Brett-James, *Conversations with Montgomery* [46], and Alan Howarth's own contribution to *Monty at Close Quarters* [193], "Monty the Author." In a review of *A History of Warfare*, American military writer S.L.A. Marshall declared, "What a relief to hear a modern soldier-scholar confess that he found Clausewitz and Jomini a waste of time!"

In the 1960s, until Churchill's death, Montgomery was a frequent visitor to Chartwell. In his book, *The Path to Leadership*, Monty wrote of his friendship with Churchill, "our true friendship began" after the war. Indeed, Churchill had once described him as "a little man on the make." But during Churchill's declining years, Monty "unfailingly cheered him up," according to Norman Rose in his excellent study, *Churchill: The Unruly Giant* [343]. Evidence of Churchill's sometimes volatile relationship with Monty is to be found in John Colville's fascinating memoir, *The Fringes of Power* [86]. As private secretary to Churchill, Colville was never far from the "fringes" of power. Mrs. Churchill was the only person that Colville knew who always succeeded in subduing Montgomery, though she became fond of him. On one occasion, Monty announced on the croquet lawn at Chartwell that all politicians were dishonest. Clementine Churchill, with flashing eyes, said that if that was his view he should leave Chartwell at once. She would arrange to have his bags packed. He apologized profusely, and stayed. In a diary entry for 1952, Colville recorded another Montgomery story: "Monty has become a mellow, lovable exhibitionist; tamed but lonely and pathetic. He is not afraid of saying anything to anybody." But Maria de Casa Valdes scored (to Monty's great delight) when she asked him: "But you tell me you don't drink, and you don't smoke: what *do* you do that is wrong? Bite your nails?"

Churchill's daughter Mary Soames (Lady Soames) presents her view of Montgomery in the essay, "A Family Friend," in *Monty at Close Quarters* [193]. edited by T. E. B. Howarth.

In 1964 he underwent prostate surgery, and his brother Brian remarked, "Physically he has never been quite the same again." Monty was in South Africa recuperating from the prostate operation when he received the news of Winston Churchill's death. Lady Churchill asked him to act as one of the pallbearers at the state funeral, but he refused, on the grounds that he had not yet recovered his health. After years of expressing his devotion to Churchill and "Clemmie", Monty's excuse did not please the Churchill family. In partial explanation of his brother's behavior, Brian Montgomery remarks in his account, *A Field-Marshal in the Family* [272], "As long as I can remember Bernard has always disliked attending funerals [he did not attend his mother's], and has avoided doing so whenever possible."

In the mid 1960s there were family difficulties. When David divorced his wife, Monty blamed his son, and cut him from his will. The unhappy episode is described by Brian Montgomery in *A Field-Marshal in the Family* [272], and by Nigel Hamilton in *Monty: Final Years of the Field Marshal* [174B]. When David remarried in 1970, to Tessa Browning, the daughter of Montgomery's wartime airborne commander, "Boy" Browning, and of Daphne du Maurier, one of Monty's favorite novelists, family wounds were healed, and David was reinstated in his father's will.

After many years of differences, Montgomery renewed his earlier friendship with B. H. Liddell Hart. He would spend the New Year holidays at the Carlton Hotel in Bournemouth. The Liddell Harts often joined him there. Brian Montgomery notes in this book, *A Field-Marshal in the Family* [272], that although his brother greatly admired the military historian and theorist, "he argued fiercely with him out of sheer delight in provocation." Historian Alex Danchev has written a warm and deserved appreciation of Liddell Hart in his book, *Alchemist of War: The Life of Basil Liddell Hart* [104]. Richard M. Swain [375] writes in *The Journal of Military History* that, "Danchev has provided a far more textured appreciation of the man behind the theories."

In the latter years of active life Montgomery delighted in making his views known in the House of Lords on a variety of subjects as diverse as the Channel Tunnel, the Vietnam War, and the Homosexual Reform Bill. At the state opening of Parliament in 1966, 1967 and 1968 Montgomery carried the Sword of State, but on the third occasion collapsed as the Queen read her speech. It was an indication that his years were numbered. His last trip abroad was to Egypt in 1967 for the 25th Anniversary of the Battle of El Alamein. In 1969 he participated in the famous BBC radio program *Desert Island Discs*. The Bible, Shakespeare's works, and his own *History of Warfare* were the books that Monty selected to be cast away with.

The last years are described in *The Lonely Leader: Monty 1944-1945* [186] by Alistair Horne with David Montgomery, and Nigel Hamilton's, *Monty: The Final Years of the Field-Marshal 1944-1976* [174B]; Alun Chalfont, *Montgomery of Alamein* [70].

Increasingly, from 1970 onwards, he took to his bed. On March 24, 1976, at the age of eighty-eight, Monty passed away at his home with his son David and brother Brian as his bedside. Historian Kenneth O. Morgan, *The People's Peace: British History 1945-1990* [286], observed that Montgomery was "a very outdated figure at the time of his death in 1976," and seemed as remote as Wellington or Marlborough.

After a state funeral at Windsor, he was buried in his local churchyard in Binsted, not far from his home at Isington Mill, Hampshire. A simple granite stone marks his grave. Drew Middleton [260], the *New York Times* World War II military correspondent, wrote at the time of Monty's death: "He had that single-mindedness of all the great captains and the inspiring simplicity of a Grant or a Wellington. 'Win?' he would say in surprise, 'Of course we'll win. It's how and at what cost that counts.'"

PART II

BIBLIOGRAPHY

1.   Adenauer, Konrad. *Memoirs 1945-53*. Vol. 1 London: Weidenfeld and Nicolson, 1966.

2.   Agar-Hamilton, J. A. L., and L. C. F. Turner. *Crisis in the Desert: May-July 1942*. London: Oxford University Press, 1952.

3.   Ahrenfeldt, Robert H. *Psychiatry in the British Army in the Second World War*. London: Routledge and Kegan Paul, 1958.

4.   Alexander, Bevin. *How Great Generals Win*. New York: W.W. Norton, 1993.

5.   Alexander, Field Marshal Earl. *The Alexander Memoirs, 1940-1945*. Edited by John North. London: Cassell, 1962.

6.   Ambrose, Stephen E. "Address to the National Press Club," Washington, D.C. April 8, 1997.

7.   Ambrose, Stephen E. *Citizen Soldiers: The U.S. Army from the Normandy Beaches to the Bulge to the Surrender of Germany June 7, 1944-May 7, 1945*. New York: Simon and Schuster, 1997.

8.   Ambrose, Stephen E. *Eisenhower: Soldier, General of the Army, President Elect, 1890-1952*. New York: Simon and Schuster, 1983.

9.   Ambrose, Stephen E. *The Supreme Commander: The War Years of General Dwight D. Eisenhower*. Garden City, N.Y.: Doubleday, 1970.

10. Andidora, Ronald. "The Autumn of 1944: Boldness is Not Enough." *Parameters: US Army War College Quarterly*, 17, No. 4 (1987): 71-80.

11.   Annan, Noel. *Changing Enemies: The Defeat and Regeneration of Germany.* New York: Harper Collins, 1995.

12.   Annan, Noel. *Our Age: The Generation That made Post-War Britain.* London: Harper Collins, 1995.

13.   Baldwin, Hanson W. *Battles Lost and Won: Great Campaigns of World War II.* New York: Harper and Row, 1966.

14.   Baldwin, Hanson W., ed. *Command Decisions.* New York: Harcourt, 1959.

15.   Barnett, Correlli. *Engage the Enemy More Closely: The Royal Navy in the Second World War.* New York: W. W. Norton, 1991.

16.   Barnett, Correlli. *The Desert Generals.* London: Allen and Unwin, 1960.

17.   Barnett, Correlli. *The Lost Victory: British Dreams, British Realities 1945-1950.* London: Pan Books, 1996.

18.   Barry, Tom. *Guerilla Days in Ireland: A First-Hand Account of the Black and Tan War (1919-1921).* New York: Devin-Adair, 1956.

19.   Bateson, Henry. *First into Italy.* London: Hodder and Stoughton, 1944.

20.   Becker, J. , and F. Knipping, eds. *Power in Europe?* New York: Walter de Grayter, 1986.

21.   Behrendt, Hans-Otto. *Rommel's Intelligence in the Desert Campaign 1941-43.* London: Kimber, 1985.

22.   Belchem, David. *All in the Day's March.* London: Collins, 1978.

23.   Belchem, David. *Victory in Normandy.* London: Collins, 1981.

24.   Belfield, E., and H. Essame. *The Battle for Normandy.* London: Batsford, 1965.

25.   Bennett, Ralph. *Ultra and Mediterranean Strategy.* New York: William Morrow, 1989.

26.   Bennett, Ralph. *Ultra in the West: The Normandy Campaign of 1944-45.* London: Hutchinson, 1979.

27.   Bharucha, P.C. *The North African Campaign, 1940-1943, Official history of* *the Indian Armed Forces in the Second World War.* Calcutta: Combined Inter-Services, Historical Section, 1956.

28.   Bidwell, Shelford. "Monty: Master of the Battlefield or the Most Overrated General?" *Journal of the Royal United Services Institute for Defence Studies,* 129, No. 2(1984): 62-63.

29.   Bidwell, Shelford, and Dominick Graham. *Firepower: British Army Weapons and Theories of War, 1904-1945.* London: Union Hyman, 1982.

30.   Blackburn, George G. *Where the Hell Are the Guns? A Soldier's Eye View of the Anxious years, 1939-44.* Toronto, Ontario: McClelland & Steward, 1997.

31.   Blake, Robert and William Roger Louis, editors. *Churchill.* New York: Oxford University Press, 1992.

32.   Blaxland, Gregory. *The Plain Cook and the Great Showman: The First and Eighth Armies in North Africa.* London: William Kimber, 1977.

33.   Blumenson, Martin. "Book Reviews," *Parameters: US Army War College Quarterly*, XXIV (Winter, 1994-95): 142-45.

34.   Blumenson, Martin. "The Most Overrated General of World War II," *Armor*, 61 (May-June 1962): 4-10.

35.   Blumenson, Martin. *Breakout and Pursuit.* Washington, D.C.: Government Printing Office, 1961.

36.   Blumenson, Martin. *Kasserine Pass.* Boston: Houghton Mifflin, 1967.

37.   Blumenson, Martin. *The Battle of the Generals: The Untold Story of the Falaise Pocket-The Campaign That Should Have Won World War II.* New York: William Morrow, 1994.

38.   Blumenson, Martin. *The Patton Papers 1885-1945.* 2 vols. Boston: Houghton Mifflin, 1974.

39.   Blumenson, Martin. *US Army in World War II: Salerno to Cassino.* Washington, D.C.: Government Printing Office, 1969.

40.   Blumentritt, Günther. *Von Rundstedt: The Soldier and the Man.* London: Odhams Press, 1952.

41.   Bond, Brian, ed. *The First World War and British Military History.* Oxford:

Clarendon Press, 1991.

42.   Bourne, J. M. *Britain and the Great War 1914-1918*. New York: Edward Arnold, 1989.

43.   Bradley, Omar N. *A Soldier's Story*. New York: Henry Holt, 1951.

44.   Bradley, Omar N. and Clay Blair. *A General's Life: An Autobiography*. New York: Simon and Schuster, 1983.

45.   Brereton, Lewis H. *The Brereton Diaries*. New York: William Morrow, 1946.

46.   Brett-James, Anthony. *Conversations with Montgomery*. London: William Kimber, 1984.

47.   Brooks, Stephen, ed. *Montgomery and the Eighth Army: A Section fromt he Diaries, Correspondence and other Papers of Field Marshal The Viscount Montgomery of Alamein, August 1942 to December 1943.* London: The Army Records Society, 1991.

48.   Brooks, Stephen. "Montgomery and the Preparations for Overlord." *History Today,* 34 (June 1984): 18-22.

49.   Bryant, Arthur, ed. *The Alanbrooke War Diaries*. Vol. I. *The Turn of the Tide*. London: Collins, 1957.

50.   Bryant, Arthur, ed. *The Alanbrooke War Diaries*. Vol II. *Triumph in the West*. London: Collins, 1959.

51.   Buckley, Christopher. *Road to Rome*. London: Hodder and Stoughton, 1945.

52.   Bullock, Alan. *Ernest Bevin*. London: William Heinemamn, 1983.

53.   Burdick, Charles. *Unternehmen Sonnenblume*. Neckargemund: Kurt Vowinckel Verlag, 1980.

54.   Butcher, Harry C. *My Three Years with Eisenhower: The Personal Diary of Captain Harry C. Butcher*. New York: Simon and Schuster, 1946.

55.   Butler, Ivan. *The War Film*. London: Tantiry Press, 1974.

56.   Butler, J. R. M. *Grand Strategy*. Vol. III, Part II, June 1941-August 1942. London: Her Majesty's Stationery Office, 1961.

57. Caccia-Dominioni, Paolo. *Alamein, 1933-1962.* London: Allen & Unwin, 1966.

58. Callahan, Raymond. "Imperfect Victory Assured," *World War II.* (May 1989): 26-33.

59. Callahan, Raymond. "Two Armies in Normandy: Weighing British and Canadian Military Performance." *D-Day in 1944.* Ed. Theodore A. Wilson. Lawrence: University Press of Kansas, 1994.

60. Calvert, Michael. *Fighting Mad.* London: The Adventurers Club, 1965.

61. Campbell, John P. *Dieppe Revisited: A Documentary Investigation.* London: Frank Cass, 1995.

62. Carr, Caleb. "The Black Knight," *MHQ: The Quarterly Journal of Military History*, Vol. 6, No. 3 (Spring 1994): 90-97.

63. Carrington, Charles. *Soldier at Bomber Command.* London: Leo Cooper, 1987.

64. Carver, Michael, ed. *The War Lords: Military Commanders of the Twentieth Century.* Boston: Little, Brown, 1976.

65. Carver, Michael. *El Alamein.* London: Batsford, 1962.

66. Carver, Michael. *Harding of Petherton.* Weidenfeld & Nicolson, 1978.

67. Carver, Michael. *Out of Step: Memoirs of a Field Marshal.* Hutchinson, 1989.

68. Carver, Michael. *The Apostles of Mobility: The Theory and Practice of Armoured Warfare.* N.Y.: Holmes & Meier, 1979.

69. Casey, R. G. *Personal Experience 1939-46.* London: Constable, 1962.

70. Chalfont, Alun. *Montgomery of Alamein.* London: Weidenfeld and Nicolson, 1976.

71. Chandler, Alfred D., Jr., ed. and Stephen E. Ambrose, assoc. ed. *The Paper's of Dwight David Eisenhower: The War Years.* 5 vols. Baltimore: The John Hopkins Press, 1967.

72. Chandler, David G., ed. *The Oxford Illustrated History of the British Army.*

New York: Oxford University Press, 1994.

73. Chandler, David G., and James Lawton Collins, eds. *The D-Day Encyclopedia*. New York: Simon and Schuster, 1994.

74. Chandos, Viscount (Oliver Lyttelton). *The Memoirs of Lord Chandos*. London: Bodley Head, 1962.

75. Churchill, Winston S. *The Second World War*. 6 vols. London: Cassell, 1948-54.

76. Clark, Mark W. *Calculated Risk*. New York: Harper, 1951.

77. Clark, Ronald W. *Montgomery of Alamein*. New York: Roy Publishers, 1960.

78. Clarke, Dudley. *The Eleventh at War*. London: Michael Joseph, 1952.

79. Clifford, Alexander. *Three against Rommel: The Campaigns of Wavell, Auchinleck, and Alexander*. London: George G. Harrap, 1943.

80. Clifton, James, M.E. *I Was Monty's Double*. London: Rider and Company, 1954.

81. Codman, Charles Russell. *Drive*. Boston: Little, Brown & Company, 1957.

82. Cole, Hugh M. *The Ardennes: The Battle of the Bulge*. Washington, DC: Office of the Chief of Military History, 1965.

83. Cole, Hugh M. *The Lorraine Campaign*. Washington, D.C.: Office of the Chief of Military History, 1966.

84. Collier, Richard. *The Sands of Dunkirk*. London: Collins, 1961.

85. Collins, J. Lawton. *Lightning Joe: An Autobiography*. Baton Rouge: Louisiana State University Press, 1979.

86. Colville, John. *The Fringes of Power*. 2 vols. London: Sceptre, 1986, 1987.

87. Connell, John. *Auchinleck*. London: Cassell, 1959.

88. Connell, John. *Wavell*. London: Collins, 1964.

89. Cooke, O.A. *The Canadian Military Experience, 1867-1995: A Bibliography*.

Ottawa: Department of History and Heritage, Monograph Series No. 2, 3rd ed., 1997.

90.   Cooling, Benjamin F. *Case Studies in the Development of Close Air Support.* Washington, D.C.: Office of Air Force History, 1990.

91.   Coultass, Clive. *Images for Battle: British Film and the Second World War, 1939-1945.* Neward, DE.: University of Delaware Press, 1989.

92.   Crawley, Aidan. *The Rise of Western Germany 1945-1972.* London: Colins, 1973.

93.   Crookenden, Napier. *Battle of the Bulge 1944.* New York: Scribner's, 1980.

94.   Cruickshank, Charles. *Deception in World War II.* New York: Oxford University Press, 1979.

95.   Cunliffe, Marcus. *The Royal Warwickshire Regiment 1919-1955.* London: Alan Sutton, 1956.

96.   Cunningham, Andrew Browne. *A Sailor's Odyssey: The Autobiography of Admiral of the Fleet Viscount Cunningham of Hyndhope.* London: Hutchinson, 1951.

97.   D'Este, Carlo. *Bitter Victory: The Battle for Sicily, July - August 1943.* New York: Harper Collins, 1991.

98.   D'Este, Carlo. *Decision in Normandy.* New York: E.P. Dutton, 1983.

99.   D'Este, Carlo. "Falaise: The Trap Not Sprung," *MHQ: The Quarterly Journal of Military History*, Vol 10, no. 4 (Summer 1994): 58-68.

100.   D'Este, Carlo. *Patton: A Genius for War.* New York: Harper Collins, 1995.

101.   D'Este, Carlo. "Review of *Brute Force* by John Ellis," *Journal of Military History*, Vol. 55, No. 2 (April 1991): 266-67.

102.   D'Este, Carlo. *World War II in the Mediterranean 1942-1945.* Chapel Hill, N.C.: Algonquin Books, 1990.

103.   Dalton, Hugh. *High Tide and After.* London: Collins, 1962.

104.   Danchev, Alex. *Alchemist of War: The Life of Basil Liddell Hart.* London: Weidenfeld and Nicolson, 1998.

105. Davies, Norman. "The Misunderstood War: A Review of *A World at Arms: A Global History of World War II.*" *The New York Review of Books* (June 9, 1994): 20-24.

106. Davis, Kenneth S. *The American Experience of War 1939-1945.* London: Secker & Warburg, 1967.

107. De Guingand, Sir Francis. *From Brass Hat to Bowler Hat.* London: Hamish Hamilton, 1979.

108. De Guingand, Sir Francis. *Generals at War.* London: Hodder & Stoughton, 1964.

109. De Guingand, Sir Francis. *Operation Victory.* London: Hodder & Stoughton, 1947.

110. Delaforce, Patrick. *Monty's Iron Sides: From the Normandy Beaches to Bremen with the 3rd Division.* London: Alan Sutton, 1995.

111. *Desert Victory.* Film produced by Army Film and Photographic Unit and Royal Air Force Film Production Unit. Chicago: Questar/Travel Network, 1989.

112. DeWeerd, Harvey A. *Great Soldiers of World War II.* N.Y.: Norton, 1944.

113. *Dictionary of National Biography, 1971-1980.* Montgomery entry by E. T. Williams.

114. "Dieppe", Canadian Broadcasting Corporation Mini-Series, 1993.

115. Divine, David. *The Nine Days of Dunkirk.* New York: W.W. Norton, 1959.

116. Dixon, Norman. *On The Psychology of Military Incompetence.* New York: Basic Books, 1976.

117. Dockrill, Saki. *Britain's Policy for West German Reamament 1950-55.* New York: Cambridge University Press, 1991.

118. Donnison, F. S. U. *Civil Affairs and Military Government, North-West Europe 1944-46.* London: HMSO, 1961.

119. Dorman-Smith, Eric. "1st Alamein: The Battle That Saved Cairo," in Purnell's *History of the Second World War.* Vol. 3 (1967).

120. Doubler, Michael D. *Closing with the Enemy: How GIs Fought the War in*

Europe 1944-1945. Lawrence, KS.: University Press of Kansas, 1994.

121. Douglas, W.A.B. and Brereton Greenhous, "Canada and the Second World War: The State of Clio's Art," *Military Affairs* Vol. XLII, No. 1 (February, 1978): 24-28.

122. Driberg, Tom. *Ruling Passions.* London: Jonathan Cape, 1977.

123. Edmonds, Martin, ed. *The Defense Equation: British Military Systems: Policy, Planning, and Performance.* London: Brassey's Defense publishers, 1986.

124. Ehrman, John, ed. *Grand Strategy.* Vols. V and VI. London: Her Majesty's Stationery Office, 1956.

125. Eisenhower, David. *Eisenhower: At War, 1943-1945.* New York: Random House, 1986.

126. Eisenhower, Dwight D. *Crusade in Europe.* New York: Doubleday, 1948.

127. Eisenhower Foundation. *D-Day: The Normandy Invasion in Retrospect.* Lawrence, KS.: University Press of Kansas, 1971.

128. Eisenhower, John S. D. *The Bitter Woods.* New York: G. P. Putman's, 1969.

129. Ellis, John. *Brute Force: Allied Strategy and Tactics in the Second World War.* New York: Viking, 1990.

130. Ellis, L. F. *Victory in the West: The Battle of Normandy.* Vol. 1. History of the Second World War. London: His Majesty's Stationery Office, 1962.

131. Ellis, L. F. with A. E. Warhurst, *Victory in the West*, Vol. II, *The Defeat of Germany.* London: Her Majesty's Stationery Office, 1962-68.

132. Ellis, William Donohue and Thomas J. Cunningham, Jr., *Clark of St. Vith: The Sergeants' General.* Cleveland: Dillon/Leiderbach, 1974.

133. Ellwood, David W., *Italy, 1943-1945.* New York: Holmes and Meier, 1985.

134. Elstob, Peter. *Hilter's Last Offensive.* London: Secker and Warburg, 1971.

135. English, John A. *The Canadian Army and the Normandy Campaign: A Study in Failure in High Command.* New York: Praeger, 1991.

136. Essame, Hubert. *Patton: A Study in Command.* New York: Charles

Scribner's Sons, 1974.

137. Essame, Hubert. *The Battle for Germany*. London: Batsford, 1969.

138. Farago, Ladislas. *Patton: Ordeal and Triumph*. New York: Astor-Honor, 1964.

139. Farquharson, John E. *The Western Allies and the Politics of Food: Agarian Management in Postwar Germany*. Dover, NH: Berg Publishers, 1985.

140. Farrar, Reginald. *Life of Dean Farrar*. London: James Nisbit, 1905.

141. Fergusson, Bernard. *The Watery Maze*. London: Collins, 1961.

142. Ferris, John. "Ralph Bennett and the Study of Ultra," *Intelligence and National Security*, 6(April, 1991): 473-86.

143. Florentin, Eddy. *The Battle of the Falaise Gap*. London: Elek Books, 1965.

144. Fraser, David. *Alanbrooke*. London: Collins, 1982.

145. Fraser, David. *And We Shall Shock Them The British Army in the Second World War*. London: Hodder and Stoughton, 1983.

146. Fraser, David. *Knight's Cross: A Life of Field Marshal Erwin Rommel*. London: Harper Collins, 1993.

147. Fraser, David. "Montgomeries," *London Review of Books*, Vol. 5, No. 24 (1983): 7-9.

148. Frost, John. *A Drop Too Many*. London: Cassell, 1980.

149. Fuller, J. F. C. *The Conduct of War 1789-1961*. New Brunswick: Rutgers University Press, 1961.

150. Fuller, J. F. C. *The Second World War: A Strategical and Tactical History*. New York: Duell, Sloan & Pearce, 1949.

151. Fussell, Paul. *Wartime: Understanding and Behavior in the Second World War*. New York: Oxford University Press, 1989.

152. Gale, Richard. *Call to Arms*. London: Hutchinson, 1968.

153. Gale, Richard. *With the 6th Airborne Division in Normandy*. London:

Sampson Low, 1948.

154. Galloway, Strome. *The General Who Never Was.* Belleville, Ont.: Mika, 1981.

155. Garland, Albert N., and H. M. Smyth. *Sicily and the Surrender of Italy.* Washington, D.C.: Government Printing Office, 1965.

156. Gavin, James M. *On to Berlin: Battles of an Airborne Commander, 1943-1946.* New York: Viking, 1978.

157. Gelb, Norman. *Ike and Monty: Generals at War.* New York: Morrow, 1994.

158. Gilbert, Martin. *Winston S. Churchill: Road to Victory.* Vol. VII. Boston: Houghton Mifflin, 1986.

159. Godwin-Austen, A. R. *The Staff and the Staff College.* London: Constable, 1927.

160. Gooch, John, ed. *Decisive Campaigns of the Second World War.* London: F. Cass, 1990.

161. Graeme-Evans, A. L. "Field Marshal Bernard Montgomery: A Critical Assessment," *Defense Force Journal.* (May-June 1978): 50-60.

162. Graham, Dominick and Shelford Bidwell. *Coalitions, Politicians, and Generals: Some Aspects of Command in Two World Wars.* London: Brassey's, 1994.

163. Graham, Dominick and Shelford Bidwell. *Tug of War: The Battle for Italy, 1943-1945.* New York: St. Martin's Press, 1986.

164. Graham, Dominick. *The Price of Command: A Biography of General Guy Simonds.* Ottawa: Stoddart, 1993.

165. Greacen, Lavinia. *Chink: A Biography.* London: Macmillan, 1989.

166. Greenfield, Kent Roberts. *Command Decisions.* New York: Harcourt Brace, 1959.

167. Greenfield, Kent Roberts. *The Historian and the Army.* New Brunswick, N.J.: Rutgers University Press, 1954.

168. Greenhous, Brereton. *Dieppe, Dieppe.* Montreal and Ottawa: Art Global in

Cooperation with the Department of National Defense, 1993.   Catalog No. 2/1993E.

169. Grigg, John. "Churchill and Lloyd George," in Robert Blake and William Roger Louis, eds. *Churchill*. New York: W. W. Norton, 1993.

170. Grigg, P. J. *Prejudice and Judgment*. London: Collins, 1948.

171. Guderian, Heinz. *Panzer Leader*. London: Michael Joseph, 1952.

172. Guedalla, Philip. *Middle East 1940-1942: A Study in Air Power*. London: Hodder & Stoughton, 1944.

173. Gunther, John. *D-Day*. London: Hamish Hamilton, 1944.

174A.   Hamilton, Nigel. *Monty: Vol. 1, The Making of a General 1887-1942*. New York: McGraw-Hill, 1981.

175A.   Hamilton, Nigel. *Monty: Vol. 2, Master of the Battlefield 1942-1944*. New York: McGraw-Hill, 1983.

174B.   Hamilton, Nigel. *Monty: Vol. 3, Final Years of the Field-Marshal, 1944-1976*. New York: McGraw-Hill, 1986.

175B.   Hamilton, Nigel. *Monty: The Battles of Field Marshal Bernard Law Montgomery*. New York: Random, 1994.

176. Harclerode, Peter. *Arnhem: A Tragedy of Errors*. London: Arms and Armour Press, 1994.

177. Harris, Sir Arthur. *Bomber Offensive*. London: Collins, 1947.

178. Harris, Kenneth. *Attlee*. London: Weidenfeld and Nicolson, 1982.

179. Harrison, Gordon A. *Cross-Channel Attack*. Washington, D.C.: The Center of Military History, 1951.

180. Hastings, Max. *Overlord: D-Day and the Battle of Normandy*. New York: Simon & Schuster, 1984.

181. Haswell, Jock. *D-Day: Intelligence and Deception*. New York: Times Books, 1979.

182. Hearnden, Arthur, ed. *The British in Germany: Educational Reconstruction* *after 1945.* London: Hamish Hamilton, 1978.

183. Hibbert, Christopher. *The Battle of Arnhem.* London: Batsford, 1962.

184. Hinsley, F. H. *British Intelligence in the Second World War: Its Influence on Strategy and Operations.* Vol. II. Part VI. New York: Cambridge University Press, 1981.

185. Hinsley, F. H. and Alan Stripp, eds. *Codebreakers: The Inside Story of Beltchley Park.* Oxford: Oxford University Press, 1994.

186. Horne, Alistair with David Montgomery, *The Lonely Leader: Monty 1944-1945.* London: MacMillan, 1994.

187. Horne, Donald. *The Australian People: Biography of a Nation.* Sydney: Angus and Robertson, 1972.

188. Horner, D.M. ed. *The Commanders: Australian Military Leadership in the Twentieth Century.* Sydney: Allen & Unwin, 1984.

189. Horrocks, Sir Brian. *A Full Life.* London: Collins, 1960.

190. Howard, Michael. "The Field-Marshal: A Review of *The Memoirs*," *New Statesman* (November 8, 1958): 643-44.

191. Howard, Michael. *The Causes of Wars and Other Essays.* London: Temple Smith, 1983.

192. Howard, Michael. *The Mediterranean Strategy in the Second World War.* London: Weidenfeld and Nicolson, 1968.

193. Howarth, T. E. B., ed. *Monty at Close Quarters: Recollections of the Man.* New York: Hippocrene Books, 1985.

194. Hughes, Thomas Alexander. *"Overlord": General Pete Quesada and the Triumph of Tactical Air Power in World War II.* New York: The Free Press, 1995.

195. Hunt David. *A Don At War.* London: Frank Cass, 1966.

196. Ingersoll, Ralph. *Top Secret.* New York: Harcourt Brace, 1946.

197. Irving, David. *The Trail of the Fox: The Life of Field-Marshal Erwin Rommel.* New York: E.P. Dutton, 1977.

198. Irving, David. *The War Between the Generals*. New York: Congdon & Lattès, 1981.

199. Ismay, Lord. *The Memoirs of General Lord Ismay*. London: Viking, 1960.

200. Jackson, W. G. F. *Alexander of Tunis as Military Commander*. London: Batsford, 1971.

201. Jackson, W. G. F. *The Battle for Italy*. London: Batsford, 1967.

202. Jackson, W. G. F. *The North African Campaign 1940-1943*. London: Batsford, 1975.

203. Jacobson, H. A., and J. Rohwer. *Decisive Battles of World War II: The German View*. New York: Putnam, 1965.

204. Johnson, Franklyn A. *Defence by Ministry: the British Ministry of Defence 1944-1974*. London: Duckworth, 1980.

205. Johnstone, Denis. *Nine Rivers from Jordan*. London: André Deutsch, 1953.

206. Kee, Robert. *The Green Flag: A History of Irish Nationalism*. London: Weidenfeld and Nicolson, 1972.

207. Keegan, John, ed. *Churchill's Generals*. New York: Grove Weidenfeld, 1991.

208. Keegan, John. *Six Armies in Normandy: From D-Day to the Liberation of Paris*. New York: Penguin Books, 1982.

209. Keegan, John. *The Battle for History: Re-fighting World War II*. New York: Vintage Books.

210. Keegan, John. *The Second World War*. N.Y.: Penguin Books, 1990.

211. Kemp, Anthony. *The Unknown Battle: Metz, 1944*. New York: Stein and Day, 1981.

212. Kennedy, Sir John. *The Business of War*. London: Hutchinson, 1957.

213. Kershaw, Robert J. *'It Never Snows in September': The German View of Market-Garden and the Battle of Arnhem, September 1944*. Marlborough: The Crowood Press, 1990.

214. Kesselring, Albert. *Memoirs*. London: Kimber, 1963.

215. Kingston-McCloughry, E.J. *The Direction of War: A Critique of the Political Direction and High Command in War*. New York: Frederick A. Praeger, 1955.

216. Kippenberger, H.K. *Infantry Brigadier*. New York: Oxford University Press, 1949.

217. Kirby, Norman, *1100 Miles with Monty*. Gloucester: Allan Sutton, 1989.

218. Lamb, Richard, *Montgomery in Europe 1943-1945: Success or Failure?*. London: Buchan & Enright, 1983.

219. Lamb, Richard. *The War in Italy, 1943-1945: A Brutal Story*. New York: St. Martin's Press, 1995.

220. Larrabee, Eric. *Commander in Chief: Franklin Delano Roosevelt, His Lieutenants, and Their War*. New York: Harper & Row, 1987.

221. Larson, Melvin G. *Field Marshal Bernard L. Montgomery: Man of Prayer*. Grand Rapids, Michigan: Zondervan Publishing House, 1945.

222. Lewin, Ronald. *Montgomery as Military Commander*. London: Batsford, 1971.

223. Lewin, Ronald. *Rommel as Military Commander*. London: Batsford, 1968.

224. Lewin, Ronald. *Ultra Goes to War*. London: Huchinson, 1979.

225. Liddell Hart, B. H., ed. *The Rommel Papers*. New York: Harcourt Brace, 1953.

226. Liddell Hart, B. H. *History of the Second World War*. New York: Putnam, 1970.

227. Liddell Hart, B. H. *The German Generals Talk*. New York: William Morrow, 1948.

228. Liddell Hart, B. H. *The Memoirs of Captain Liddell Hart*. 2 vols. London: Cassell, 1965.

229. Liddell Hart, B. H. *The Other Side of the Hill: Germany's Generals, Their Rise and Fall, with Their Own Account of Military Events, 1939-1940*. London: Macmillan, 1993.

230. Linklater, Eric. *The Campaign in Italy*. London: His Majesty's Stationery Office, 1951.

231. Lovat, Lord. *March Past: A Memoir*. London: Weidenfeld and Nicolson, 1978.

232. Lucas, James and James Barker. *The Battle of Normandy: The Falaise Gap*. New York: Holmes & Meier, 1978.

233. Luck, Hans von. *Panzer Commander: The Memoirs of Colonel Hans von Luck*. New York: Dell, 1989.

234. MacDonald, Charles B. *A Time for Trumpets*. New York: Morrow, 1985.

235. MacDonald, Charles B. *The Decision to Launch Operation Market-Garden*. Washington, D.C.: Center of Military History, 1990.

236. MacDonald, Charles B. *The Last Offensive*. Washington, D.C.: Office of the Chief of Military History, 1973.

237. MacDonald, Charles B. *The Mighty Endeavour: American Armed Forces in the European Theater in World War II*. New York: Oxford University Press, 1969.

238. MacDonald, Charles B. *The Siegfried Line Campaign*. Washington, D.C.: Office of the Chief of Military History, 1963.

239. MacIntyre, Donald. *The Battle of the Mediterranean*. London: Batsford, 1964.

240. Macksey, Kenneth. *Crucible of Power: The Fight for Tunisia 1942-1943*. London: Hutchinson, 1968.

241. Maguire, Eric. *Dieppe, August 19*. London: Cape, 1963.

242. Majdalany, Fred. *The Battle of El Alamein*. London: Weidenfeld and Nicolson, 1965.

243. Majdalany, Fred. *The Fall of Fortress Europe*. London: Hodder and Stoughton, 1969.

244. Mallaby, Sir George. *Each In His Office*. London: Collins, 1972.

245. Malone, Dick. *Missing from the Record*. Toronto: Collins, 1946.

246. Manning, Olivia. "The Flap" in Purnell's *History of the Second World War*. Vol. 3, (1967).

247. Manvell, Roger. *Films and the Second World War*. London: Dent, 1974.

248. Marshall-Cornwall, Sir James. *Haig as Military Commander*. New York: Crane, Russak, 1973.

249. Martel, Sir Giffard. *An Outspoken Soldier*. London: Sifton Praed, 1949.

250. Mason, David. *Breakout: Drive to the Seine*. New York: Ballantine Books, 1969.

251. Maughan, Barton. *Tobruk and El Alamein: Australia in the War of 1939-1945*. Canberra: Australian War Memorial, 1966.

252. McCallum, Neil. *Journey With A Pistol: A Diary of War*. London: Victor Gollancz, 1959.

253. McGill, Michael C. And William D. Flackes. *Montgomery, Field-Marshal: An Ulster Tribute*. Belfast: The Quota Press, 1946.

254. McNish, Robin. *Iron Division: The History of the 3rd Division*. London: Ian Allen, 1978.

255. Meese, Giovanni. *Come Fini La Guerra in Africa: La "Prima Armata" Italiana in Tunisia*. Milan: Rizzoli, 1946.

256. Mellenthin, F.W. von. *Panzer Battles: A Study of the Employment of Armor in the Second World War*. New York: Ballantine Books, 1956.

257. Merriam, Robert E. *Dark December: The Full Account of the Battle of the Bulge*. Chicago: Ziff-Davis, 1947.

258. Merriam, Robert E. *The Battle of the Ardennes*. London: Souvenir Press, 1958.

259. Middlebrook, Martin. *Arnhem 1944: The Airborne Battle, 17-26 September*. New York: Viking, 1994.

260. Middleton, Drew. "Montgomery, Hard to Like or Ignore," *New York Times*, 25/3/76.

261. Miller, Edward G. *A Dark and Bloody Ground: The Hürtgen Forest and the*

Roer River Dams, 1944-1945. College Station: Texas A&M University Press, 1995.

262. Millett, Allan R. Review of "Battle of the Bulge." *Journal of American History.* Vol. 82, No. 3 (December 1995): 1325-26.

263. Molony, C. J. C. *The Mediterranean and Middle East.* Vol. 5. London: HMSO, 1973.

264. Montgomery, Bernard Law. *A History of Warfare.* New York: World Publishing Company, 1968.

265. Montgomery, Bernard Law. *An Approach to Sanity.* London: Collins, 1959.

266. Montgomery, Bernard Law. *El Alamein to the Sangro.* London: Hutchinson, 1948.

267. Montgomery, Bernard Law. *Forward to Victory.* London: Hutchinson, 1946.

268. Montgomery, Bernard Law. *The Memoirs of Field Marshal The Viscount Montgomery of Alamein, K.G.* London: Collins, 1958.

269. Montgomery, Bernard Law. *Normandy to the Baltic.* London: Hutchinson, 1947.

270. Montgomery, Bernard Law. *The Path to Leadership.* New York: G. P. Putnam's Sons, 1961.

271. Montgomery, Bernard Law. *Three Continents.* London: Collins, 1962.

272. Montgomery, Brian. *A Field-Marshal in the Family.* London: Constable, 1973.

273. Montgomery, Brian. *Monty: A Life in Photographs 1887-1976.* Poole: Blandford Press, 1985.

274. Montgomery, Maude. *Bishop Montgomery-A Memoir.* London: Society for the Propagation for the Gospel in Foreign Parts, 1933.

275. Moore, J. H. *Morshead-A Biography of Lieutenant-General Sir Leslie Morshead.* Sydney: Haldane, 1976.

276. Moorehead, Alan. *African Trilogy.* London: Hamish Hamilton, 1944.

277. Moorehead, Alan. *Eclipse*. London: Hamish Hamilton, 1945.

278. Moorehead, Alan. *Montgomery*. London: Hamish Hamilton, 1946.

279. Moorehead, Alan. *Montgomery*. Newport Beach, CA.: Books on Tape, 1988 (Cassettes of Book).

280. Moran, Lord. *Churchill: The Struggle for Survival 1940-65*. London: Constable, 1966.

281. Mordal, Jacques. *Dieppe: The Dawn of Decision*. London: Souvenir Press, 1963.

282. Morelock, J. D. *Generals of the Ardennes: American Leadership in the Battle of the Bulge*. Washington, D.C.: National Defense University Press, 1993.

283. Morgan, Kay Summersby. *Past Forgetting: My Love Affair with Dwight D. Eisenhower*. New York: Simon and Schuster, 1975.

284. Morgan, Sir Frederick. *Overture to Overlord*. London: Hodder & Stoughton, 1950.

285. Morgan, Sir Frederick. *Peace and War: A Soldier's Life*. London: Stodder and Stoughton, 1961.

286. Morgan, Kenneth O. *The People's Peace: British History 1945-1990*. New York: Oxford University Press, 1992.

287. Morison, Samuel Eliot. *Sicily-Salerno-Anzio*. Boston: Little, Brown, 1954.

288. Morris, Eric. *Salerno: A Military Fiasco*. New York: Stein and Day, 1983.

289. Muggeridge, Malcolm. *Like It Was*. London: Collins, 1981.

290. Murray, G. E. Patrick. *Eisenhower versus Montgomery: The Continuing Debate*. Westport, CT.: Praeger, 1996.

291. Murray, Williamson. "Overload," *MHQ: The Quarterly Journal of Military History*, Vol. 6, No. 3 (Spring 1994): 6-21.

292. Murray, Williamson, MacGregor Knox and Alvin Bernstein. *The Making of Strategy: Rulers, States, and War*. New York: Cambridge University Press, 1994.

293. Myers, Frank. "Conscription and the Politics of Military Strategy in the

Attlee Government," *The Journal of Strategic Studies*, Vol. 7 (1984): 55-73.

294. Namier, Sir Lewis. *In the Nazi Era*. London: Macmillan, 1952.

295. Neillands, Robin. *The Desert Rats: 7th Armored Divsiion, 1940-45*. London: Weidenfeld and Nicolson, 1991.

296. Nichols, H.G., ed., *Washington Despatches 1941-1945: Weekly Political Reports from the British Embassy*. Chicago: The University of Chicago Press, 1981.

297. Nicholson, G. W. L. *The Canadians in Italy 1943-1945*. Ottawa: Queen's Printer, 1966.

298. Nicolson, Harold. *Diaries and Letters*. Vol. II, *The War Years 1939-1945*. London: Collins, 1967.

299. Nicolson, Nigel. *Alex*. London: Weidenfeld and Nicolson, 1973.

300. Nobécourt, Jacques. *Hilter's Last Gamble*. London: Chatto and Windus, 1967.

301. North, John. *Northwest Europe, 1944-1945: The Achievement of 21st Army Group*. London: Her Majesty's Stationery Office, 1953.

302. Orange, Vincent. *Coningham: A Biography of Air Marshal Sir Arthur Coningham*. London: Methuen, 1990.

303. Overy, Richard. *Why the Allies Won*. New York: W.W. Norton, 1996.

304. Owen, Roderic. *Tedder*. London: Collins, 1952.

305. Pack, S. W. C. *Operation HUSKY: The Allied Invasion of Sicily*. New York: Hippocrene Books, 1977.

306. Pack, S. W. C. *Cunningham the Commander*. London: Batsford, 1974.

307. Parkinson, Roger. *Blood, Toil, Tears and Sweat*. London: Hart-Davis MacGibbon, 1973.

308. Parrish, Thomas, ed. *The Simon and Schuster Encyclopedia of World War II*. New York: Simon and Schuster, 1978.

309. Paschall, Rod. "Tactical Exercises: The Failure of *Market-Garden*," *MHQ*,

(Spring 1994): 88-89.

310. Patton, George S. *War as I Knew It.* New York: W. H. Allen, 1950.

311. Peacock, Lady. *Montgomery.* London: Hutchinson, 1951.

312. Peden, G. C. "The Burden of Imperial Defence and the Continental Commitment Reconsidered," *The Historical Journal,* 27, No. 2 (1984): 405-23.

313. Pelly, M.E. and H.J. Yasamee. *Documents on British Policy Overseas.* Series I, Vol. V. London: Her Majesty's Stationery Office, 1990.

314. Peniakoff, Vladimir. *Private Army.* London: Cape, 1950.

315. Perret, Geoffrey. *There's a War to be Won: The United States Army in World War II.* New York: Random House, 1991.

316. Phillips, C. E. Lucas. *Alamein.* London: Heinemann, 1962.

317. Playfair, I.S.O. *The Mediterranean and Middle East,* Volumes III and IV. London: HMSO, 1960 and 1966.

318. Pocock, Tom. *Alan Moorehead.* London: The Bodley Head, 1990.

319. Pogue, Forrest C. *George C. Marshall.* Vol. III, *Organizer of Victory 1943-1945.* New York: Viking, 1973.

320. Pogue, Forrest C. *The Supreme Command.* Washington, D.C.: Office of the Chief of Military History, 1954.

321. Pond, Hugh. *Salerno.* London: William Kimber, 1961.

322. Pond, Hugh. *Sicily.* London: William Kimber, 1962.

323. Powers, Stephen T. "The Battle of Normandy: The Lingering Controversy," *The Journal of Military History.* 56 (July 1992): 455-71.

324. Price, Frank James. *Troy H. Middleton: A Biography.* Baton Rouge: Louisiana State University Press, 1974.

325. Pugh, Michael. Review of Vincent Orange's "Coningham," *The New Zealand Journal of History,* Vol. 28, No. 1 (April, 1994): 114-15.

326. Raugh, Jr., Harold E. *Wavell in the Middle East, 1939-1941: A Study in*

Generalship. New York: Brassey's 1993.

327. Rees, Goronwy. *A Bundle of Sensations: Sketches in Autobiography.* New York: MacMillan, 1961.

328. Reid, Brian Holden. *J.F.C. Fuller:Military Thinker.* London: Macmillan, 1987.

329. Reynolds, David. *Britannia Overruled: British Foreign Policy and World Power in the Twentieth Century.* New York: Longman, 1991.

330. Reynolds, Michael. *Steel Inferno: ISS Panzer Corps in Normandy.* New York: Sarpedon, 1997.

331. Reynolds, Quentin. *The Curtain Rises.* New York: Random House, 1944.

332. Richards, Denis, and H. St. George Saunders, *Royal Air Force, 1939-1945.* London: Her Majesty's Stationery Office, 1954.

333. Richards, Denis. *Portal of Hungerford.* New York: Holmes & Meier, 1990.

334. Richards, Jeffrey and Dorothy Sheridan, eds. *Mass Observation at the Movies.* London: Routledge and Regan Paul, 1987.

335. Richardson, Sir Charles. *Flashback: A Soldier's Story.* London: Kimber, 1985.

336. Richardson, Sir Charles. *Send for Freddie.* London: Kimber, 1987.

337. Ridgway, Matthew B. *Soldier: The Memoirs of Matthew B. Ridgway.* New York: Harper, 1956.

338. Roberts, G.P.B. *From the Desert to the Baltic.* London: Kimber, 1987.

339. Robertson, Terence. *Dieppe: The Shame and the Glory.* Boston: Atlantic-Little, 1962.

340. Rohmer, Richard. *Patton's Gap: An Account of the Battle of Normandy 1944.* New York: Beaufort Books, 1981.

341. Rollins, Peter. "Document & Drama in *Desert Victory,*" *Film and History.* Vol. 4, No. 2 (1974): 11-13.

342. Rooney, Andy. *My War.* New York: Random House, 1995.

343. Rose, Norman. *Churchill: The Unruly Giant.* New York: The Free Press, 1994.

344. Roskill, Stephen W. *The War at Sea 1939-1945,* Vol. III, Part I, *The Offensive.* London: Her Majesty's Stationery Office, 1960.

345. Roskill, Stephen. *Churchill and the Admirals.* New York: Morrow, 1978.

346. Ryan, Cornelius. *A Bridge Too Far.* New York: Simon and Schuster, 1974.

347. Ryan, Cornelius. *The Last Battle.* London: Collins, 1966.

348. Ryan, Cornelius. *The Longest Day.* London: Gollancz, 1960.

349. Ryder, Rowland. *Oliver Leese.* London: Hamish Hamilton, 1987.

350. Scarfe, Norman. *Assault Division: A History of the 3rd Division from the Invasion of Normandy to the Surrender of Germany.* London: Collins, 1947.

351. Scoullar, J. L. *Battle for Egypt: The Summer of 1942.* Wellington: Department of Internal Affairs, 1955.

352. Seldon, Anthony. *Churchill's Indian Summer: The Conservative Government 1951-55.* London: Hodder and Stoughton, 1981.

353. Serle, Geoffrey. *John Monash: A Biography.* Melbourne: Melbourne University Press, 1982.

354. Shepperd, G. A. *The Italian Campaign 1943-45: A Political and Military Reassessment.* New York: Frederick A. Praeger, 1968.

355. Shinwell, Emanuel. *I've Lived Through It All.* London: Victor Gollancz, 1973.

356. Shulman, Milton. *Defeat in the West.* London: Secker & Warburg, 1947.

357. Sixsmith, E. K. G. *Eisenhower as Military Commander.* London: Batsford, 1973.

358. Sixsmith, E.K.G. *British Generalship in the Twentieth Century.* London: Batsford, 1970.

359. Slessor, Sir John. *The Central Blue: The Autobiography of Sir John Slessor, Marshall of the RAF.* New York: Frederick A. Praeger, 1957.

360. Slowe, Peter. *Manny Shinwell: An Authorized Biography.* Boulder, Colorado: Pluto Press, 1993.

361. Smyth, Sir John. *Bolo Whistler.* London: Frederick Muller, 1967.

362. Sorel, Nancy Caldwell. "Dwight Eisenhower and Bernard Montgomery," *The Atlantic Monthly*, Vol. 275, No. 3 (March 1995): lll.

363. Sosabowski, Stanislaw. *Freely I Served.* London: William Kimber, 1960.

364. Speidel, Hans. *Invasion 1944: Rommel and the Normandy Campaign.* Chicago: Henry Regnery, 1950.

365. Stacey, C.P. *A Date with History: Memoirs of a Canadian Historian.* Ottawa: Deneau, 1982.

366. Stacey, C.P. *Arms, Men and Governments: The War Policies of Canada 1939-1945.* Ottawa: Queen's Printer, 1970.

367. Stacey, C.P. *The Victory Campaign: The Operations in North-West Europe, 1944-1945.* Vol III, *Official History of the Canadian Army in the Second World War.* Ottawa: Queen's Printer, 1960.

368. Strang, William. *Home and Abroad.* London: Deutsch, 1956.

369. Strawson, John. *El Alamein: Desert Victory.* London: J. M. Dent, 1981.

370. Strawson, John. *Gentlemen in Khaki: The British Army 1890-1990.* London: Secker & Warburg, 1989.

371. Strawson, John. *The Battle for North Africa.* London: Batsford, 1969.

372. Strong, Sir Kenneth. *Intelligence at the Top.* Garden City, N.Y.: Doubleday, 1969.

373. Sulzberger, C. L. *World War II.* Boston: Houghton Mifflin, 1987.

374. Summersby, Kay. *Eisenhower Was My Boss.* New York: Prentice-Hall, 1948.

375. Swain, Richard M. "Review of Alchemist of War by Alex Danchev," *Journal of Military History*, Vol. 63, No. 2 (April 1999): 468-70.

376. Taylor, A.J.P. *English History 1914-1945.* New York: Oxford University

Press, 1965.

377. Taylor, R.J. *Kiwis in the Desert: The North African Campaign, 1940-1943.* Wellington: New Zealand Military Studies Centre, 1992.

378. Tedder, Lord. *With Prejudice: The War Memoirs of Marshal of the Royal Air Force, Lord Tedder.* London: Cassell, 1966.

379. Terraine, John. *A Time of Courage: The RAF 1939-1945.* New York: Macmillan, 1985.

380. Thompson, R. W. "Massacre at Dieppe," *Purnell's History of the Second World War.* Vol 3, No. 8(1967).

381. Thompson, R. W. *Montgomery the Field Marshal.* London: Allen & Unwin, 1969.

382. Thompson, R. W. *The Montgomery Legend.* London: George Allen & Unwin, 1967.

383. *Time: The Weekly News Magazine.* "The Eighth Army's Montgomery: The Lord and John Bunyan were with him." (February 1, 1943): 26-28.

384. *The Times*(London). "What Monty Saw." (January 8, 1999): 23.

385. Toland, John. *Battle: The Story of the Bulge.* New York: Random House, 1959.

386. Toland, John. *The Last 100 Days.* New York: Random House, 1966.

387. Truscott, Lucian K., Jr. *Command Missions.* New York: E. P. Dutton, 1954.

388. Tugwell, M. A. J. *"Arnhem: The Ten Germs of Failure,"* Royal United Service Institution Journal. (December 1969).

389. Tuker, Sir Francis. *Approach to Battle.* London: Cassell, 1963.

390. Urquhart, Brian. *A Life in Peace and War.* New York: Harper and Row, 1987.

391. Urquhart, R. E. *Arnhem.* London: Cassell, 1958.

392. Van Creveld, Martin. *Supplying War: Logistics from Wallenstein to Patton.* New York: Cambridge University Press, 1977.

393. Verney, Gerald L. *The Desert Rats*. London: Hutchinson, 1954.

394. Villa, Brian Loring. "Mountbatten, the British Chiefs of Staff and Approval of the Dieppe Raid," *The Journal of Military History*. 54(April 1990): 201-26.

395. Villa, Brian Loring. *Unauthorized Action: Mountbatten and the Dieppe Raid*. New York: Oxford University Press, 1989.

396. Warner, Oliver. *Cunningham of Hyndhope: Admiral of the Fleet*. London: John Murray, 1967.

397. Weigley, Russell F. "Book review," *The Journal of American History*, Vol. 74 No. 4 (March 1988):1383.

398. Weigley, Russell F. *Eisenhower's Lieutenants: The Campaign of France and Germany, 1944-45*. Bloomington: Indiana University Press, 1981.

399. Weinberg, Gerhard L. *A World at Arms: A Global History of World War II*. New York: Cambridge University Press, 1994.

400. Weingartner, Steven, ed. *The Greatest Thing We Have Ever Attempted: Historical Perspectives on the Normandy Campaign*. Wheaton, Ill.: Cantigny First Division Foundation, 1998.

401. Westphal, Siegfried. *The German Army in the West*. London: Cassell, 1951.

402. Whitaker, Denis and Shelah Whitaker, *Dieppe: Tragedy to Triumph*. Toronto: McGraw-Hill Ryerson, 1992.

403. Whitaker, W. Denis, and Shelagh Whitaker. *Rhineland: The Battle to End the War*. New York: St. Martin's Press, 1989.

404. Whiting, Charles. *The Last Battle: Montgomery's Campaign April-May 1945*. Marlborough: Crowood, 1989.

405. Whitlock, Flint. "Imperfect Victory at Falaise," *World War II*, Vol. 12, No. 1 (May 1997): 26-32, 73.

406. Willkie, Wendell L. *One World*. New York: Simon and Schuster, 1943.

407. Wilmot, Chester. *The Struggle for Europe*. New York: Harper, 1952.

408. Young, Desmond. *Rommel*. London: Collins, 1950.

409. Young, F. W. *The Story of the Staff College 1858-1958.* Staff College, Camberley, 1958.

410. Young, Kenneth, ed. *The Diaries of Sir Robert Bruce - Lockhart.* New York: St. Martin's Press, 1974.

411. Younger, Carlton. *Ireland's Civil War.* New York: Taplinger, 1969.

412. Ziegler, Philip. *Mountbatten.* London: Collins, 1985.

413. Zuckerman, Solly. *From Apes to Warlords.* London: Hamish Hamilton, 1978.

Index

About the Compiler

COLIN F. BAXTER is Professor of History at East Tennessee State University. His earlier books include *The Normandy Campaign, 1944: A Selected Bibliography* (Greenwood, 1992) and *The War in North Africa, 1940–1943: A Selected Bibliography* (Greenwood, 1996).

ISBN 0-313-29119-5

90000>

HARDCOVER BAR CODE